Thomas Hobbes

Thomas Hobbes

Turning Point for Honor

Laurie M. Johnson Bagby

LEXINGTON BOOKS

A division of
ROWMAN & LITTLEFIELD PUBLISHERS, INC.
Lanham • Boulder • New York • Toronto • Plymouth, UK

LEXINGTON BOOKS

A division of Rowman & Littlefield Publishers, Inc.
A wholly owned subsidary of The Rowman & Littlefield Publishing Group, Inc.
4501 Forbes Boulevard, Suite 200
Lanham, MD 20706

Estover Road
Plymouth PL6 7PY
United Kingdom

British Library Cataloguing in Publication Information Available

Library of Congress Cataloging-in-Publication Data

Bagby, Laurie M.
  Thomas Hobbes : turning point for honor / Laurie M. Johnson Bagby.
    p. cm.
  Includes bibliographical references and index.
  ISBN-13: 978-0-7391-2637-0 (cloth : alk. paper)
  ISBN-10: 0-7391-2637-7 (cloth : alk. paper)
  ISBN-13: 978-0-7391-3605-8 (electronic)
  ISBN-10: 0-7391-3605-4 (electronic)
 1. Hobbes, Thomas, 1588–1679. 2. Honor. I. Title.
  B1248.H66B35 2009
  192—dc22   2008050908

Printed in the United States of America

∞™ The paper used in this publication meets the minimum requirements of American
National Standard for Information Sciences—Permanence of Paper for Printed Library
Materials, ANSI/NISO Z39.48-1992.

To Tim and Hunter—honor!

Contents

Acknowledgments

My great appreciation and thanks to Ms. Kathy MacKenzie, my graduate research assistant, who helped with the research and editing for this book, as well as formatting the text to the publisher's specifications. Ms. MacKenzie has worked efficiently and in the most helpful manner in this and other research over several years, and she has my gratitude. I also wish to thank Professor Marsha Frey for her initial reading and critique of this book, and also for the very helpful comments and suggestions of the anonymous reviewer. In addition, I must express my gratitude to Kansas State University for allowing me a half-year sabbatical in which I did the lion's share of writing on this project.

Introduction

Recently there has been a small but noticeable surge of interest in the idea of honor, and the question of what our society makes of this idea in the twenty-first century. In 2004, Brad Miner's *The Compleat Gentleman: The Modern Man's Guide to Chivalry* was published.[1] This book was aimed at a popular audience and did not use scholarly citations. Nonetheless, it was noticed by some elements of the intellectual class, notably by conservative commentators for whom the revival of honor resonated as a worthwhile project. Indeed, Miner's purpose in writing the book was to revive, especially for men, the sense of honor developed during the Middle Ages, a project that for many scholars would seem anachronistic at best.

Early in his book, Miner recounts the decision by men on the *Titanic* to adhere to the principle of "women and children first" and discusses the response of many men today that such gentlemen are . . . "chumps." Contemporary men, in Miner's view, have no reliable and positive idea of what it means to be a man. But without this type of ideal, men become less responsible, less of a positive force in society. Miner clearly believes that men in particular are missing something very important—the desire and sense of duty that compels those who are stronger to protect those who are weaker. Even more important, the very idea of nobility, of noble motivations and actions, does not seem recognizable to many people today. Rather than spending much time trying to figure out why this has happened, Miner spends most of his book reacquainting his audience with medieval ideals of chivalry: courage, love, and piety, or the virtues of the warrior, lover, and monk. Miner's book reads mainly like nostalgia (much like, for a younger audience, does *The Dangerous Book for Boys*). Obviously someone still had to try to explain what if any real harm occurred with the loss of the concept of honor, and how and why that loss occurred.

Next came James Bowman's *Honor: A History*.[2] Bowman is a journalist who takes a scholarly interest in literature, and is also a resident scholar at the Ethics and Public Policy Center. He frames his discussion of honor in light of the new enemy, radical Islam, whose idea of honor seems so foreign to the West as to be incomprehensible. Bowman traces the changes in and eventual demise of the Western ideal of honor. He does this mainly through an examination of popular culture—novels, plays, movies—to show how the Western mind came to reject, as antiquated and even silly, the old-fashioned "manly" view of honor as courage, and the willingness to risk one's life for the sake of principles or reputation. He also pinpoints major cultural and political changes in Western society that provided the foundation for these changes in popular culture. Bowman looks at the impact of mechanized, impersonal warfare in the First and Second World Wars, which reduced or at times even eliminated the opportunity to see war as a stage for honor and heroism. He also examines the impact of the feminist movement, as well as the trend toward seeing the world's problems in terms of psychological disorders with the need for therapeutic solutions (i.e., his chapter on "Vietnam: War as Social Therapy and Psychological Trauma").

Bowman shows his own form of courage in his last chapter, when he attempts to ask what it would take to revive our sense of honor. There is a real urgency in his writing, because Bowman thinks that the Western world is so out of touch with the mentality of honor that it may not be able to defend itself against those for whom a perverse and invidious love of honor is all that matters. But Bowman's recommendations for change, as he himself admits, are hard to imagine. Speaking of a social movement to bring back honor, Bowman writes:

> It would . . . have to create a new subculture capable of breaking free of the gravitational pull of the celebrity-culture death star and looking down upon it with the kind of amused contempt that was last possible in the 1950s. Finally, it would have to revamp and revitalize our political, social and intellectual assumptions about the differences between the sexes, in particular making the traditional role of women as wives, mothers and nurturers not only respectable again but the most honorable of female aspirations.[3]

But such changes are probably not possible, as Bowman admits. Also, proposals such as women returning to an acceptance of their private role, where men take the helm of public action and women embrace the domestic nurturing role, may not really get to the heart of the problem, because the problem may be bigger than gender and gender roles. Bowman's analysis, having to do mainly with popular culture and fairly recent historical events, limits his ability to find the true source of changes in our conception of honor. It is a valiant attempt, and adds to our understanding of recent cultural changes in American society, but because of its sources and its focus on recent times, it is necessarily circumscribed in its ability to find the root cause of these changes and thus to pinpoint solutions. Still, Bowman says something in his concluding chapter, "Honor's Revival," that clearly gets to the heart of the matter: "Honor Mark II would first have to defeat our hatred and fear of war, our conviction that it is the worst of human conditions and the growing corollary assumption that peace is worth having at any price."[4]

The idea that peace is worth having at any price is exactly the idea that Thomas Hobbes wishes us to adopt after following his reasoning in *Leviathan*. It is the very practical idea that without survival nothing else is possible, so the primary aim of political life must be survival at almost any cost. To this end, Hobbes counsels nearly complete obedience to the government no matter who is in charge or what laws are in force. Bowman and Hobbes are polar opposites on the question of the value of human life for the sake of life, of whether survival should be the top priority, or whether a particular way of life is necessary for it to be worth living. Depending upon how one answers these questions, one either mourns the loss of the idea of honor in our society, or one may even be inclined to mockery of those who still cling to the idea of honor.

In the same year as Bowman's book was published came Harvey Mansfield's *Manliness*, which raised more controversy largely because Mansfield is a prominent and sometimes controversial figure in academia. Unlike the other two authors, Mansfield is an academic, indeed a professor of government at Harvard University with a long list of widely discussed books and scholarly articles to his credit. Whereas Miner dealt mainly with medieval ideals, hoping to revive them as a guide for more gentlemanly, that is to say honorable, conduct from men, Mansfield spent more time in explanation. Just how had society lost the ideal of manliness, which Mansfield associated with virtues of (at least the old-fashioned model of) leadership—aggressiveness, decisiveness, toughness, courage. Whereas Bowman stayed at the level of popular culture and current history, Mansfield dug deeper. Of course, the women's movement was a part of Mansfield's discussion, because this movement sought to erase gender roles that previously had enforced the ideal of manliness and manly behavior, including honor. But Mansfield is a scholar of political philosophy, not literature. So though he spent some time in his book on popular culture, he also examined the history of political thought to explain the changes that have taken place at a deeper level.

Pertinent to the topic of this book, Mansfield saw in Thomas Hobbes someone who wished to create the "sensitive male," a man who finally understood the consequences of his own nature and willingly submitted to an absolute sovereign whom he would obey no matter what he was asked to do or not do.

Mansfield explained succinctly the conflict that one of my students had instinctually uncovered when he called Hobbes a "coward." Mansfield said that
there were two competing human motivations, "love of liberty and desire for
security." "If we look at them from the aspect of manliness, they *necessarily*
conflict."[5] Hobbes, arguably the father of classical liberalism, came down almost entirely on the side of the desire for security. Mansfield pointed out that
Hobbes deliberately left out courage in his list of virtues.[6] He argued that
Hobbes's state of nature was the "manly extreme," and that Hobbes included
everyone in that extreme—both men and women—in order to show how un-
tenable life would be if manly vainglory was left unchecked. Hobbes thus
shows why we have to reject what Mansfield identified as the primarily male
virtue of glory or pride.[7] Explaining Hobbes's reasoning, Mansfield wrote:
"Anticipating your violent death by a violent chance encounter puts you in
the frame of mind to want to avoid all such chances. Being in the right frame
of mind is a moral as well as an intellectual duty, according to Hobbes. You
reach this frame of mind through fear, not through shame."[8]

Mansfield thus starts but does not finish the discussion this book will undertake. His primary focus is on the devolution of the concept of manliness,
not the larger and related concept of honor per se. However, while the theme
of this book is not manliness or gender but the idea of honor, it is unnecessary to ignore the intersection between gender and honor. This is especially
true because at the time Hobbes was writing, the two were so explicitly tied
together. So we will have to look at what Hobbes has to say about "gentlemen" and the notion of "chivalry," because these get to the heart of his views
on honor. We will be able to see in Hobbes's thought on these matters the
modern shift away from the virtue of glory or honor, and the fundamental reasons behind that shift. Inevitably, we will see this partly as a movement from
the claims of particularly male virtues to a universalizing of virtues. Mansfield has pointed out the modern rejection of pride, and its opposite shame, in
motivating men to take certain actions, relying instead on a more lowly foundation of fear and self-interest. Through examining Hobbes's thoughts on
honor in a variety of ways, we can begin to see how and why this foundational shift took place and what its implications are, for men and women.
Though the concept of honor has been tied up mainly with masculinity in the
past, it is not necessarily growing gender equality that threatens to extinguish
it. I believe the roots run deeper, and that Mansfield himself understood this
when he brought up Hobbes and liberal political thought. Thus his book invites the type of lengthier exploration that I am undertaking.

The concept of honor is a large one, even if narrowed down to an examination of one particular thinker's analysis of it, especially if that thinker is a
good representative, as I believe Hobbes is, of a large intellectual and cultural

shift in the understanding of honor in the modern Western mind. Indeed, I believe that Hobbes's thought represents a clear turning point in Western society's conception of honor. For this reason, Hobbes's idea of honor has to be approached from several directions, or through several lenses, before it can be fully understood.

I will begin in chapter 1 with an analysis of how Hobbes used the term itself. I will avail myself of the considerable work of Gabriella Slomp on Hobbes and glory to show that Hobbes's idea of honor can be distinguished from his references to glory, and to show how the two terms are related. Next, I will explore Hobbes's early views on honor by looking at how he uses the term in three brief works, made available to us through the persistence of Arlene Saxonhouse.[9] Because these early works are not political treatises, and as we will see, their authorship is still somewhat in doubt, I will rely more on his earliest political treatise, *The Elements of Law*. In early works, we find that Hobbes has one foot in the past and one in his future critique of honor. After exploring the evolution of his thought at intermediate stages, I will turn to what Hobbes has to say explicitly about honor in his mature thought, especially in *De Cive* and *Leviathan*, where he most thoroughly deals with the term and tries to define it. Here he seems to deconstruct the very concept, leaving it hollow, or rather having largely collapsed it into what he calls "vainglory" or harmful "pride." While Hobbes is almost notorious for his desire for consistency, when it comes to the idea of honor, there are instances where it appears that he uses the term in a traditional way even in his later works. The thrust of his mature writing devalues and indeed deconstructs honor, however. Through a thorough exploration of how he uses the term, we may begin to understand why he wishes to undermine it. Hobbes's cynical and almost mocking tone will perhaps surprise the reader, but it may also remind him or her of attitudes such as the three authors discussed above find in critics of honor today: for Hobbes, someone who believes in the reality of honor instead of understanding it as foolish vanity does not really understand the world and thus plays the part of the fool.

In the next chapter, I will look at what Hobbes says about the heroic ideal, specifically what he has to say about the nobles and gentlemen of his day. In order to understand Hobbes's views in context, I will spend some time on the development of the ideas of chivalry and the gentleman prior to and up to Hobbes's time. I have chosen to use the work of medieval author Geoffroi de Charny as a classic example of chivalric writing, not because Hobbes explicitly acknowledges his work (he does not) or has any specific connection to such work, but because it provides a very clear and useful contrast between the medieval admiration for chivalry and Hobbes's early modern rejection of the same. I will also take a look at Hobbes's own social status, including his eventual entry into gentlemanly status. Despite his friendly relations with members of the nobility and his own ascension in status as a result of these relations, in his political philosophy, Hobbes provides an account of the origins of nobility that takes away any special moral status from the noble class, and his use of the term "gentleman" suggests that it no longer signifies for him any special moral status. Rather, for Hobbes, gentlemanly status is a matter of the opinion of those in power, no more and no less. It has nothing to do with character, and everything to do with proximity to power. Thus he appears to peel away or "cut through the rhetoric" of gentlemanliness and see the foundation underneath it: relative power regardless of moral worth. He is a gentleman whom the *king says* is a gentleman. Hobbes deals with hereditary titles and coats of arms in the same way, demystifying them, effectively undermining their special allure. His treatment of the gentlemen's role in the English Civil War is almost entirely critical, revealing these supposed high-minded men to be mere egotistical manipulators, out to empower and enrich themselves with no higher purpose or goal. This effective rejection of aristocratic virtues as so much rhetoric or misty-eyed sentimentalism is certainly emblematic of the modern social view. And if we remember that the aristocracy was necessarily the embodiment of the ideal of honor at Hobbes's time, we can see how tearing down its special status also affects the status and understanding of honor generally.

In addition to examining Hobbes's critique of gentlemen and the aristocracy in chapter 2, I will take a look at what Hobbes has to say about another heroic figure, this one accorded great honor in Christianity, the martyr. The martyr, of course, obtains his special status by laying down his life for God's truth. He or she is not willing to lie or submit to false religions simply to survive, and (key to Hobbes's dislike) is admired for centuries as the very definition of courage and sacrifice. Martyrs seemingly prove the superiority of honor, the idea that life is *not* worth living at any cost. Hobbes's views on martyrdom could simply be seen as a part of his overall criticism of otherworldly zeal, which they are. But in the context of the discussion of gentlemen and aristocracy, his treatment of these Christian role models takes on a more significant meaning. Hobbes wishes to undermine any idea of heroism, because it contradicts so dramatically his insistence that fear of death should be the decisive factor in our political and religious choices. The Christian hero is the most significant barrier in the way of Hobbes's designs, because in his view it is precisely religious zeal (stirred up by those who simply want power) which makes men most indifferent to the survival imperative, which makes them even go gladly to their deaths. One could argue that Hobbes, despite his seeming deconstruction of Christianity, is actually a Christian thinker in the sense that he makes humility the top, and really the only, virtue that a believer should have. However, his treatment of martyrdom may suggest to us that Christianity is not really about Hobbes's version of humility, in which the desire for peace dictates complete surrender to the stronger, and that other virtues such as courage and conviction are important aspects of Christianity that cannot be so easily dismissed.

In chapter 3, I will turn to Hobbes's thoughts on human nature, the state of nature, and the social contract. These are the most famous parts of his theory, so crucial for the development of Western liberal thought, and they have a profoundly destructive influence on the older ideals of honor and courage. The damage is done not directly, as it is in the other lenses through which we will approach Hobbes's views of honor. But the damage done by these central Hobbesian ideas is more profound, because their rationale veritably eliminates the possibility of honorable motivation and action. Here we see honor as the enemy of safety, the very motive that must be stamped out in order to bring peace. It is the man who would fight over an insult to himself or his loved ones, the man who would go to battle over high-minded principles, who is the most dangerous to peace and safety in Hobbes's view. It is the mentality of honor, or what he frames as dangerous and sinful pride, which must be overcome once and for all by Hobbes's political science. In place of honor, he puts fear of violent death and individual self-interest. He debunks the Aristotelian notion of man as social and political, and depicts him as radically individualistic and entirely self-interested. These ideas about human nature make honor, inextricably tied up with moral obligations to other individuals and to society, impossible. Honor is exposed as entirely unnatural and thus irrational. In the social contract, human beings acknowledge their only rational interest, survival, and the crucial role government has in protecting them from violent death. At the end of this chapter, I will explore the ramifications of this conclusion for the issue of military service in Hobbes's thought. Hobbes struggled mightily it seems with how to establish any obligation to stand and fight for one's country, and his reasoning revealed the tension between his social contract and the necessity of national defense. In the end, he could not justify any reason for obligating a soldier to face imminent death for a chance to preserve his country.

Finally, in my conclusion, I will discuss the implications of the rejection of honor for modern political thought after Hobbes. Many thinkers as diverse as Strauss, Macpherson, Coleman, and Kraynak have identified Hobbes as the founder or at least intellectual precursor of classical liberal theory. Indeed, the core ideas of Hobbes's theories *are* liberal. The acceptance of political equality in the state of nature; the ignoring of all remaining actual inequalities for the purposes of peaceful politics; the idea that governments are formed for the natural right of the individual; the dispelling of religious authority as superstition;

the rejection of eternal truths in favor of human perspective; the critique of political rhetoric as motivated by power and pride; the questioning of the war-making powers of the state as motivated by political or personal ambitions; the power of education to socialize citizens to accept alternative political, religious, and social schemes are all liberal ideas that come to fruition during the Enlightenment a century later. Even the idea of gender equality can be found in Hobbes's thought, an idea that was only finally realized in Western societies in the twentieth century. For these reasons, Hobbes's thought can be seen as a "turning point," a pivot on which the mind of Western European society began to change. With the transformation of classical liberal politics into egalitarianism, we can trace the destruction of the ability to make distinctions among people, an ability crucial to a serious understanding of honor. With the development of classical liberal values, or what some call the "bourgeois virtues" of the Western world, we can trace the slow diminishment of honor into what Bowman depicts as a cultural shadow from the past, sometimes wistfully dreamed of in cowboy fairy tales, but not really understood or seriously wanted anymore. The conclusion will entertain some possibilities and ask some questions, such as, if we admit that some inequality does matter after all, such as inequality of strength, intelligence, or character, would we have to admit that some individuals (and even some countries) might have more responsibility for the common welfare than others? If we admit that sometimes the call to fight is sounded for genuine and compelling reasons, such as preservation of family, society, and way of life, and not simply for political or personal advantage, might we have to evaluate each call more carefully and contemplate making a painful sacrifice? Hobbes begins an attitude of cynicism that becomes so great and deep that it is now difficult for citizens of democracies to see the claims of anyone in leadership as worthy of objective consideration. But we now find ourselves confronted by a foe that does not appreciate many of what we consider to be admirable aspects of liberal society, such as democratic participation, gender equality, and religious tolerance. In the face of this type of foe, we may at some point have to fall back on a deeper sense of belonging and loyalty than that produced by obligation based on individual self-interest, an alternative sense of obligation which causes people to protect their own because it is basically good and because it is their own.

Hobbes's thought sets us down the path of radical moral uncertainty. As a society we have accepted his idea that disputes about values can never be resolved by reason, either by us as individuals, or by higher authorities, even if we have not accepted his conclusion that we must therefore submit to the arbitrary judgments of a sovereign power. Can we reevaluate his assumption of uncertainty about basic values while still keeping the benefits of liberalism?

With hopefully the same courage evinced by Miner, Bowman, and Mansfield, I will attempt a discussion of why the diminishment of the old-fashioned concept of honor is an actual loss, and even maybe as Bowman suggests, a dangerous loss in today's world. In tandem, I will have to discuss the possibilities for a revival of honor that is compatible with our thoroughgoing liberal society, though this is always the most difficult and dangerous undertaking for anyone writing on this subject. Can understanding the philosophical origins of the loss help us repair it? Is there any way to make liberalism compatible with honor? Can gender equality be reconciled with ideals that for so long were associated only with men (a woman's honor previously having been confined to chastity and obedience)? I can only hope to make an attempt at answering these questions. I also hope that this book will form part of a growing discussion and debate on this topic of great importance for our culture and, potentially, our survival.

A FINAL NOTE: WHY NOT MACHIAVELLI?

Leo Strauss placed the beginning of modern political thought first in Hobbes, but then changed his mind and argued that Machiavelli should have the title of first modern political philosopher. It is true that by openly rejecting ancient and medieval Christian idealism, most importantly the idea that the state should be morally good and promote the good life in its citizens, Machiavelli deserves this title. Hobbes follows Machiavelli in the assumption that better motives are not to be counted upon, that true statesmen in Plato's sense are difficult if not impossible to find, and that politics is most often an arena of amoral manipulation and misleading rhetoric. But it is in this last point that we begin to detect a difference between them, a difference that turns out to be of crucial importance to the topic of this book, honor.

Machiavelli and Hobbes both view politics and its sometime extension, war, as an arena of selfish ambition, deception, and immorality, and they both differ from the ancients in accepting this state as the norm instead of trying to persuade their readers to adopt better motivations. But Machiavelli embraces these things—selfish ambition, deception, and immorality—as good when wielded by the virtuous leader. Machiavelli still admires the ancient heroic ideal, albeit devoid of Platonic/Aristotelian and Christian moralism. He longs for a prince who is amoral, but bold, ambitious, courageous, daring, and yes, interested in everlasting fame and glory. This leader can and should be allowed to use the common people like building materials in pursuit of his personal glory. Machiavelli admires republican government because it provides an arena in which ambitious men can compete without ruining the state, their regulated competition providing some stability for the state. He would certainly have no problem with them displaying their talents in the arena of war, for war is a prominent way for a nation to obtain safety and prosperity.

It is this admiration for, even reliance upon, the selfishly ambitious leader with warlike virtues, that separates Machiavelli from Hobbes. It is Hobbes's rejection of this human type entirely that makes his thought, not Machiavelli's, the point of departure when it comes to honor. Vickie Sullivan, in *Machiavelli, Hobbes, and the Formation of a Liberal Republicanism in England*, sums up the difference nicely when she writes of Machiavelli: "War is to be cultivated in his view, and those most hungry for its honors must be embraced, despite the dangers such individuals present when they turn their aggressive instincts on the state itself."[10] Hobbes, however, was unwilling to make the same concession, and indeed aimed his most powerful argumentative weapons against this very type of person. Sullivan argues that the difference is brought about by Hobbes's insistence on natural equality and his denial of inherent differences among men:

> Because Europe's monarchies were supported by aristocratic families who were distinguished from the remainder of subjects by their social status, wealth, and education—if not by God's special grace—Hobbes's assertion of human equality challenged centuries of custom. Moreover, the members of these aristocratic families were skilled in the martial arts, having originally received their holdings of land in exchange for their military service to the king. The members of this exalted class had very much of which to be proud. Trained to seek honor on the battlefield, they are likely to advocate for war abroad; disposed to view themselves as superior in strength and resolve, they are likely to defend their honor vigorously, even violently, from insults and slights, and are, as a result, the source of disturbances in the realm.[11]

While this does not argue for Hobbes being, after all, the first modern philosopher, it does argue for Hobbes, and not Machiavelli, as the philosopher who questions honor. Hobbes even blames for much of society's problems the ancient and medieval heroic/chivalric values that men in leadership positions had previously thought ideal. I hope to show that Hobbes ends up rejecting honor as an admirable goal for men because it is too destructive. In doing so, he sets the stage for the modern skepticism about honor and the men and women who still admire and pursue it, in and beyond the military arena. It is Hobbes who starts us down the path that ends in questioning the very possibility of honor, in a world so uncertain of ideals that "every man for himself" seems the smarter and more admirable code of conduct. In this sense, I hope to show that Hobbes's thought is truly the turning point for honor.

NOTES

1. Brad Miner, *The Compleat Gentleman: The Modern Man's Guide to Chivalry* (Dallas: Spence Publishing, 2004).

2. James Bowman, *Honor: A History* (New York: Encounter Books, 2006).

3. Bowman, *Honor*, 307.

4. Bowman, *Honor*, 307.

5. Harvey C. Mansfield, *Manliness* (New Haven, Conn., and London: Yale University Press, 2006), 165.

6. Mansfield, *Manliness*, 166.

7. Mansfield, *Manliness*, 167.

8. Mansfield, *Manliness*, 169.

9. There is some dispute about whether or not these are Hobbes's works, as I will make clear in chapter 1.

10. Vickie B. Sullivan, *Machiavelli, Hobbes, and the Formation of a Liberal Republicanism in England* (Cambridge: Cambridge University Press, 2004), 80.

11. Sullivan, *Machiavelli*, 98.

Chapter One

What Honor Meant to Hobbes

Examining Hobbes's use of the term "honor" is a commonsense starting point for this investigation. While his definition is not the "full story," it is certainly important, especially because Hobbes himself placed such an emphasis on establishing proper definitions in building his political theory. First, we should take the time to get an idea of what honor meant to others prior to Hobbes's interpretation of it. In particular, we should know what it meant to his immediate medieval predecessors. Next, we will need to distinguish his concept of honor from his frequent use of "glory." While related, these two terms are distinct for Hobbes because they refer to different human experiences. After this, we should take a look at how Hobbes used the word "honor" in his early works so that we can see if his ideas on the subject developed and changed over time, and if so, how. As a result, we will come to a close examination of Hobbes's most sustained treatment of the idea of honor in *Leviathan*, especially in chapter 10 of that work, where he takes great pains to fully define and describe it. By doing all these things, we should have a firmer understanding of Hobbes's ideas on honor and know a little about why the idea of honor was so important to him. We will have to go farther, of course, to fully understand its political and social significance and its place in his larger political theory.

PRIOR UNDERSTANDINGS OF HONOR

By understanding what honor meant to previous generations we can get a fuller appreciation for how Hobbes's views differed with them as well as his contemporaries. We have to know who Hobbes was arguing with and why, in order to understand fully his intent in his mature analysis of honor. Hobbes contrasted his own thoughts most frequently with that of the ancients, particularly with Aristotle, who promoted the idea of the good life as that of the good man and citizen. For Aristotle, the honorable and thus happy life was one of fulfilling moral obligations to oneself, one's friends, and one's community. In a way, Aristotle and his teacher Plato rebelled against the popular view of honor in their time as primarily about military and political success, by promoting the primacy of moral virtue in living the good life. Hobbes criticized medieval scholastics who combined Aristotelian teachings with Christian theology. Their primary aim was the good life, defined by them as the life of Christian virtue. Hobbes's real problem with these teachings was not the advocacy of morality itself, but the idea that the individual could decide what morality he would follow, even if this meant rebelling against authority. This is why Hobbes had as many complaints against those who promoted honor as military or political prowess as those who promoted it as moral virtue. He had as many problems with those who taught that men should follow the Church's lead as those who taught that individuals must follow their spiritual inspiration. In both cases, men could be led into disobedience to their government. The fault of the ancients was that they had argued that reason on these matters should prevail over authority, and that it was possible and even incumbent upon the thinking person to criticize government or authority if it did not conform to what he thought was right. This mistake was, in his view, carried over through the Middle Ages and into his own time by theologians and other scholars of the Catholic Church and then the Anglican and other Protestant churches, whose leaders tried to argue that what was morally right in their eyes should prevail over existing authority. With this in mind, we should look more closely at the thinking Hobbes opposes.

The medieval understanding of honor can be seen in the code of chivalry, which slowly developed with the feudal order and which matured by the fourteenth century. In chivalric literature, honor was imbued with Christian moral meaning. It also was associated with noble breeding and refined character, as well as prowess in arms and the martial virtues. There was little to no cynicism attached to the concept of honor. Instead, contrasts between honorable and dishonorable were clearly and sincerely made, and men were judged accordingly either to be good or bad men.

Geoffroi de Charny's *Le Livre de chevalerie* (The Book of Chivalry) reflects this simpler understanding of honor. While there is no evidence that Hobbes read this book or was informed directly by de Charny's ideas, this "mirror" book is exemplary of the chivalric frame of mind, and provides many useful examples of contrast with Hobbes's thought. The reason for referring to it here is that it provides an excellent view of the medieval chivalric ideal with which to contrast Hobbes's rejection of that ideal. Many of the ideals that de Charny writes about with such passion have parallels in Hobbes's own analysis, which rejects those older ideals. This is not as true of perhaps the more obvious choice of Baldassare Castiglione's book, *The Courtier*, a work closer to Hobbes's time, having been published in 1528.[1] While *The Courtier* contains much advice for the women and men at court, Castiglione's work had already become infected by the growing emphasis on the acceptability of self-interest, which Hobbes's own work represents. The focus in *The Courtier* is self-promotion through learning the political and social arts of advancement, and there is less concern for the genuineness of conviction and more concern for the semblance of it. It represents a reinterpretation (some might even say a rejection) of the older chivalric code itself, and thus it cannot provide the kind of contrast that a work like de Charny's can, representing, as it tries to do, true religious conviction and love of honor for its own sake.[2]

De Charny was a knight of the fourteenth century, who served France during the first part of the Hundred Years' War, both in that conflict with England and in the crusades. Well respected as both a knight and a counselor in his own country, his fame spread throughout Europe, with de Charny considered as a model of military prowess, noble character, and moral rectitude. As a result of his military record and reputation, Jean II chose de Charny to found a new order of chivalry, the Company of the Star, in 1352. It was because of this charge that de Charny wrote three books on chivalry. He died in battle at Poitiers in 1356, defending the king, a death that served as a glorious ending for a man considered by many the very model of chivalry.

De Charny's *The Book of Chivalry* is short, well written, and unambiguous. He repeatedly weighs various knightly acts and ways of life on the scales of honor, to show which are the most and which are the least honorable, this with the idea of encouraging young knights to strive for the highest ideals. It is honorable and admirable to display one's military prowess in tournaments, for instance, if one does so without too much ostentatious display. But it is still more honorable to display one's skills in actual battle.

> And as soon as they [the knights] realize this, they give up participating so frequently in exercising their skill at arms in local events and take up armed combat in war. They look around, inquire, and find out where the greatest honor is to be found at that particular time. Then they go to that place and, in keeping with their natural good qualities, are keen to discover all the conditions of armed combat in war, and cannot be satisfied with themselves if they do not realize to the full their wish to find themselves there and to learn.[3]

De Charny associates honor with good birth and nobility, not exclusively, but with the idea that those born into greatness have greater opportunities and also greater responsibilities because of their lofty positions. Unlike Hobbes's mature reaction to the hereditary nobility, de Charny's understanding is that noble birth is a source of actual superior qualities, not simply the result of the kingly power to hand out benefits to those who support him or those he fears. De Charny accepts without question the idea of social rank as a measure of worthiness and indicator of appropriate role. The nobles are the beneficiaries of God, "So it must seem to everyone that such people should strive with the utmost diligence to ensure that they suffer no reproach against themselves nor against the bounties God has bestowed on them." Because of the gifts God has given the nobles, they bear greater responsibilities toward their lessers and those in need, and must see themselves always as moral examples, who can either uplift or debase the entire community through their actions. De Charny says, "it is necessary that in all the respects mentioned above, in no way can anything dishonorable be perceived nor said concerning them; for there will be much greater talk and notoriety about their shortcomings than there would be concerning some one without such a great reputation."[4] De Charny then goes on to discuss all the things the nobles must avoid, including avarice, gambling, and gluttony. He puts forth a manly ideal in which overindulging or caring too much about appearance is considered effeminate, unbecoming, a sign of poor character in a man. He also takes pains to point out that soft living in a man makes him unfit in times when his military services are actually needed. So he continually reminds his readers that the reason they should practice the arts of chivalry comes down to the fundamental need for defense of the country, not simply display.

De Charny is not afraid to call soft men cowards. In contrast with Hobbes's thought on fear of death and the imperative to survive, de Charny writes, "And while the cowards have a great desire to live and a great fear of dying, it is quite the contrary for the men of worth who do not mind whether they live or die, provided that their life be good enough for them to die with honor."[5] What would be seen as sheer folly by Hobbes, the desire for honor over life itself, is seen by de Charny as an absolute necessity for a life worth living. For de Charny, this is because the ultimate source of honor is God. "You can see clearly and understand that you on your own can achieve nothing except what God grants you. And does not God confer great honor when he allows you of His mercy to defeat your enemies without harm to yourself? . . . And if you are in a state of grace and you die honorably, does not God show you great mercy when He grants you such a glorious end to your life in this world and bears your soul away with Him into eternal bliss?"[6]

De Charny's view of the afterlife is a traditional one, in which God reigns supreme in this world and the next, rewarding those of good character and punishing those who are evil. He does acknowledge the fame of this world, and even treats it as well worth desiring. But if a man focuses only on this and does not remember to value God's honor more, he should not win the greatest admiration. As we will see, while not writing God out of the equation entirely, Hobbes will rewrite scripture in such a way that the kind of courage which de Charny thinks God admires can be seen as unnecessary, even against God's will.

De Charny treats women and children differently than men. For instance, where it is unattractive for men to make a fuss over their appearance and put on much finery, it is understandable and admirable in women, who cannot be too active in the outside world and thus have a smaller arena in which to display their refinement and virtue. Likewise, women and children are physically weaker and more in need of protection than men. In true chivalric tradition he spends much time in his work establishing the moral duty to defend them. "And again, if some people wanted to seize the land and inheritance of defenseless maidens or widows and could not be dissuaded from this except by war or combat, one ought to embark on this confidently in regard to one's personal reputation and the saving of one's soul, and the same is true in relation to the defense of orphans."[7]

Shame is an important concept for de Charny, who employs it liberally as an incentive to do the right thing. A notion almost completely absent in Hobbes's mature works,[8] shame is the worst punishment this life can mete out, at least for a man who understands honor. De Charny writes that one "should not fear to die in order to avoid all shame,"[9] and shame comes from dishonorable actions. In fact, shame becomes a prominent theme at the end of de Charny's work, as the ultimate motivation to do honorable deeds. The dandy, who bedecks himself with ornaments, or is so concerned with his appearance that he girds his midsection in order to look good in his armor, but then cannot move well in battle, should simply be ashamed of himself. "And it is to be expected that the excessive adornments with which they deck themselves out make them neglect to perform many great deeds; and there are many who forget all shame, and just as they forget all shame, so is all honor forgotten."[10]

Obviously, not being able to stand firm (or stand at all!) in battle and face death would be cowardice for de Charny, and cowardice would reap deserved criticism in this world and punishment in the next. An honorable man could never be a coward. The medieval view of honor is inextricably linked with death: that is, being able to show that one is not afraid to die for a worthy cause. This type of courage is again linked to the existence of God and a cosmic order that rewards such disregard for life in favor of honorable deeds. As we will see, Hobbes must break these linkages in order to establish what he believes to be more solid foundations for political order. Hobbes does not want to rely upon the good character of nobles, kings, or commoners, and for this reason, he must deconstruct the medieval concept of honor represented in de Charny's work.

NOTE: GLORY AND HONOR

Hobbes's political thought is full of warnings against glory, or more specifically, vainglory and "glorying," which can lead to the irrational desire for supremacy over others instead of the rational desire for self-preservation. It is easy to think that Hobbes meant the same thing when writing of honor. That is why it is necessary to briefly explain the difference between honor and glory. At one point, Hobbes does say that "glory is like honor," because "if all men have it no man hath it, for they consist in comparison and precellence."[11] But this is to say that they are similar because of their relative nature: glory and honor are both only considered good if men do not have an equal share of them. But when it comes to glory, the important thing is the individual's perception of enjoying more than others, even though it is possible for others to feel that they too are experiencing more, for glory is an entirely subjective thing—it is an internal quality, a feeling. While Hobbes occasionally uses the term glory in a way similar to honor, for the most part he does make this distinction.[12]

Gabriella Slomp's study of Hobbes's view of glory supports this distinction. For instance, she writes:

> In the *Elements of Law* the pleasure of observing one's power in attaining one's objectives is called by Hobbes "glory." As in *Anti-White*, so in the *Elements of Law*, Hobbes maintains that the power of man to achieve his objectives is not absolute, but determined by the difference with the power of others (*Elements of Law*, 34). Thus, a more precise description of glory in the *Elements of Law* is the pleasure of superior power with respect to others (*Elements of Law*, 36–37).[13]

Slomp goes on to show that Hobbes distinguishes among "true, vain, and false glory," but all three share the inward pleasure at one's own supremacy over others.[14] In a later publication, Slomp argues that Hobbes's view of glory remained fairly stable from the *Elements of Law* to *Leviathan*, but whereas it was treated as a universal motivation for conflict in earlier works, in *Leviathan* he argues that *some* people both in nature and in civil breakdown are motivated by glory, and this motivation causes them to challenge others, with the end result that all must prepare for war.[15]

Honor can be an inward feeling toward another, and also an outward sign. When we honor someone else, we can do so without any outward show of it.

But in order for that honor to mean anything to another person, signs of it must be given. So, while glory is an internal feeling about oneself, honor is a person's estimation of someone else, and that someone else only has honor when others give it to him. "For honor . . . is nothing else but the estimation of another's power; and therefore he that hath least power, hath always least honour."[16] This idea that honor is given by others runs fairly consistently from Hobbes's early to his mature works.[17]

HOBBES'S EARLY UNDERSTANDING

Leo Strauss, in his *Political Philosophy of Hobbes, Its Basis and Genesis*, argued that Hobbes's ideas on honor evolved from a humanistic view in his early works to a modern utilitarian view of honor in his mature works. He argued that, at first, Hobbes was able to pay homage to honor as a warlike virtue, thereby still acknowledging an older aristocratic understanding of the term. But as he developed his theory further, his emphasis on the primacy of fear would not allow him to give any recognition to honor as a useful or socially admirable quality. Strauss writes:

> While Hobbes could still say in the *Elements* "the only law of actions in war is *honour*," in the *Leviathan* he says: "*Force and Fraud*, are in warre the two Cardinall vertues." When Hobbes replaces "honour" by "force and fraud," he gives us to understand that what he formerly esteemed as "honour" he has now detected as fundamentally unjust and a pretext for injustice.[18]

Devin Stauffer further explains Strauss's view that the

> antithesis between vanity and the fear of violent death is a "moral and humanist antithesis," . . . insofar as it expresses a distinction between moral and immoral intentions. The moral judgment expressed by Hobbes's crucial antithesis guided his ever more emphatic rejection, over the course of his life, of all notions of virtue that praise valor and insist that men are sometimes morally obligated to risk their lives. In particular, Hobbes became increasingly critical of the principle of honor as he developed "a progressively more and more decided criticism of aristocratic virtue." . . . At the same time, Hobbes came increasingly to see the fear of violent death as the "sufficient motive for right behavior," as the "power which makes men see" by piercing through the "cocoon of vain dreams" that man weaves about himself in his effort to deceive himself about "the horror of his natural situation."[19]

This contrast between the older aristocratic view of honor as admirable and necessary, and the modern, more "utilitarian" view of honor as hollow, useless, and perhaps even dangerous, is helpful for us as we try to place exactly what Hobbes's views on honor were, and especially as we try to understand their significance for political thought. In this section, I will trace Hobbes's use of the term honor, and related terms such as valor, courage, and shame, from Hobbes's early to late works. My goal is to further the project of tracing Hobbes's idea of honor through time, to develop a better understanding of how and why he arrived at such a forthright dismissal of honor in his later works.

EARLY WORKS

The *Horae Subsecivae* (Idle Hours) was a book that appeared in 1620 by an anonymous author or authors, and it was on this work that Arlene Saxonhouse had written her dissertation. She suspected that Hobbes was the author of at least some of this work. If Hobbes was the author of some or all of it, the *Horae Subsecivae* could provide unique insight into the early development of his political thought (prior to 1640), much earlier than previously thought possible.[20] Later in her career, Saxonhouse had the opportunity to collaborate with Noel Reynolds to conduct statistical wordprint analysis of the works in the *Horae Subsecivae*, and the results were encouraging. Three discourses could be "confidently attributed to Hobbes" because the vocabulary and syntax were so similar to Hobbes's known works.[21] These three discourses were, "A Discourse upon the Beginning of Tacitus," "A Discourse of Rome," and "A Discourse of Laws." I will not attempt a complete analysis of these discourses. But the three works uncovered by Reynolds and Saxonhouse, especially the "Discourse on Tacitus," do provide some insights into Hobbes's early use and understanding of honor.

While the determination of authorship is still controversial, the argument of Saxonhouse and Reynolds is a fairly convincing one, resting not only on Reynolds's statistical analysis but also on Saxonhouse's content analysis. From my own reading, I believe that there is good reason to suspect that these are Hobbes's works. Robert Kraynak, reviewing the book, was likewise convinced that at least two of the three works were Hobbes's, primarily because of Saxonhouse's content analysis. But, "While the discourses on Tacitus and the laws seem like embryonic Hobbes, the discourse on Rome does not."[22] For Kraynak the latter discourse seems to be written by a devout Protestant, not a skeptic such as Hobbes. I am not as convinced by this counterargument, since it is possible that Hobbes's attitude toward religion was in transition, and it is also true that Hobbes even in his mature years could sound fairly devout when he wanted to, especially when criticizing Catholics. Todd Butler has made a persuasive argument that this discourse is very characteristic of Hobbes because of its focus on the power of image and rhetoric to move people for good or for ill.[23] John C. Fortier likewise has questioned Hobbes's authorship of the "Discourse of Laws," indicating that the authors did not successfully rule out the authorship of Francis Bacon using statistical word print analysis, and indeed that their analysis may lend more weight to the idea that Bacon wrote that particular essay. He also musters evidence that the "Discourse of Laws" contains up to 30 percent content from a previously unknown essay by Bacon whose authorship has been established, again calling into question Saxonhouse's and Reynolds's methodology. He reasonably points out that "wordprint analysis may be foiled when the most serious candidates for authorship worked together as closely as did Hobbes, Bacon [for whom Hobbes briefly served as secretary] and Cavendish."[24]

At any rate, it is fair to say that while we cannot be absolutely certain about the authorship of these essays even now, there is enough evidence to merit their analysis as a *part* of this study. If we were to use them alone as evidence of Hobbes's early position, they would not be enough. But as a source of supplementary information, they are useful. Therefore, for purposes of this study, I will treat them as if they were Hobbes's, but alongside other works whose authorship has not been disputed. It is important to acknowledge the efforts of Saxonhouse and Reynolds and put their scholarship to good use as providing supplementary texts that, *in addition to other more known works*, add more to our knowledge of Hobbes's early frame of mind. As Butler writes, it is important to read these works alongside others whose authorship has never been disputed:

> Rather than looking immediately ahead to such texts, I contend that it is more fair and productive to read the discourses alongside Hobbes's first major publication and their near contemporary, his translation of the *Eight Books*, published in 1629 though likely completed much earlier. Doing so provides additional and substantive grounds for considering these essays as Hobbes's work, for together the discourses and the translation of Thucydides share a common concern over how, owing to the nature of the human mind, any image—verbal or visual—could influence political action.[25]

In some ways, these discourses reveal that Hobbes's thinking on important topics such as civil breakdown and the role of government was already quite formed, well before the impact of the English Civil War.[26] This may have had a lot to do with his early interest in Thucydides' *History of the Peloponnesian War*. As noted, Hobbes's first published work in his own name was his translation of Thucydides' *History*. The three discourses show that Hobbes had learned political lessons from Thucydides that he would carry forward into his more mature political thought. For instance, in the "Discourse on Tacitus" he opines "The manifold miseries that do accompany Civil Wars, and the extreme weakness which follows them, do commonly so deject and expose a State to the prey of ambitious men, that if they lose not their liberty, it is only for want of one that has the courage to take the advantage of their debility."[27] Time and again he treats civil breakdown in this way, as lamentable, not admirable, even if in the name of liberty. As he says, "civil war is the worst thing that can happen to a State."[28]

Yet in other respects, Hobbes's tone does seem different from that in his more mature works. For instance, just within the first discourse, there are two references to "feminine" or "effeminate" qualities in people, and these descriptions are decidedly negative in a way that resonates with earlier chivalric notions of courageous manhood. For instance, he refers to Antony as "already vanquished with effeminate passions, and [having] his heart chained to the delight of a woman."[29] In "A Discourse of Rome," he uses the term in much the same way when he writes that, "a life of pleasure does so besot and benumb the senses, and so far effeminate the spirits of men, that though they be naturally prone to an active life, yet custom has brought them to such a habit, that they apprehend not any thing farther than the compass of their own affections; think nothing beyond their present enjoyments."[30] Of course, Hobbes was still capable of using the word "effeminate" in much later works, but with less of a sense of stigma attached to it. In *Leviathan*, he excuses both women and men of "feminine courage" for running away in battle (more on this topic in chapter 3). In this case, the reader does not sense that "effeminate" is terribly pejorative, but more descriptive.

Likewise, in these early discourses, Hobbes uses the term "valor" in a way that thinkers like de Charny, as well as many of Hobbes's contemporaries, would have understood, as descriptive of manly courage and skill. For instance he comments that, "Soldiers are most commonly needy, and next to valor, they think there cannot be a greater virtue than liberality."[31] It is treated as entirely positive when Hobbes writes that, "in the opinion of Augustus, when a Prince has a Minister of valor, and worth, which may make him capable of great place, the meanness of his birth ought to be no bar to his rising."[32] In "A Discourse of Rome," Hobbes associates valor with bravery in a very traditional way when he writes, "a place of hardness, and a life exercised in actions of valor and not idleness, has ever produced the bravest men, and arrived at the greatest fortune."[33] This is nothing if not a confirmation of the traditional manly and heroic ideals, similar enough to words de Charny employed. As Hobbes writes of the Italian countryside, pointing out his impression of its relative lack of fertility, and wondering along with his fellow Englishmen how such a place produced the great Roman Empire, he argues that it takes this type of poor environment to produce men tough enough to display such "worthiness, and Valor."[34]

When it comes to the use of the term "honor" itself, Hobbes provides a straightforward definition in one place in the "Discourse on Tacitus" when he writes, "Besides, Agrippa, in that he was a good Soldier, deserved to have the reward of his virtue, which is honor."[35] Agrippa was the minister that Augustus esteemed as having valor and worth. From this, one would think that Hobbes adopted the rather traditional view that honor was a result of virtue, indeed as he said, virtue's reward. Clearly Agrippa's virtue was not strictly moral virtue but martial virtue and loyalty to Augustus. "For men reward the success of actions done on their behalves, rather than the labor, and virtue, or the danger which they expose themselves unto in the same."[36] This bit of cynicism at the end reminds us that we are probably dealing with Hobbes, who even at this point winked at the value of moral virtue and kept his eye mainly on success and failure. Nonetheless, in this passage honor is not simply about power but about the recipient's worth, based upon his valor. Augustus is shown bestowing honors on others for different reasons, however. In one case, Augustus makes Livia's son Nero heir to his throne instead of his own son, whom he allows to be driven into exile. Hobbes says that Augustus bestowed on Nero this "honor." And yet, Hobbes passes judgment on this decision in his next paragraph:

> I have not found so great a defect in Augustus's judgment, in all his former actions, as in this, so far to follow her will, as to banish and confine his own blood, for the advancement of hers. But, as Tacitus says, he was now grown old, and so the weakness that accompanies old age may excuse that fault, which in his younger, and more mature judgment, peradventure he would never have committed.[37]

Later in the same paragraph, Hobbes characterizes Augustus's decisions as "the weak judgment of an old man." His entire treatment of this episode smells of shame. Hobbes judges that Augustus had become an unmanly, doddering fool, able to be led around by his scheming wife. Any honor he gave to Nero was no real honor because of the source of it, not to mention the character of the recipient.

Hobbes also associates honor with defense of country in the Tacitus discourse, making a bold statement after translating a passage about Roman war against the Germans: "Wars are necessary only where they are just, and just only in case of defense. First, of our lives, secondly, of our right, and lastly, of our honor."[38] "Our lives" is self-explanatory. Presumably "our right" refers to what is rightfully ours but has been taken. But what of honor? Hobbes explains that the honor of states is more important than the honor of even great leaders, and it becomes clear that by honor he means "reputation." He notes that often a country is made more strong and secure by its military reputation than its actual military power. It is a necessity to uphold your country's honor or reputation so that it will not be tried by its enemies. In this example, Hobbes's thought seems not too far from where it would end up, because honor is to be equated with others' estimation of a country's power. Interestingly, war for empire or other gain is discounted by Hobbes as against the "Law of God."

In "A Discourse of Laws," Hobbes only uses the word "honor" twice, and in both cases in a way similar to that discussed above. In fact, he again closely associates a country's honor with its reputation, saying, "it is the greatest honor and reputation, a Kingdom, or commonwealth can be ambitious of, and enjoy, to have Justice justly distributed, and people obedient to the Laws" and, "Next to the honor of a Kingdom, is the safety of the King."[39] In this case, though the cause of the honor is the internal strength and tranquility of the people, nevertheless, Hobbes refers to international reputation as the fruit of this internal harmony, holding that any commonwealth that neglects its internal order "gives advantage to their enemies, and causes their disreputation to spread through the world."[40] This is a very similar argument to one he would make later in *Leviathan* and elsewhere, placing the responsibility for peace among nations squarely on their governments' strength and ability to deter their enemies. David Boucher notes, "In *A Dialogue between a Philosopher and a Student of the Common Laws of England*, the philosopher contends that 'the most visible advantage is then, when the one Nation is obedient to their King, and the other not.' This, of course, is a salutary warning that internal security has profound implications for external security."[41]

Again, and even dealing with the honor of individuals, Hobbes seems closer than first appears to his more mature view of honor. He makes a distinction between honor and virtue, with honor being the outward esteem shown by others, and virtue being an inner motivation which may or may not gain honor:

> Honors sometimes be of great power, to change a man's manners and behavior into the worse, because men commonly measure their own virtues, rather by the acceptance that their persons find in the world, than by the judgment which their own conscience makes of them, and never do, or think they never need to examine those things in themselves which have once found approbation abroad, and for which they have received honor. Also honor many times confirms in men that intention wherewith they did those things which gained honor; which intention is as often vicious as virtuous. For there is almost no civil action, but may proceed as well from evil as from good; they are the circumstances of it (which be only in the mind, and consequently not seen and honored) that make

virtue. Out of all these things, I suppose, may be gathered, that honor nourishes in light and vain men a wrong opinion of their own worth, and consequently, often changes their manners into the worse, but especially that it increases their pride and insolence.[42]

Clearly in this passage, Hobbes is removing moral qualities, or considerations of virtue, from honor. Hobbes is saying that honor does not have to coincide with actual virtue, but can actually foster viciousness in its recipient, depending upon the person's initial character. Still, in Hobbes's words and tone there is the sense that the type of character who responds to honor in this way is not admirable, or that it would be better to be virtuous, which is not quite the same as the position Hobbes adopted later in which honor was almost entirely rhetorical, devoid of moral content. Nevertheless, Hobbes had already come quite far in developing his cynicism about honor in this passage. Likewise, in "A Discourse of Rome," Hobbes's treatment of the pope and other Catholic officials includes the use of the term "honor" in much the same way as he would use it in *Leviathan* and *Behemoth*, as the esteem of others based upon power and influence. He depicts these officials as selfishly vying for honor due, and not having honor bestowed upon them due to their piety.[43] But there is a tone of shaming in his writing, as though this is not the best attitude for men of the cloth.

In sum, if the discourses discussed above are Hobbes's works, we can conclude that even in 1620, Hobbes's ideas were in some ways quite characteristic of his later views, but not completely. He recognizes true manly valor and true honor as admirable, but also recognizes that men often deal in honor cynically. At this point, he has not developed a political theory for tackling this human weakness that causes so much turmoil. In other words, the discourses show a mixed treatment of the idea of honor, but they are not indisputably Hobbes's. Luckily, we have two other early works to consider.

HOBBES'S TRANSLATION OF THUCYDIDES

We can find some corroboration for Hobbes's having a mixed definition of the word "honor" in his early career in his commentary on Thucydides, which was published with his 1640 translation of the *History of the Peloponnesian War*. In his dedicatory letter to the younger Sir William Cavendish, the term "honor" abounds, as is to be expected, and it is always used sincerely. It is associated with good birth and fine character qualities. He tells William, for instance, "I had the honour to serve him [William's father], I know this: there was not any, who more really, and less for glory's sake favoured those that studied the liberal arts liberally, than my Lord your father did."[44] Here,

Hobbes distinguishes honor from glory, and indeed almost makes the two opposites in worthiness: honor is something Hobbes has been given by being associated with a man of good character, and partly what distinguishes a man of good character is that he *does not* pursue learning and accomplishments for the feeling of glory, but presumably for their own sake. Hobbes depicts the elder Cavendish as a magnanimous man, an aristocrat who treated equals equally and "inferiors familiarly; but maintaining his respect fully, and only with the native splendour of his worth. In sum, he was one in whom might plainly be perceived, that *honour* and *honesty* are but the same thing in the different degrees of persons."[45] The term "honor" here seems to hold genuine moral worth. It is not an empty rhetorical shell that really signifies power, but instead it is the result of real moral qualities in the individual. Hobbes even mentions at one point the "heroic virtues," presumably of the elder Cavendish, from which his son was able to benefit. In commending Thucydides to William, Hobbes writes:

> For in history, actions of *honour* and *dishonour* do appear plainly and distinctly, which are which; but in the present age they are so disguised, that few there be, and those very careful, that be not grossly mistaken in them. But this, I doubt not, is superfluously spoken by me to your Lordship.[46]

Again, honor and dishonor are moral qualities, deserving William's attention and pursuit. Hobbes distinguishes between the past understanding of honor, which was straightforward, and the current state of honor—its true qualities are lost upon most people. William is depicted as astute enough to be able to distinguish between honor and dishonor in a morally confused age, and he is commended for his natural preference for honor.

As he did in his commentary on the elder Cavendish (which was only to be expected), so (and more significantly) in his treatment of Thucydides, Hobbes associates honor partly with good birth. He mentions more than once that Thucydides was honorable because of his aristocratic lineage, and would have been remembered for that fact alone, even if he had not written a history. Thucydides, he notes, was descended from Thracian kings, and "was of the house of Miltiades, that famous general of the Athenians against the Persians at Marathon." Expressing himself in a way reminiscent of writers like de Charny, Hobbes argues that Thucydides' name would have been well known for that reason alone, "in regard of his honour and nobility."[47]

In this brief life of Thucydides, Hobbes often uses the words "honor" and "dishonor" in the traditional sense, as when he comments that nothing Thucydides wrote about Athens brought "dishonour" upon Athenians as such, but upon particular people,[48] making dishonor a moral judgment against them.

Defending Thucydides against the criticism of Dionysius Halicarnassius, Hobbes further refines his understanding of honor to include the idea of intellectual honesty. Dionysius criticized Thucydides for not portraying Athens in a positive light in his *History* and therefore being disloyal. Thucydides argued, for instance, that the war was instigated by Athens because of her threatening growth in power. But Hobbes staunchly defends Thucydides, stating that honor does not require blind loyalty, nor does it require Thucydides to lie about his country's actions in the war. Instead, Hobbes characterizes such honesty as honorable. Hobbes favorably compares Thucydides to Herodotus (whom Dionysius prefers), noting that Thucydides did his country more of a service through telling the truth than Herodotus did through his stories, because Thucydides' arguments were "profitable to posterity,"[49] that is, useful for avoiding future mistakes. Thucydides' action in writing the *History* was honorable, even if he depicted Athenian actions "that were not to the honour of his country."[50] The latter reference to dishonor certainly refers to the military losses Athens suffered, but also to some of Athens's more morally dubious actions, including Athens's harsh treatment of the small island city of Melos. Dionysius claims Thucydides puts Athens in a bad light by making Athenians seem unjust and ruthless. But Hobbes answers that he does not doubt that the Athenians treated cities like Melos this way, and that Thucydides was simply portraying events honestly.[51]

We should not take the point too far, however, and argue that Hobbes's view was totally in line with a traditional, moral view of honor. Clearly he learned a great deal from Thucydides' Athenians who, especially in their dialogue with the Melians, discounted the value of honor and seemed to do what Hobbes would do more clearly later, make raw power the real source of honor. At the end of his commentary on Thucydides' life, Hobbes implies that the reason Dionysius praised Herodotus (a Halicarnassian and therefore Dionysius's countryman) over Thucydides is that Dionysius wanted to knock Thucydides' reputation down so that his own reputation could rise, and "by this computation he saw the honour of the best historiographer falling on himself."[52] Here, honor is clearly selfishly pursued without reference to moral virtue. The modern sense also comes out in Hobbes's footnotes to the *History*, as when he comments in book 1 that in ancient times robbing was an honorable profession, a point about the relativity of perceptions of honor that he continued to make throughout his scholarly career.[53] The modern sense is also apparent when Hobbes comments on a speech by Spartan ambassadors in book 4. The ambassadors call for a peace treaty because many of their best men have been captured in Pylos by the Athenians. At the end of their speech, the Spartans say, "Wherein consider how many commodities are like to ensue. For if we and you go one way, you know the

rest of Greece, being inferior to us, will honour us in the highest degree."
Hobbes's note reads:

> Conveying to the understanding of the wiser sort of hearers, the consideration
> of tyrannizing the rest of Greece. For by the highest honour, he means tyranny;
> but avoiding the envy of the word. Because if he had said it plainly, the confed-
> erates would see, that they which termed themselves the *Deliverers of Greece*,
> would now out of private interest, be content to join with the Athenians to tyr-
> annize it.[54]

Here, Hobbes notices that the term honor is used rhetorically as a cover for
the desire for power stemming from self-interest. But in another note, Hobbes
says about the Athenians "having made a necessary league with Perdiccas,"
that the term "necessary" meant "or scarce honorable,"[55] which seems to use
the term in the more traditional sense—that is, an alliance made out of necessity (rather than right) is not honorable.

As in the discourses, we see in *Hobbes's Thucydides* a mixed treatment of
the idea of honor, with both the more traditional view and the more modern
view commonly associated with Hobbes's later works. This confirms the impression made upon us by the discourses: Hobbes still admired true honor, but
noticed that much of the world did not. He had not yet provided a solution to
this problem.

THE ELEMENTS OF LAW

Hobbes completed *The Elements of Law* in 1640. In it, he explored human
physiology and explained the way people think and communicate with each
other on the basis of that physiology. He defined human nature and developed
his theory of the state of nature. He proposed the social contract, advocated
absolutism, and dealt with the obstacles in the way of good government. Most
parts of his mature political thought were in place at this point, though they
would be modified and elaborated upon as Hobbes continued to write, the effort of a lifetime culminating in his *Leviathan* of 1651.

At the beginning of *Elements*, Hobbes used the term "honor" in the traditional sense, in his dedicatory letter to William, Earl of Newcastle, calling
him "My Most Honoured Lord," and stating that "I desire no greater honour
than I enjoy already in your Lordship's known favour."[56] But in the first part
of the book itself, where Hobbes is dealing with human physiology and human nature, he treats honor as a natural human desire to which man has an
appetite. He uses it as an example of how the mind moves from one thought
to the next, "As when a man, from the thought of honour to which he hath an

appetite, cometh to the thought of wisdom, which is the next means thereto; and from thence to the thought of study, which is the next means to wisdom."[57] This is interesting because, while Hobbes does treat honor here as an object of natural desire instead of a quality of character others recognize, he also says that the means of obtaining honor (just as an example, though) is study which produces wisdom. As we will see, this does not reflect his later stance that, at least in civil society, honor comes from power—for instance, that those whom the sovereign wants to give honor will have honor, quite regardless of whether they are somehow intellectually or morally qualified.

As we will see, Hobbes's position hardens in *Leviathan*, though it does not ever become completely solidified in the sense of entirely rejecting older meanings. But in *The Elements of Law*, Hobbes's first serious treatment of honor comes before he clearly defines what it is, and the use of it in his example reflects the older notion, that honor is something earned through merit, in this case the merit of having obtained wisdom, which is something a man can obtain by himself without reference to having power himself or having powerful associates. This is closer to the traditional view of a thinker such as de Charny. However, de Charny goes much further with that core thought than Hobbes does, by holding that the strong can be unwise and unjust and therefore dishonorable, and that the separation of honor from power is the main political problem.

In chapter 7 of the first part of *Elements*, discussing the endlessness of man's appetites, Hobbes again puts honor into the category of human desires, this time along with riches, "or other power." So it would seem here that honor is a form of power, (which is not the same as his eventual view that honor *emanates* from power). Near the end of the chapter Hobbes states that "labour and honour" are inseparable, "for the most part."[58] This would imply that, at least most of the time, honor is not simply an artifact of who you know, or how powerful or rich you are, but in this case, what you actually do. But it is in chapter 8 that we come to that part of the *Elements* that corresponds the most to Hobbes's treatment of honor in chapter 10 of *Leviathan*.

In chapter 8 of the *Elements*, a discussion of honor is preceded by a discussion of sensual pleasures, and the conception of power. Hobbes considers three kinds of conception: present (sense itself), past (remembrance of sensory experiences), and thought of the future (extrapolating from past sensory experiences what the future may hold). He proceeds through an analysis of the senses, observing that our pleasure or displeasure in various sensual experiences is a result more of our individual perspective than a direct result of the thing sensed. He then hones in on our thoughts about the future, declaring that in order to hope for pleasure in the future, a man must conceive of some power within himself that can bring these pleasures to him. By power here he means "the same with the faculties of body and mind, mentioned in the first chapter, that is to say, of the body, nutritive, generative, motive; and of the mind, knowledge. And besides those, such farther powers, as by them acquired (viz.) riches, place of authority, friendship or favour, and good fortune."[59] He then makes power relative, observing that one man's power can hinder another's, so that "power simply is no more, but the excess of the power of one above that of another."[60]

Next, Hobbes says that the sign by which we know our own power is our very actions, but the sign by which others acknowledge our power is through their actions, attitude and speech toward us. This is when honor is introduced in the chapter, because "the acknowledgment of power is called HONOUR; and to honour a man (inwardly in the mind) is to conceive or acknowledge, that that man hath the odds or excess of power above him that contendeth or compareth himself. And HONOURABLE are those signs for which one man acknowledgeth power or excess above his concurrent in another."[61]

Still, while Hobbes's discussion of honor is very much tied to power, the power Hobbes is referring to here is power that comes from within—the actual abilities and attributes of the person under discussion. This is clear from the examples that follow. For instance, beauty can bring honor, because beauty is a sign of health and ability to reproduce. Actions of bodily strength are honorable because they are signs of physical power that can bring victory in battle. Teaching and other powers to persuade are honorable "because they be signs of knowledge."[62] Gifts, clothing, and great houses are honorable because they are signs of riches. Hobbes has argued (above) that riches are acquired by personal traits such as strength and knowledge. Nobility is honorable because it is a sign of powerful ancestors (past prestige). Interestingly, authority is honorable "because a sign of strength, wisdom, favour or riches by which it is attained."[63] Finally, good fortune is honorable "because a sign of the favour of God . . ."[64]

Hobbes is saying that authority comes from a wide variety of sources. Strength is listed first, but next is wisdom. Wisdom is listed alongside favor and riches, as though equal to them. While previous thinkers might not approve of the equivalency in this statement, as though strength, social connections, and riches are on a par with wisdom as qualifications for authority, from the point of view of Hobbes's later work, this relative openness to the independent authority of knowledge is telling. It shows that Hobbes's thought on honor had not yet been reduced to seeing it as solely a product of physical power.

But Hobbes is consistent with his later work in defining glory as the pleasure men have in the signs of honor others give them, a topic that he discusses extensively in the ninth chapter. Whereas honor is something external to ourselves, something others must give, glory is the "internal gloriation or triumph of the mind," a passion "which proceedeth from the imagination or conception of our own power, above the power of him that contendeth with us."[65] While Hobbes does say that glory can be justified if it is based upon a true experience of our own actions, most of his treatment of glory is negative, playing up that part of human nature that is vain and presumptuous. Signs of glorying he lists include "ostentation in words, and insolency in actions."[66] Fame and trusting other people's evaluation (which may be mere flattery) Hobbes calls false glory, whereas he defines vainglory as the imagination that a man has done great things which he has not done, thinking that things unrelated to his own actions should be attributed to him. Hobbes treats vainglory here as a sort of delusion of the mind, whereas false glory is a delusion caused by others. In contrast with Hobbes's treatment of honor, where his tone is fairly neutral or even positive, his treatment of glory is mainly negative. We know from understanding Hobbes's thought as a whole that it is glorying or pride which he believes to be the main source of political instability in his world.[67]

But in a surprising concurrence with earlier chivalric thought like de Charny's, Hobbes contrasts men who are motivated by sensual delights with those who are motivated by honor and glory. He describes the former men as "addicted" to ease, food, and the like, and while he does not call them unmanly, he does call them dishonorable. They pursue fleeting pleasures which "taketh away the inclination to observe such things as conduce to honour; and consequently maketh men less curious, and less ambitious, whereby they less consider the way either to knowledge or to other power; in which two consisteth all the excellency of power cognitive."[68] This certainly shows that Hobbes had not yet let go of his admiration for truly honorable men.

An interesting development in chapter 17 of *Elements* has Hobbes sounding more like the Hobbes of *Leviathan*, at least on the issue of hereditary privilege and/or wisdom as sources of honor. Here he starts by saying, "The question, which is the better man, is determinable only in the estate of government and policy, though it be mistaken for a question of nature, not only by ignorant men, that think one man's blood better than another's by nature; but also by him, whose opinions are at this day, and in these parts of greater authority than any other human writings (Aristotle)."[69] In so saying, Hobbes seems to question what he previously had said about honor, in the *Elements* and in earlier works, that both birth and wisdom could be independent sources of honor and authority. Here he argues that whenever anyone thinks that some special quality makes him more qualified to have authority over others, that some are born to lead and others to serve, he has invented a means to disturb the peace.

This is because human beings will never be able to agree on who is qualified to have influence and who is not.[70] Hobbes reminds his readers of the history of sedition and civil wars in ancient times, when usually those of "coarser wits" eventually won in conflicts started by the presumption of those of "finer" wits. Because of this natural human reaction to presumption, "as long as men arrogate to themselves more honour than they give to others, it cannot be imagined how they can possibly live in peace: and consequently we are to suppose, that for peace sake, nature hath ordained this law, *That every man acknowledge other for his equal.* And the breach of this law, is that we call PRIDE."[71] Here we see the logic for rejecting honor as not socially and politically useful, an argument which Hobbes would retain and elaborate upon in later works.

Notice that Hobbes is not denying that we can distinguish between finer and coarser wits, or even that ideally the finer should rule the coarser sorts, but only that men will not easily accept any such claim to superiority. Because of this unwillingness, aristocratic claims are bound to lead to social conflict. So here the quest for honor appears presumptuous and prideful—one might even say undemocratic, except we know that democracy is not where Hobbes is taking us. Instead, he is heading toward his argument for absolute monarchy as the best form of government, a monarchy built upon his new ideas of equality in the state of nature and the fear it produces, a monarchy which through its absolute power will level everyone else in society.[72]

While honor may ultimately be out of place in civil society even in this early political treatise, we have seen that Hobbes still clung to it as something admirable when it was genuine. Additionally, in this work, Hobbes does seem to reserve a positive place for honor in the midst of war. Whereas in civil society the law of nature dictates sociability, justice, equity, and peace, in war Hobbes acknowledges that a man's only protection is "to be formidable" through his own power. So while civil society consists of "equity and justice, the latter [war] consisteth in actions of honour."[73] Hobbes's use of the term "honor" when it comes to war reverts back to the older medieval definition— honor in the sense of physical strength and prowess, a sense that de Charny would easily recognize. In chapter 19 of *Elements*, we can see some evidence that Hobbes used the term to mean restraint in warfare. Again writing of war, Hobbes teaches that the "law of nature commandeth in war: that men satiate not the cruelty of their present passions, whereby in their own conscience they foresee no benefit to come."[74] David Boucher comments "In *The Elements of Law*, Hobbes contends that the law of nature commands us in war not to be carried away by our passions and indulge in gratuitous cruelty with no prospect of future benefit. A mind disposed to cruelty without necessity is at variance with the law of nature."[75]

Hobbes gives an example of honorable fighting from ancient times, when marauders spared not only their enemies' lives but also their means of subsistence. Again, Hobbes identifies honor in war with restraint:

> For nothing but fear can justify the taking away of another's life. And because fear can hardly be made manifest, but by some action dishonourable, that bewrayeth the conscience of one's own weakness; all men in whom the passion of courage or magnanimity have been predominant, have abstained from cruelty; insomuch that though there be in war no law, the breach whereof is injury, yet there are those laws, the breach whereof is dishonour. In one word, therefore, the only law of action in war is honour; and the right of war providence.[76]

Just as when Hobbes distinguished between the soft man addicted to sensual pleasures and the man motivated by honor and power, we get the sense that Hobbes's comments here reflect traditional chivalric ideas of warfare. His words have the effect of shaming much as did de Charny's, and conversely of setting up an ideal of manly behavior—that of courage and magnanimity. By inference, cruelty is associated with cowardice. So, whereas honor may be a problem in civil society insomuch as it causes conflict among those who make their claims for it, honor in war, where there is no civil society, is the closest thing to law possible. In war, honor is actually enjoined by the law of nature; but in civil society, humility is enjoined instead. In fact, the competition of men within civil society for honor can actually make that society weaker not only domestically but in foreign affairs. This is because "by the diversity of judgments and passions in so many men contending naturally for honour and advantage one above another: it is impossible, not only that their consent to aid each other against an enemy, but also that the peace should last between themselves, without some mutual and common fear to rule them."[77]

It remains for us to wonder how men, used to being leveled and made peaceable due to fear of the absolute power of a sovereign, will have the character to exercise honor on the battlefield, but that subject will be taken up in another chapter.[78] We find in *The Elements of Law*, still, a mixed treatment of honor. Hobbes treats honor as coming from real character qualities, such as wisdom and courage. But he also sees honor as a harmful object of desire. He acknowledges that honor-seeking for many men without good character devolves into glory-seeking, or vainglory, and he is able to see this as a source, if not the main source, of domestic conflict. Even before the English Civil War, Hobbes was aware that honor was so often falsely and selfishly pursued that it was more a source of conflict than of self-restraint, at least in domestic relations. While he still accepts the idea of honor as being the only restraint possible in warfare, he is not willing to rely upon it as a source of restraint in civil society. Instead, people must submit to an all-powerful

sovereign that will keep them in check. So, in the *Elements*, we see Hobbes
still capable of appreciating true honor, but already choosing the path that
would lead to the cynical treatment of honor that appears so prominently in
his mature works.

DE CIVE AND LEVIATHAN

Hobbes published *De Cive* (The Citizen) in Latin in 1642, but translated it
into English in 1651, the same year he published *Leviathan*. The English
translation of *De Cive*, then, can be seen as contemporaneous with *Leviathan*,
and, if anything, is even more forthright about the place it assigns honor. In
De Cive, honor is the source of mankind's antisocial sociability—it draws
men together for competition, not over material things but over status. In his
account of how man compares to the animals (an answer to Aristotle's assessment of human nature), Hobbes makes it abundantly clear that desire for
honor is precisely what makes us different from the animals. "For, first,
among them there is a contestation of honour and preferment; among beasts
there is none: whence hatred and envy, out of which arise sedition and war, is
among men; among beasts no such matter."[79] Most of the other differences
with the animals Hobbes mentions next, such as the desire for eminence, the
love of showing off our wisdom, and so on, refer back to the natural human
desire for honor.[80] Also in *De Cive*, Hobbes states that it is often those who
do the least, and thus do not deserve it, who want honor the most. All men
want honor, he writes, "but chiefly they, who are least troubled with caring
for necessary things."[81] As we will see in the next chapter, these types of comments fit quite well with Hobbes's overall assessment of the role of the gentry and nobility in the English Civil War.

Recall that in *The Elements of Law*, we were able to see Hobbes arguing in
places that honor can come from personal qualities of character and talent. In
chapter 10 of *Leviathan*, the chapter in which Hobbes attempts at length to
define honor, he does, through some of his definitions, argue that power can
come through personal qualities not related to force. But unlike in *The Elements of Law*, he makes a clear distinction in the same chapter between natural powers (and the instrumental powers that flow from them) and those that
are artificially created, thus drawing more attention to the distinction and its
political significance.[82] "*Natural power*, is the eminence of the faculties of
body, or mind: as extraordinary strength, form, prudence, arts, eloquence, liberality, nobility. *Instrumental* are those powers, which acquired by these, or
by fortune, are means and instruments to acquire more: as riches, reputation,
friends, and the secret working of God, which men call good luck."[83] So far,

Hobbes's discussion of natural powers seems fairly in agreement with his argument in *Elements*, which makes personal qualities sources of power, apart from the will of a sovereign or of law. Hobbes continues listing personal qualities, even mentioning personal good form, which meets with the approval of women, giving men power over them!

Still writing in the section that deals with natural powers, Hobbes discusses the relative quality of power from all these sources. At least ideally, from the older aristocratic point of view, a man was honorable because of his wisdom and moral qualities, and we have seen that Hobbes's earlier works represented this older view part of the time. An honorable man was worthy because of the type of person he was—his quality, his character, his courage, that is, worthy in an absolute sense, regardless of whether others recognized him as such. However, as we have also seen, he does discuss honor's relative quality in earlier works as well, the idea that honor is something others give, and thus dependant upon their opinion, and not always deserved. However, Hobbes plays up the relative quality of power even more in *Leviathan*, chapter 10, where he argues that the "*value*, or WORTH of a man, is as of all other things, his price; that is to say, so much as would be given for the use of his power: and therefore is not absolute; but a thing dependant on the need and judgment of another."[84]

After making this statement, he then proceeds to define honor:

> The manifestation of the value we set on one another, is that which is commonly called honouring, and dishonouring. To value a man at a high rate, is to *honour* him; at a low rate, is to *dishonour* him. But high, and low, in this case, is to be understood by comparison to the rate that each man setteth upon himself.[85]

So, honor is relative not only because it is dependant on others' opinions of us, but also because it is dependant on our own estimation of self-worth. After making this observation, Hobbes proceeds to describe all the ways that people can show honor and dishonor to each other. Still in the section discussing natural power, Hobbes argues that to ask someone for help is to honor him. To obey is to honor, too, because in both cases, there is an acknowledgement of the superior power of another.[86] In all the examples Hobbes uses, the common denominator is the acknowledgement of superior power, which Hobbes sometimes refers to as "valuing" another. For instance, Hobbes writes, "To show any sign of love, or fear of another, is to honour; for both to love, and to fear, is to value."[87] Sometimes Hobbes uses the word "approve" as well as "value" in the same way. "To imitate, is to honour; for it is vehemently to approve."[88] So Hobbes begins to emphasize the idea that power flowing from personal qualities is dependent upon others recognizing and valuing or approving of these qualities in a way that makes them want to obey or follow a person. All of this is discussed before he turns to civil power. He makes it clear that up until this point, he has been discussing sources of power that can and do exist apart from civil society, but that the matter changes once civil society has been established.

In the same chapter in which he discusses natural powers, he introduces civil power: "All these ways of honouring, are natural; and as well within, as without commonwealths. But in commonwealths, where he, or they that have the supreme authority, can make whatsoever they please, to stand for signs of honour, there be other honours."[89] Hobbes turns to a discussion of the various ways that a sovereign can define honor and bestow honors on his subjects. He calls this "civil honour,"[90] presumably to distinguish it from the natural honor he previously outlined. Here, the terms "honorable" and "dishonorable" are clearly products of power:

> *Honourable. Honourable* is whatsoever possession, action, or quality, is an argument and sign of power.
>   *Dishonourable.* And therefore to be honoured, loved, or feared of many, is honourable; as arguments of power. To be honoured of few or none, *dishonourable.*[91]

Whereas personal qualities were sources of natural power that led to honor in the first part of his argument, here it is power that bestows the quality of honor on someone, preferably in Hobbes's view the power of the sovereign, but possibly the power of anyone able to wield it. Hobbes states this idea very simply in *De Cive*, where he seems, even more clearly than in *Leviathan*, to argue that honor is a sign of power. "For honour, as hath been said in the section above, is nothing else but the estimation of another's power; and therefore he that hath the least power, hath always least honour."[92] Hobbes briefly discusses gifts, such as titles and coats of arms, that are dependent upon the will and design of the sovereign.

Hobbes explains that what is considered honorable in civil society can and does change, depending upon who is in power. He explains the existence of the nobility in this context—"Nobility is power, not in all places, but only in those commonwealths, where it has privileges: for in such privileges consisteth their power."[93] Hobbes includes in his discussion a brief explanation of various ranks, titles, insignia, and coats of arms. He is familiar with the history of the feudal system, but his main point is to show its conventional nature. Differing completely with the ideal of the nobility put forth by de Charny, at this point Hobbes concludes that there is nothing natural about the social order of superiors and inferiors, nobles and commoners. All such ranks and titles relate back to the taking of land, and the granting of privileges to those who helped to take it. Later, these ranks and privileges were assigned politically, as rewards to those whom the prince or monarch favored.

To further clarify his point about the relationship of power to the worth of a person, and to make it clear that honor in civil society is solely dependent on sovereign will, Hobbes comments at the end of chapter 10 on the difference between worth and worthiness or fitness for a particular task. Plato would argue that the person most suited to the task based upon his understanding and moral worth should undertake it. In his view, the person most suited to rule was the one who was wisest.[94] But here, Hobbes overturns that idea, echoing what he said earlier in chapter 10 of *Leviathan* on worth, and instead, arguing that fitness to do a task is no argument that one *should* do it:

> WORTHINESS, is a thing different from the worth, or value of a man; and also from his merit, or desert, and consisteth in a particular power, or ability for that, whereof he is said to be worthy: which particular ability, is usually named FITNESS, or *aptitude*.
>
> For he is worthiest to be a commander, to be a judge, or to have any other charge, that is best fitted, with the qualities required to the well discharging of it; and worthiest of riches, that has the qualities most requisite for the well using of them: any of which qualities being absent, one may nevertheless be a worthy man, and valuable for something else. Again, a man may be worthy of riches, office, and employment, that nevertheless, can plead no right to have it before another; and therefore cannot be said to merit or deserve it. For merit presupposeth a right, and that the thing deserved is due by promise: of which I shall say more hereafter, when I shall speak of contracts.[95]

The reason why Hobbes argues in this way, separating *worthiness for* and *right to* power, is clear when we remember his main agenda. Hobbes wishes to remove any reason people might have to wield independent judgment against their sovereign. If critics can argue that government is illegitimate because it is not just, or not ruled by a wise man but a selfish and craven man, there is an argument for revolt, a disaster which, even in *The Elements of Law*, Hobbes wanted to avoid at all costs. Hobbes argues that the sovereign must be firmly in charge of distributing honors, "For in sovereignty is the fountain of honour."[96] Men should not be able to put a value on themselves in a well-ordered commonwealth—the value of each man should be set by the sovereign. It is necessary, he argues, that there be "laws of honor" and that the sovereign determine what the criteria will be "to appoint what order of place, and dignity, each man shall hold; and what signs of respect, in public or private meetings, they shall give to one another."[97] Hobbes's comments are in agreement with those in *De Cive*, in his chapter on the duties of rulers:

> But because ambition and greediness of honours cannot be rooted out of the minds of men, it is not the duty of rulers to endeavor it; but by constant application of rewards and punishments, they may so order it, that men may know

that the way to honour is, not by contempt of the present government, nor by factions and the popular air, but by the contraries.[98]

Certainly Hobbes would prefer a sovereign who handed out honors based upon actual merit and loyalty, so that the commonwealth would be well served by a system of incentives. But throughout *Leviathan*, Hobbes argues strongly against holding the sovereign to any expectations for just or equitable treatment—he is the source, the very definition of justice and equity. If he wants to give undeserving cronies all the honors of the kingdom, it would be his right.

In sum, because power in civil society must be obtained from its ultimate source in the sovereign, it stands to reason that natural powers and the honors that may come from them are not relevant, or at least can be trumped by the sovereign, once civil society is established. Through reducing honorable qualities to affects of power, he makes their meaning and use as descriptors less relevant. For instance, "Covetousness of great riches, and ambition of great honours, are honourable; as signs of power to obtain them."[99] He further uncouples honor from any intrinsic moral value by distinguishing it from justice—"Nor does it alter the case of honour, whether an action, so it be great and difficult, and consequently a sign of much power, be just or unjust: for honour consisteth only in the opinion of power."[100] Hobbes must argue this because it is obvious to readers that he whom the sovereign chooses to honor may not be moral or just, but needs to be respected and honored nonetheless. He goes on to give some lengthy examples to back up this uncoupling, including noting that the ancients honored gods who did very unjust things, including rapes and adulteries. He mentions the example of pirates and highway thieves, whose occupation was once considered honorable, as well as the example of duels (which are considered honorable though they are illegal, but which Hobbes believes could be labeled dishonorable if the sovereign firmly penalized such behavior). Both of these examples are designed to show honor dependent upon sovereign power, and thus changeable, and are also found in *The Elements of Law*, and a similar example of ancient marauders is found in *De Cive*.[101]

Further proof that Hobbes is reducing honor to a consequence of power in civil society may be found in his list of classical virtues, all of which he reduces in the same way: "Magnanimity, liberality, hope, courage, confidence, are honourable; for they proceed from the conscience of power. Pusillanimity, parsimony, fear, diffidence, are dishonourable."[102] In *Leviathan* and *De Cive* both, power is the key to understanding all of the opinions men hold of each others' honor in civil society. If a man is powerful, he will be well regarded, and he will have all these other positive qualities, many of them moral, attributed to him. These are, of course, qualities to which others might give concrete definitions and treat as separate from the issue of power. The ancients, as well as medieval authorities such as de Charny, would argue that a poor and powerless man (such as Socrates or Diogenes, or a disfavored knight-errant) could have many virtuous qualities, whereas the tyrant might have none, despite his superior power. This type of observation, of course, formed the means of a critique of existing governments and leadership. For de Charny, the worth of a man was not his price or his power, but rested in his level of justice and wisdom. Good and evil had concrete meanings that may or may not have been reflected in law and leadership. Because of this, it was possible for previous thinkers to critique and judge government. But this is precisely why Hobbes dislikes the ancient and medieval views so much. This is the reason he repeatedly attacks the universities for promoting upheaval through Aristotelian moral and political philosophy.

Leviathan reflects all the ways in which Hobbes's previous thought promoted cynicism about honor, and goes beyond those works to remove more but not all inconsistencies, arguments in which honor might still be said to have some independent force. What about the issue of honor in warfare? At first, Hobbes seems to make an exception for honor in warfare in *Leviathan*, as he did in previous works. In part 2 of that *Leviathan*, Hobbes again observes that even the marauders of old (which he had previously employed as examples of the relativity of honor to power) observed the "laws of honour; that is, to abstain from cruelty, leaving to men their lives, and instruments of husbandry."[103] This seems to reflect the notion of honor as restraint in battle, an idea clearly voiced in *The Elements of Law*, chapter 19, where Hobbes states that the law of nature commands restraint in war, and that the only law of action in war is honor.[104] In *De Cive* he notes that "in the war of nation against nation a certain mean was wont to be observed," at least in ancient times.[105] However, this seems about as far as Hobbes goes with this idea of restraint in warfare in *De Cive* or *Leviathan*, and it is not as strong a statement on this topic as that made in *Elements*, as Hobbes makes these observations about the past, but not about the present.

Instead of focusing on honor as a source of restraint in warfare, Hobbes turns the tables and accuses honor of being a source of irresponsibility and extremism. "Competition of riches, honour, command, or other power, inclineth to contention, enmity, and war: because the way of one competitor, to the attaining of his desire, is to kill, subdue, supplant, or repel the other."[106] Along these lines, Hobbes's words no longer carry such a critical tone when discussing man's tendency to desire "ease, and sensual delight." Such desire does not make them unmanly, but "disposeth men to obey a common power,"[107] which is exactly what they should do. Those who *seek* honor in

war are the problem. Those who shun it are the solution. Fear of death makes
men want to be peaceful:

> On the contrary, needy men, and hardy, not contented with their present condi-
> tion; as also, all men that are ambitious of military command, are inclined to
> continue the causes of war; and to stir up trouble and sedition: for there is no ho-
> nour military but by war; nor any such hope to mend an ill game, as causing a
> new shuffle.[108]

This passage reminds readers of the view so often expressed in contemporary debates over war and national security, that it is precisely those concerned
with honor, and the display of virtues like courage (or more crudely, those who
want to express their *machismo*), who are actually responsible for wars, civil as
well as international. Hobbes could no longer afford to encourage his readers to
admire honor, even as it was expressed in battle, because he had concluded that
war is most often a result of the desire for honor—providing a sort of perverse
incentive to do things that cause destruction instead of construction. The overriding theme in *Leviathan* is that if all people could simply remember to fear
death more than they love honor, they would be able to enjoy lasting peace. In
The Elements of Law, honor was treated as a source of humanity in battle, the
difference between restraint and wanton cruelty. Here it is primarily treated as
a sign of outward worth to be desired for selfish reasons and with destructive
results—a completely different perspective on honor in society and in war.

Even in *Leviathan*, there is still the occasional ambiguity in Hobbes's treatment of honor, as when he derides vainglorious men because they are "inclined to rash engaging; and in the approach of danger, or difficulty, to retire
if they can: because not seeing the way of safety, they will rather hazard their
honour, which may be salved with an excuse; than their lives, for which no
salve is sufficient."[109] Hobbes still has some problem (as we'll see even more
in the third chapter) with running away in battle, even though he cannot rationally justify staying in the face of death. But the main problem for him is
not the running away itself, though his suggestion remains that it is cowardly,
but rather that such men are "inclined to rash engaging" in the first place.
Hobbes is showing that such men are often full of bravado until they are faced
with a real threat, and then they cower, endangering others in the process. He
is pointing out their hypocrisy and undermining the arguments men might use
to justify taking up arms and pursuing honor in battle.[110]

CONCLUSION

While Hobbes's attitude toward honor was far from wholly positive in his
earlier works, by the time he wrote *De Cive* and *Leviathan*, it was almost en-

tirely negative. Hobbes's mature thought on natural honor taught that honor was dependent on other people's perceptions. This was radically different from the views of ancient and medieval thinkers, who taught that true honor was something that many people sadly did not recognize but which did not depend on others' perceptions, because it was an absolute. Likewise, civil honor was not born from individuals' intrinsic character qualities for Hobbes, but was exclusively given by the sovereign in the forms of rank and title, and could just as easily be taken away. Hobbes concluded that both in nature (or war) and in civil society, honor was separable from morality and justice, a point he clearly stated early in his career in *The Elements of Law*, but made even more emphatically in *Leviathan*. In this way, his views on honor diverged further from previous thinkers like de Charny, who more or less equated the honorable with the moral and just life, and were willing to critique established laws and social practices on this basis.

Though Hobbes retained his views on natural powers that come from intrinsic human qualities, in his mature thought, any power that came from these qualities, and might lead to honor, was trumped by the necessity of civil order. Civil order had become such an overriding concern for Hobbes, that what at first appeared admirable, namely honor in battle, was eventually seen by him solely as a source of conflict to be eliminated. By the time he wrote *Leviathan* there was no reason, at least no reason for the development of his political science, to admire the honorable man. The honorable man was too often the troublesome man, the prideful man, the man who risked his and others' lives for false convictions and thinly veiled self-love. This is not to say that Hobbes denied that true honor, which did not start battles over insults or shallow ambitions, did not exist. As we will see, Hobbes continued to acknowledge that true honor was possible, but he came to believe it was very rare and so politically unreliable.[111] In the next chapter, we will explore how Hobbes viewed the "gentlemen" of his day (including himself), and how he viewed their role in the English Civil War. The Civil War, which intervened between his early works, such as his translation of Thucydides and *The Elements of Law*, and later works like *De Cive* and *Leviathan*, is perhaps the most important source of the hardening of his views on honor. But to truly understand why this experience pushed Hobbes in the direction of his final, modern, view of honor, we will need to examine, among other things, his analysis of the war itself.

NOTES

1. The work Hobbes would have most likely read is the Thomas Hobby translation of *The Courtier*. See *The courtier of Count Baldessar Castilio: deuided into foure bookes. Verie necessarie and profitable for young gentlemen and gentlewomen abiding*

in court, pallace, or place, done into English by Thomas Hobby (London: Iohn Wolfe, 1588).

2. There is also the problem that *The Courtier* invites a variety of interpretations, probably because of its conversational format. On this problem, see Joann Cavallo, "Joking Matters: Politics and Dissimulation in Castiglione's Book of the Courtier," *Renaissance Quarterly* 52, no. 2 (Summer 2000): 402–24. Douglas Northrup argues that this problem of differing interpretations existed when the book was first published and disseminated as well. Douglas A. Northrup, "'The Ende Therfore of a Perfect Courtier' in Baldassare Castiglione's *The Courtier*," *Philological Quarterly* 77, no. 3 (Summer 1998): 295–305.

3. Geoffroi de Charny, *The Book of Chivalry*, ed. Richard W. Kaeuper and Elspeth Kennedy (Philadelphia: University of Pennsylvania Press, 1996), para. 16–45, p. 103.

4. De Charny, *The Book of Chivalry*, para. 19–21, p. 109.

5. De Charny, *The Book of Chivalry*, para. 22–45, p. 127.

6. De Charny, *The Book of Chivalry*, para. 23–77, p. 133.

7. De Charny, *The Book of Chivalry*, para. 35–203, p. 165.

8. Shame is mentioned only seven times in *Leviathan* and several of those appear in Biblical quotations. He defines it as "Grief, for the discovery of some defect of ability." Thomas Hobbes, *Leviathan*, ed. Michael Oakeshott (New York: Simon and Schuster, 1997), part 1, ch. 6, p. 52. By contrast, honor is mentioned 287 times and fear is mentioned 297 times in the same work.

9. De Charny, *The Book of Chivalry*, para. 35–225, p. 167.

10. De Charny, *The Book of Chivalry*, para. 42–179, p. 189.

11. Thomas Hobbes, *De Cive*, ed. Sterling P. Lamprecht (Westport, Conn.: Greenwood Press, 1982), part 1, ch. 1, sect. 2, p. 24.

12. For an example of where he seems to use the two terms more loosely, see *De Cive* part 2, ch. 9, sect. 15, p. 112, where he writes "Furthermore, because by natural necessity all men wish them better, from whom they receive glory and honour, than others; but every man after death receives honour and glory from his children, sooner than from the power of any other men." It is hardly possible to imagine a man who is dead feeling glory (especially in Hobbes's system) and so it seems equated with honor here.

13. Gabriella Slomp, *Hobbes and the Political Philosophy of Glory* (New York: St. Martin's Press, 2000), 34. See Michael Oakeshott, *Hobbes on Civil Association* (Berkley: University of California Press, 1975), 35, for a similar emphasis on the distinction between honor and glory.

14. Slomp, *Hobbes*, 35.

15. Gabriella Slomp, "Hobbes on Glory and Civil Strife," in *The Cambridge Companion to Hobbes's Leviathan*, ed. Patricia Springborg (Cambridge: Cambridge University Press, 2007), 181–98.

16. Hobbes, *De Cive*, part 2, ch. 9, sect. 8, pp. 108–9.

17. "In Hobbes's works, whereas glory is one's joy to be superior to others, honour is the recognition of one's power by other individuals. Thus glory and honour are two types of reaction to an agent's power, respectively by the agent himself and by others" (Slomp, *Hobbes and the Political Philosophy of Glory*, 39).

18. Leo Strauss, *The Political Philosophy of Thomas Hobbes, Its Basis and Genesis* (Chicago: University of Chicago Press, Midway Reprint, 1984), 114.

19. Devin Stauffer, "Reopening the Quarrel between the Ancients and the Moderns: Leo Strauss's Critique of Hobbes's 'New Political Science,'" *The American Political Science Review* 101, no. 2 (May 2007): 225–26.

20. Opposed to this view where scholars who, in their attempt to critique Strauss's arguments, based their own views on the belief that *A Short Tract on First Principles* was Hobbes's first known work. Robert Gray, "Hobbes' System and His Early Philosophical Views," *Journal of the History of Ideas* 39, no. 2 (April–June 1978): 199–215. Gray used the *Tract*, some of Hobbes's letters, and his prose biography, among other sources, to argue that Hobbes's mechanistic psychology developed alongside his humanism, instead of representing a clear break. In this case, Strauss's argument would be wrong. Even as late as 1993, Peter Zagorin referred to Hobbes's *A Short Tract on First Principles* as Hobbes's "first extant" work, which could be used as "a documentary source for the roots of his metaphysics and the formation of his scientific ideas." Peter Zagorin, "Hobbes's Early Philosophical Development," *Journal of the History of Ideas* 54, no. 3 (July 1993): 505. The *Short Tract* was probably published circa 1630, but it does not contain Hobbes's political thought. It is a work of physical science and biology, so it is not as relevant here, even if it was authored by Hobbes, the position Zagorin takes. See also Arlene Saxonhouse's earlier article on how Hobbes's thought did and did not change from the *Horae* to his later political treatises, "Hobbes and the 'Horae Subsecivae,'" *Polity* 13, no. 4 (Summer 1981): 541–67.

21. Thomas Hobbes, *Three Discourses: A Critical Modern Edition of Newly Identified Work of the Young Hobbes*, ed. Noel B. Reynolds and Arlene Saxonhouse (Chicago: University of Chicago Press, 1995), viii.

22. Robert P. Kraynak, "Review: Speculations on the Earliest Writings of Hobbes," *The Review of Politics* 58, no. 4 (Autumn 1996): 815.

23. Todd Butler, "Image, Rhetoric, and Politics in the Early Thomas Hobbes," *Journal of the History of Ideas* 67, no. 3 (July 2006): 465–87.

24. John C. Fortier, "Hobbes and 'A Discourse of Laws': The Perils of Wordprint Analysis," *The Review of Politics* 59, no. 4 (Autumn 1997): 887.

25. Butler, "Image, Rhetoric, and Politics in the Early Thomas Hobbes," 467.

26. Arlene Saxonhouse wrote in 1981, "The evidence of the *Horae* would suggest that, contrary to the standard biographies, Hobbes did not spend his twenties reading romances with occasional attempts to improve his Latin style. Instead, it would appear that he was already busy analyzing political issues and laying down the foundations which the discovery of Euclid some fifteen years later could build on but not obliterate" (566). For instance, "He . . . could not accept in the *Horae* Machiavelli's positive appraisal of glory" (559). And, Hobbes characterized human nature (at least aristocratic nature) as being unable to be content with the status quo, but always wanting more, a thought that is echoed in *Elements of Law* and in *Leviathan* (applying then to all mankind) (560). "Hobbes and the 'Horae Subsecivae,'" *Polity* 13, no. 4 (Summer 1981): 541–67.

27. Thomas Hobbes, "A Discourse on Tacitus," in *Three Discourses: A Critical Modern Edition of Newly Identified Work of the Young Hobbes*, ed. Noel B. Reynolds and Arlene W. Saxonhouse (Chicago: University of Chicago Press, 1995), 37.

28. Hobbes, "A Discourse on Tacitus," 37.

29. Hobbes, "A Discourse on Tacitus," 42.

30. Thomas Hobbes, "A Discourse of Rome," in *Three Discourses: A Critical Modern Edition of Newly Identified Work of the Young Hobbes*, ed. Noel B. Reynolds and Arlene W. Saxonhouse (Chicago: University of Chicago Press, 1995), 73.

31. Hobbes, "A Discourse on Tacitus," 44.

32. Hobbes, "A Discourse on Tacitus," 50.

33. Hobbes, "A Discourse of Rome," 74.

34. Most of the "Discourse of Rome" is a critique of what Hobbes considered the superstitious Roman Catholic culture. Hobbes, "A Discourse of Rome," 75.

35. Hobbes, "A Discourse on Tacitus," 50.

36. Hobbes, "A Discourse on Tacitus," 50.

37. Hobbes, "A Discourse on Tacitus," 56.

38. Hobbes, "A Discourse on Tacitus," 59.

39. Thomas Hobbes, "A Discourse of Laws," in *Three Discourses: A Critical Modern Edition of Newly Identified Work of the Young Hobbes*, ed. Noel B. Reynolds and Arlene W. Saxonhouse (Chicago: University of Chicago Press, 1995), 108.

40. Hobbes, "A Discourse of Laws," 108.

41. David Boucher, "Inter-Community & International Relations in the Political Philosophy of Hobbes," *Polity* 23, no. 2 (Winter 1990): 226–27.

42. Hobbes, "A Discourse on Tacitus," 64–65.

43. Hobbes, "A Discourse of Rome," 97. This could be credited to Hobbes's general anti-Catholicism except he uses much the same language in later works to describe Anglican and Dissenting ministers as well.

44. Hobbes, "To the Right Honourable Sir William Cavendish," in *Hobbes's Thucydides*, ed. Richard Schlatter (New Brunswick, N.J.: Rutgers University Press, 1975), 3.

45. Hobbes, "To the Right Honourable Sir William Cavendish," 4.

46. Hobbes, "To the Right Honourable Sir William Cavendish," 4–5.

47. Hobbes, "Of the Life and History of Thucydides," in *Hobbes's Thucydides*, ed. Richard Schlatter (New Brunswick, N.J.: Rutgers University Press, 1975), 10–11.

48. Hobbes, "Of the Life and History of Thucydides," 17.

49. Hobbes, "Of the Life and History of Thucydides," 20.

50. Hobbes, "Of the Life and History of Thucydides," 22.

51. Hobbes, "Of the Life and History of Thucydides," 24–25.

52. Hobbes, "Of the Life and History of Thucydides," 26.

53. Hobbes, *Hobbes's Thucydides*, Hobbes's footnote 6 in book 1, p. 576.

54. Hobbes's footnote 3 in book 4, p. 581; referenced passage in book 4, para. 20, p. 255 of *Hobbes's Thucydides*.

55. Hobbes's footnote 37 in book 1, p. 577; referenced passage in book 1, para. 61, p. 61 of *Hobbes's Thucydides*.

56. Hobbes, *The Elements of Law*, 2nd ed., ed. Ferdinand Tonnies (London: Frank Cass and Company Limited, 1969), xv–xvi.

57. Hobbes, *The Elements of Law*, part 1, ch. 4, para. 2, pp. 13–14.

58. Hobbes, *The Elements of Law*, part 1, ch. 7, para. 8, p. 30.

59. Hobbes, *The Elements of Law*, part 1, ch. 8, para. 4, p. 34.

60. Hobbes, *The Elements of Law*, part 1, ch. 8, para. 4, p. 34.

61. Hobbes, *The Elements of Law*, part 1, ch. 8, para. 5, pp. 34–35. Hobbes says again on p. 35 "The signs of honour are those by which we perceive that one man acknowledgeth the power and worth of another."

62. Hobbes, *The Elements of Law*, part 1, ch. 8, para. 5, p. 35.

63. Hobbes, *The Elements of Law*, part 1, ch. 8, para. 5, p. 35.

64. Hobbes, *The Elements of Law*, part 1, ch. 8, para. 5, p. 35.

65. Hobbes, *The Elements of Law*, part 1, ch. 9, para. 1, pp. 36–37.

66. Hobbes, *The Elements of Law*, part 1, ch. 9, para. 1, p. 37.

67. As a sidebar, in this chapter he treats the passion of shame, which is the discovery in oneself of a defect of some kind. Coyly, Hobbes observes that "This passion, as it is a sign of infirmity, which is dishonour; so also it is a sign of knowledge, which is honour." Again, knowledge is treated here as a separate source of honor. Hobbes, *The Elements of Law*, 38. I will return to this theme in another chapter.

68. Hobbes, *The Elements of Law*, part 1, ch. 10, para. 3, p. 49.

69. Hobbes, *The Elements of Law*, part 1, ch. 17, para. 1, pp. 87–88.

70. Hobbes warns frequently in his works of men who "must needs take it ill, and be grieved with the state, as find themselves postponed to those in honour, whom they think they excel in virtue and ability to govern." *The Elements of Law*, part 2, ch. 8, para. 3, p. 169.

71. Hobbes, *The Elements of Law*, part 1, ch. 17, para. 1, p. 88.

72. Even then, the problems that honor can cause do not come to an end. The sovereign must guard against his own court, whose members will strive for honor through their ability to sway him with their advice—even to the point of knowingly giving destructive advice simply to thwart their competitors. See *The Elements of Law*, p. 143. An intelligent sovereign will reward those who serve the commonwealth "within the bounds of modesty" instead of those who are obviously ambitious. *The Elements of Law*, part 2, ch. 9, para. 7, p. 182.

73. Hobbes, *The Elements of Law*, part 1, ch. 17, para. 15, p. 95.

74. Hobbes, *The Elements of Law*, part 1, ch. 19, para. 2, p. 100.

75. Boucher, "Inter-Community & International Relations in the Political Philosophy of Hobbes," 220.

76. Hobbes, *The Elements of Law*, part 1, ch. 19, para. 2, p. 101.

77. Hobbes, *The Elements of Law*, part 1, ch. 19, para. 4, pp. 101–2.

78. As we will see, Hobbes's treatment of the position of the soldier in war, in light of his view that the right to self-preservation is absolute, and therefore running away in fear of one's life is justified, is problematic to say the least.

79. Hobbes, *De Cive*, part 2, ch. 5, sect. 5, p. 65.

80. Oakeshott agrees with this analysis on pages 86–87 of his *Hobbes on Civil Association* (Indianapolis: Liberty Fund, 1975).

81. Hobbes, *De Cive*, part 2, ch. 12, sect. 10, p. 136.

82. In *The Elements of Law*, Hobbes does make this distinction but he does so in a separate chapter, chapter 17, where he deals with honor within civil society. There he deals with it as wholly a creation of sovereign power.

83. Hobbes, *Leviathan*, part 1, ch. 10, p. 72.

84. Hobbes, *Leviathan*, part 1, ch. 10, p. 73.

85. Hobbes, *Leviathan*, part 1, ch. 10, p. 73.

86. Many of these reflect Hobbes's natural laws.
87. Hobbes, *Leviathan*, part 1, ch. 10, p. 74.
88. Hobbes, *Leviathan*, part 1, ch. 10, p. 74.
89. Hobbes, *Leviathan*, part 1, ch. 10, p. 75.
90. Hobbes, *Leviathan*, part 1, ch. 10, p. 75.
91. Hobbes, *Leviathan*, part 1, ch. 10, p. 75.
92. Hobbes, *De Cive*, part 2, ch. 9, sect. 8, pp. 108–9. Hobbes repeats this idea in part 3, ch. 15, para. 9, when he writes "Honour to speak properly, is nothing else but an opinion of another's power joined with goodness; and to honour a man, is the same with highly esteeming him" (180). What exactly Hobbes means by "joined with goodness" is unclear here, but perhaps it means that when we honor someone we impute goodness to them, an idea that Hobbes repeats in one way or another many times in his analyses of honor.
93. Hobbes, *Leviathan*, part 1, ch. 10, p. 73.
94. This idea comes out very clearly, of course, in Plato's *Republic*.
95. Hobbes, *Leviathan*, part 1, ch. 10, p. 79.
96. Hobbes, *Leviathan,* part 2, ch. 18, p. 141.
97. Hobbes, *Leviathan*, part 2, ch. 18, p. 139.
98. Hobbes, *De Cive*, part 2, ch. 13, sect. 12, p. 149.
99. Hobbes, *Leviathan*, part 1, ch. 10, p. 76.
100. Hobbes, *Leviathan*, part 1, ch. 10, p. 76.
101. Hobbes, *The Elements of Law*, ch. 19, para. 2, and *De Cive*, ch. 5, sect. 2, pp. 63–64.
102. Hobbes, *Leviathan*, part 1, ch. 10, p. 75. One way to interpret this passage is that we see these virtues as honorable because they belong to a person who is powerful. They are indications of power. Likewise, the following vices are usually signs that a person does not have power and knows it. On the other hand, Hobbes may be saying that these virtues come out in someone who is powerful because he is not burdened by fear and want. If that is the case, Hobbes's interpretation is closer to the classical point of view than it first appears.
103. Hobbes, *Leviathan*, part 2, ch. 17, p. 129.
104. Boucher also notes that Hobbes retains his teaching on honor and warfare in *Leviathan* through his treatment of honor among confederates in the state of nature, a situation that can be likened to international relations. In addition to a prohibition against cruelty, the law of nature demands honor in agreements among these confederacies: "Even in this crude condition a code of honor appears to be evident. To enter into a confederacy with others in which everyone expects the same degree of defense is an expedient measure, but to then attempt to deceive your confederates and thus break the covenant is an act of folly which leaves you in a position where your only means of safety and defense is your individual power. If you were to be allowed entry into another confederation, it would only be by the error of the confederates, an error which cannot be relied upon. The most likely scenario is that you will be cast out of the confederation you deceived by breaking your covenant and left to perish as an outcast unable to procure the protection of another confederation because it is publicly known that you give your word lightly." Boucher, "Inter-Community & International Relations in the Political Philosophy of Hobbes," 220.

105. Hobbes, *De Cive*, part 2, ch. 5, sect. 2, p. 63.

106. Hobbes, *Leviathan*, part 1, ch. 11, p. 81. Hobbes lists competition for honor as the first way in which human beings differ from animals, competition which leads to more hostilities among men. See *Leviathan*, part 1, ch. 6, para. 34, p. 51.

107. Hobbes, *Leviathan*, part 1, ch. 11, p. 81.

108. Hobbes, *Leviathan*, part 1, ch. 11, p. 81.

109. Hobbes, *Leviathan*, part 1, ch. 11, p. 82.

110. Still in part 1 of *Leviathan*, he again associates love of honor with the worst actions rather than the best. Discussing the Greek gods, he writes that they displayed "anger, revenge, and other passions of living creatures, and the actions proceeding from them, as fraud, theft, adultery, sodomy, and any vice that may be taken for an effect of power, or a cause of pleasure; and all such vices, as amongst men are taken to be against law, rather than against honour" (92).

111. Keith Thomas's argument in "The Social Origins of Hobbes's Political Thought," chapter 9 in *Hobbes Studies* (Oxford: Basil Blackwell, 1965), shows that Hobbes maintained an understanding for and appreciation of old-fashioned honor throughout his career.

Chapter Two

Gentlemen and Martyrs

The figure of the "gentleman" was the manly ideal in Hobbes's time, having eclipsed, but to a certain extent incorporated, the earlier ideal of the chivalrous knight. The other heroic ideal that survived (enough for Hobbes to want to challenge it) was the figure of the Christian martyr. Hobbes's treatment of gentlemen and martyrs will be the subject of this chapter. His treatment of them clearly shows his determination to alter older notions of honor, and will help us discern his plan and purpose. First, we will examine Hobbes's own rise to gentlemanly status, which may have influenced his thinking on this issue. Next we will take a step back and look at the social milieu of Hobbes's day, the complex layering of social and economic classes, and how that affected the common understanding of the term "gentleman." Then, we will look specifically at gentlemanly values—what constituted the ideal gentlemanly character of the time, for Hobbes and his contemporaries. We will then turn to Hobbes's treatment of actual gentlemen and how they behaved during the English Civil War. We will see that Hobbes retained a personal ideal of how a gentleman should behave, but the behavior of real-life gentlemen of his time made extending personal expectations to others in his society unrealistic. Their behavior during the war proved what Hobbes had already concluded by that time, that one could not rely upon good character for proper political leadership. We will look at some of the chief actors in the war and examine their motivations as Hobbes saw them. We will then turn to his solution, particularly his focus on the importance not just of absolute sovereignty, but on the type of education for gentlemen the sovereign should promote. Finally, we will briefly visit the issue of martyrdom as a way of understanding the difference between the type of religious education and understanding once considered honorable, and that which Hobbes desires. The type of Christianity

49

which Hobbes wants taught at the universities, and eventually in the pulpits, is a type stressing meekness and abject obedience, not the stiff-necked refusal to bend from principle and willingness to die for the truth of the martyred heroes of old (or of the new would-be martyrs of his own day).

THOMAS HOBBES, ESQUIRE

Before exploring what the gentlemanly ideal was for seventeenth-century English society and for Hobbes, it makes sense to take a look at Hobbes's personal experience as he developed friendships with gentlemen, and eventually became a gentleman himself. Hobbes came from obscure, somewhat embarrassing, origins. Hobbes's father, also Thomas, was an Anglican minister from Westport. As a low-ranking minister, he would have been considered a mere commoner. He was most likely an alcoholic and had been called to task by his church for not always fulfilling his basic duties. He abandoned his family when Hobbes was sixteen, after a rivalry with another minister escalated into a physical fight. Hobbes's father knew the authorities would seek to arrest him. Aubrey writes that Hobbes's father died "in obscurity beyound London," where he had fled to avoid the police.[1]

Left with the care of three children (in addition to Thomas, there was an older brother and a younger sister), Hobbes's mother turned to her husband's brother, Francis. Francis was wealthy, a burgess and alderman, and made his living as a glover.[2] He helped keep the family afloat financially, and paid Thomas's tuition to primary school. Francis continued in this role, providing Thomas with tuition to attend Magdalen Hall, Oxford. It is safe to say that without the unfortunate antics of Hobbes's father, and the presence of a stable and wealthy substitute in Francis, Hobbes's future might have looked very different. The education that Hobbes's uncle provided changed his life forever. But it was not the content of the education that would lead to Hobbes's rejection of humanism in favor of science. Of his entire education, Miriam M. Reik writes that:

> It is important for a correct perspective on Hobbes's life to recall that had he died before his forty-first year, he would probably be remembered today only as a rather minor representative of the last generation of Tudor humanists and translators who did so much to appropriate classical culture to the English language. This humanistic achievement of the Elizabethan period stood firmly grounded on the institution of its grammar schools; and Hobbes, like everyone else who attended them, acquired there a basic education in the learned languages, entailing in itself an introduction to classical thought and expression.[3]

It was Hobbes's classical education that allowed him to leave his less-than-optimal origins behind and begin a long process of social advancement. He took the route of many promising intellectuals of his time, of seeking and finding wealthy and noble patrons who could support and protect him. His relationships with these patrons not only provided him sustenance but also gave him higher status in society, openings to relationships with other philosophers and scientists, and thus intellectual companionship.

Hobbes's first position after finishing his education was with William Cavendish, First Earl of Devonshire (from now on "Devonshire"), who hired him to tutor his son, also William. "Hobbes must have been a good and respectable student, because the principal of Magdalen Hall recommended him to the rich and influential Cavendish family of Hardwick Hall, probably in early 1608."[4] Lisa T. Sarasohn has provided a useful analysis of Hobbes's relationship with both Devonshire and another and related William Cavendish, Duke of Newcastle, and how these relationships helped Hobbes socially and intellectually. Clearly, in her view (and she also argues in Hobbes's view) his first position was more like that of a distinguished domestic servant than an equal. Hobbes had not yet achieved the status of gentleman, but worked "filling the roles of tutor, advisor, and retainer to the second and third earls [of Devonshire]."[5] While in the employment of Devonshire, Hobbes began to develop a social and intellectual relationship with Newcastle, who was more engaged in intellectual circles, especially in scientific investigations. It was his ability to discuss scientific and philosophical matters of great interest that enabled him to engage Newcastle and other social superiors in a more collegial, less subservient way. Hobbes maintained frequent correspondence with Newcastle and occasionally provided a service for him while still employed with Devonshire. His status began to change because of his growing association with Newcastle, allowing Hobbes to obtain the title of "esquire" and the status of a gentleman. From that point on, both Devonshire and Newcastle were Hobbes's patrons. Because of these relationships, others were able to see Hobbes as a gentleman and not simply a domestic servant. The fruit of these relationships and his elevated status was Hobbes's increasing ability to devote more time to writing books and interacting with others as a scholar.

Toward the end of Hobbes's career, mid-seventeenth century, the source of scholarly status began to change. Whereas noble patronage had been the main route to social and intellectual status in the early seventeenth century, by mid-century, with the advent of the Royal Society as an independent scholarly organization whose membership began to develop standards independent of the noble class, old-fashioned patronage became less of a factor in the acceptance of scholarly ideas.[6] Hobbes was never granted membership in the Royal Society, despite the attempts of his friend and biographer John Aubrey to reconcile some of the differences between Hobbes and those scholars who blocked him.[7] Because patronage was the dominant mode of upward mobility for scholars for much of Hobbes's career, this snubbing from the Royal Society did him little real harm. Sarasohn argues that patron-client relationships such as he enjoyed were mutually beneficial to both parties. The client was elevated by the support and admiration of his patron, and was allowed into social circles that would otherwise be closed. The patron's status was also advanced by being seen as a supporter and source of learning and scholarship. The patron was more able to fully engage in intellectual circles through the activities of his client.[8]

Hobbes experienced both the reality of social hierarchy and the experience of collegiality with those of higher social rank and status, because of their appreciation of his intellect. He understood in a very personal way that there was no necessary difference among various ranks of men—that the visible differences among them were caused by social agreements, not by nature. Slomp writes, "In his daily frequentation of the aristocracy, Hobbes must have realised that their superiority was merely a human artefact. Indeed in his three main political works, Hobbes repeats almost *verbatim* the claim that equality is natural and that '[t]he inequallity that now is, has bin introduced by the Lawes civill.'"[9]

Interestingly, because of his association with William Cavendish, Hobbes also may have glimpsed the potential for the female sex to be more than it was. William's wife Margaret was somewhat of a philosopher in her own right, and while her works were roundly criticized by many of her contemporaries, even some female ones, for being sometimes too radical or unsupported by facts, William defended his wife's scholarly activities and her right to engage in such speculations even though she was a woman. Sara Hutton convincingly shows that Margaret was acquainted with Hobbes's ideas, even though she denied much contact with this member of her household, and that she openly disagreed with some of Hobbes's arguments in her own published writings.[10] While she was not allowed access to the scholarly circles Hobbes enjoyed, nonetheless, William supported his wife's scholarly attempts to the best of his ability, considering the social limitations of the day.[11] The relationship between William and Margaret might have helped form Hobbes's opinion, set forth in his political philosophy, that there was also nothing inherent in men and women which led to their inequality, but rather that inequality was caused by social agreement.

NOBLES AND GENTRY

Given that Hobbes was of common origins, but was able to rise to a relatively high social status because of his native intelligence and access to education, it should come as no surprise that Hobbes's views on the nobility were mixed and complex. Hobbes was supported and appreciated by the noble class, and yet Hobbes's political philosophy came to be critical of anyone who esteemed themselves above others, especially those who considered themselves legitimate judges of the sovereign, and so he could not help but find fault with those nobles who were haughty, interfering, and ignorant of their place.

Vickie Sullivan sums up his reaction to the nobility in his political philosophy when she writes:

> He . . . attempts to undercut the central assumption of those who seek self-promotion: the assumption that some human beings are inherently superior to others. In its stead, Hobbes assumes equality, and he makes the acceptance of his equality a necessary condition for the overcoming of the state of nature. To this end, he preaches that human beings are equal in the faculties of the body as well as of the mind.[12]

Hobbes's own social mobility was emblematic of the times in which he lived. Lawrence Stone's seminal work on this topic, *The Crisis of the Aristocracy, 1558–1641*, is still a particularly useful resource for understanding the varied economic, social, and cultural dynamics changing the status and attitudes of social classes at this time.[13] He explains that at the bottom of the social hierarchy were the common peasants, laborers, servants, and other working people. Small businessmen, artisans, and small landlords were a step above. Hobbes saw these common men as rather innocent (but not harmless) in the larger scheme of things. They were certainly not the cause of the social calamity of the Civil War that befell England. Their biggest problem was their relative ignorance, which made them vulnerable to manipulation by those who were better educated. In *Behemoth*, Hobbes describes their situation, and explains why they were led to disapprove of their sovereign:

> there are few, in respect of the rest of the men, whereof many cannot read: many, though they can, have no leisure; and of them that have leisure, the greatest part have their minds wholly employed and taken up by their private businesses or pleasures. So that it is impossible that the multitude should ever learn their duty, but from the pulpit and upon holidays; but then, and from thence, it is, that they learned their disobedience.[14]

Common men could not be expected to teach themselves, and they had not been taught their duty by the only people who could do the job: their ministers. Hobbes also depicts the commoners as having been made fairly cynical by the antics of the upper classes jockeying for power, which shows that commoners were capable of some astute observations. "King, they thought, was but a title of the highest honour, which gentleman, knight, baron, earl, duke, were but steps to ascend to, with the help of riches."[15] Hobbes believed the people had lost much of the respect they had instinctually held for the upper classes for centuries, and had come to think of the nobles as no better than themselves. They were essentially correct in this observation, but they did not know what to do with this information. They turned toward more democracy at the behest of the rhetoricians in their midst instead of turning toward the great leveler which could protect them best, in Hobbes's view: absolute sovereignty.

Wealthy merchants (like Hobbes's uncle) lived on the edge of being considered gentlemen. Those who aspired to gentlemanly status included "small landed proprietors but also in part professional men, civil servants, lawyers, higher clergy, and university dons."[16] The newly emerging and strengthening merchant class was challenging the older aristocratic structure in some ways, but reinforcing that structure in others. Land-ownership was a prerequisite for membership in the House of Commons and for political and social influence generally, and so it was pursued by the wealthiest merchants. Land sales burgeoned as aristocrats began to sell off some of their property to men with newer money, in exchange for much-needed income to maintain their lifestyles. The sale of titles was rampant at this time (up until 1640 when it was stopped by the king in an attempt to reinforce social lines), and the wealthy merchants were not above trying to invent lineages to allow themselves to obtain a dubious gentlemanly status.[17] More than any division of the nobles and gentry, Hobbes notes the division between city and country, particularly the tendency of the Southeast and London to side with the Parliament and reforms generally, the merchant class in London, in particular, being very concerned about taxation. Also, there was a large concentration of Presbyterians in London,[18] and there was a tendency of those in the country, both nobles and gentry, to remain Anglican and support the Royalist position. Even this division was not always reliable, but made a fairly strong general rule.[19]

Next were the "country elite—many of the esquires and nearly all the knights and baronets, titular categories which expanded enormously in numbers in the early seventeenth century and which in purely economic terms have an awkward tendency to merge into one another."[20] Display of heraldry, creatively obtained if necessary, was all the rage, and, "Genuine genealogy was cultivated by the older gentry to reassure themselves of their innate superiority over the upstarts; bogus genealogy was cultivated by the new gentry in an effort to clothe their social nakedness, and by the old gentry in the internal jockeying for position in the ancestral pecking order."[21] Because of the rise of a class of men whose wealth was earned, "The Commons emerged as a far more important political assembly than the Lords, and peers were unable to exercise that influence over parliamentary elections which they had wielded under Elizabeth, and were to wield again under the Hanoverians."[22] Their rise was critical in the eventual civil war and revolution that Hobbes so despised. Nevertheless, Hobbes had to devise a political philosophy that accepted some of these social and economic changes but mitigated their destructive possibilities.

> During the early seventeenth century these authoritarian attitudes were having to complete with what can only be described, for lack of a better word, as the concept of individualism. The growth of population faster than food supplies or employment opportunities and the increased use of money and credit led to a more cut-throat competitive society, first in the towns and more slowly in the countryside. The ideal of a society in which every man had his place and stayed in it was breaking down under a combination of material and ideological pressures. Many no longer had a place in which to stay, and those who had were less willing to accept their lot as eternally ordained by God.[23]

Alison Wall's study on politics in England 1558–1625 shows that the vying of various factions within the gentry, based upon religion, bloodlines, history, and so on, had been going on for a long time, leading to the disunion of the upper class in Hobbes's time. Competition for control of offices among the gentry was fierce in many counties.

> All the troubled counties we have considered had ambitious and power-hungry gentry, willing to spend energy and legal costs, seeking local prominence and hence Court notice. The specific issues in contention varied: the pretensions of a peer; party dominance of the commission of the peace and of appointments to subsidy or militia office; differences in religion; and particular local problems . . . counted in varying degree.[24]

At the very top, of course, were members of the aristocracy, the peerage, especially those closest to the court. Stone argues that the social and moral values of the day continued to be set by the aristocracy then and for some time to come. Rather than trying to change those values in favor of a more egalitarian system, most members of the merchant class and gentry still wanted to fit in to the social framework established and maintained by the aristocracy. The nobles made every effort to keep the social lines drawn neatly in the minds of all, even going so far as to pass laws regulating who could wear certain types of clothing or engage in certain types of activities. Inferiors were treated harshly, with punishments like flogging and the use of stocks to inflict public humiliation and remind malefactors of their place.

The issue of whether socioeconomic class was really the fundamental cause of the English Civil War has been debated by numerous scholars. Some, like C. B. Macpherson, have argued in a Marxist vein that seventeenth-century England had become a "possessive market society" and that Hobbes was aware of this development. Macpherson is able to cite the few places in Hobbes's theory where he seems to discuss labor as a commodity, property interests, and the rejection of customary status in ways similar to someone who understands society in terms of the market.[25] Macpherson writes that Hobbes "treated the war as an attempt to destroy the old constitution and replace it with one more favourable to the new market interests."[26] While this sounds plausible, a closer examination of Hobbes's works does not reveal a clear foundation for Macpherson's position. In fact, time and again, Hobbes argues that property, wealth, and status, are all and should all be dependent upon the king's will. Representative of Hobbes's views is his statement in *De Cive*: "that only is proper to each man, which he can keep by the laws, and the power of the whole city, that is, of him on whom its chief command is conferred."[27] As Keith Thomas points out, Hobbes is "unequivocal in his view that all class differences stem from convenience and agreement, rather than from innate differences of blood, race or capacity."[28] Other scholars, such as Leo Strauss, have argued that the struggle was not, for Hobbes, about property, but about power itself, and that this is why Hobbes's solution is not an economic one, but a political one.[29] It is not that elements of the future market economy were not there, or that Hobbes did not recognize them, but that Hobbes did not attribute to them the source of the conflict, nor did he point to economics as a solution. Deborah Baumgold, considering both points of view, summed up the direction of most scholars since that debate in the 1960s: "Revisionist historians are currently putting forward the anti-teleological, 'high politics' view that the Civil War was a struggle for power among political elites—as opposed to an ideological or a class conflict."[30]

Keith Thomas argues that the values of the time, which Hobbes drew upon, were very mixed, emblematic of a society in transition:

> the economy is somewhat less advanced than is usually suggested; the social hierarchy, although largely contractual, still retains marked traces of patriarchalism; and the concern for reputation and honour in the upper reaches of society is more marked than any desire for riches. Nevertheless, the growth of capitalism is reflected in the emancipation of individuals from many of the old customary bonds and in the obvious presence of acquisitive appetites.[31]

So it is a stretch to see within Hobbes a class-based theorist, or a mere representative of the "bourgeoisie." Indeed, Hobbes views political conflict as a competition for power for its own sake. This is why he places so much emphasis on the dangers of ambition and pride, which have nothing directly to do with wealth. As we have seen in the first chapter, wealth, in fact, seems to be sought because of the political and social power and thus the honor it brings the owner. Hobbes is not primarily an economic theorist, but on the other hand, he does speak in terms of nobles, gentry, merchants, and yeomen. He is aware of class, but in the final analysis, it does not explain what happened in the English Civil War, or what drives most people in any conflict. As we will see, in that war, nobles often acted contrary to their economic interests, siding with the members of the gentry and merchant classes in order to exact revenge upon a king whom they felt had slighted them somehow. Commoners and other classes of men could be found on either side of the conflict. As we will also see, the rhetorical dividing line of religion was not the real issue for Hobbes either, since he sees leading men of all religious stripes as using their religion in an attempt to gain more power. In the end, Baumgold is right that Hobbes attributes conflict not to economic class, or to ideology, but to the desire for power itself, an intrinsic psychological attribute.

GENTLEMANLY VALUES

In order to understand what *moral* meaning Hobbes's contemporaries wished to convey when they used the term "gentleman," it is useful to know what the manly ideal was earlier and how it had been changing. Generally speaking, the earlier manly ideal was aristocratic and chivalrous, with a high value placed upon martial valor, as exemplified in the last chapter by Geoffroi de Charny's work. Reaching a period of real influence in the late twelfth century, chivalry was an ideal fostered by the church and by literary writers in an effort to protect the weak from strong young men capable of much destruction. It was not at first a particularly humble code. Like the Aristotelian idea of magnanimity, the early chivalric code fostered a generous pride of place, in which kindnesses done to others were done to display one's own greatness and generosity, not mainly out of a sense of moral duty. This is why chivalry in its heyday was often not courteous in practice, at least not toward the lower class. "The world centers around the knight," writes Elias. "Hungry dogs, begging women, rotting horses, servants crouching against the ramparts, villages in flames, peasants being plundered and killed—all this is as much a part of the landscape of these people as are tournaments and hunts. So God made the world: some are rulers, the others bondsmen. There is nothing embarrassing about all this."[32] Nevertheless, the concept of chivalry was continually refined. It emphasized more and more the moral obligation that superiors had to protect inferiors, especially women, children, and the elderly. As the ideal of chivalry continued to develop, it incorporated more and more of the Christian values of charity and kindness toward all, especially the weakest, as de Charney's work demonstrated.

During the late Middle Ages and Renaissance, the chivalric ideal began to change again. Around this time, "the dominant social ideal became the landed gentleman rather than the professional soldier," and the ideal qualities began to center much more around manners or courtesy, and good form.[33] As Bornstein explains, out of feudalism in the sixteenth century came a new social order. This was court society, which kept the elite nobles, who lived and served at court, close physically and politically to the sovereign, taking away their independent power. The change in the behavior and values of the upper class was due in large part to the policy of the Tudors, who between 1485 and 1530 centralized government and prohibited private armies, taking away much of the power of the nobility, and concluding an alliance with the gentry instead.[34]

Going along with this move to centralize power and organize society, at the level of intellectual discourse, was what David Burchell describes as the Stoic revival. Neostoicism emphasized the disciplined and orderly life, and the suppression of passions in a way congruent with the Puritan ethos of the time. Burchell points out that Hobbes cites one of the leading fathers of the Stoic revival, Dutch humanist Justus Lipsius, in the introduction to his translation of Thucydides (one of the few times he cites any thinker, especially a contemporary), thus joining his admiration of Thucydides with his approval of Lipsius. Neostoicism emphasized military discipline and organization in both the actual military and in society, and criticized any pursuit of individual glory, especially in battle.[35] Another and related reason for the revision of the earlier chivalric ideals was the advent in the fifteenth century of effective artillery and handguns and the mustering of professional armies, which began to replace the armed and independent nobility. Chivalry did not seem of much use in these circumstances for any class of men, "for armour was no protection against a hail of bullets."[36]

For a new social arrangement, a new definition of the gentleman was necessary. "The concept of *civilité* acquired its meaning for Western society at a time when chivalrous society and the unity of the Catholic Church were disintegrating."[37] This new emphasis on civility or polite manners at court departed from and even rejected some of the chivalric code. The gentleman was measured by his loyalty to the crown, not his lady's attention. His excellence was not so much in his honesty as it was in his discretion. The sign of his worth was less his inner character than the exterior appearance of his success and status.[38] Baldassare Castiglione's *The Courtier*, 1528,

> set the tone for many of the attitudes of the knight's successor, the gentleman. The gentleman's ideals are often assumed to stem from those of chivalry; but in the main this is untrue. The gentleman's models hark back either to the classical world, or to the great men of contemporary life, and many writers of the six-

teenth century are harsh critics of the chivalrous code, condemning dueling and attacking the ethics of the romances.[39]

Elias credits Erasmus for much of the inspiration surrounding the values of this new civilité, especially his book *On Civility in Children* (*De civilitate morum puerilium*, 1530), which was mainly about outward propriety, that is, good manners, and was written to instruct boys on how to become gentlemen. As far as the activities of the nobility were concerned, the bridge between older knightly chivalry and the gentleman of Hobbes's day were the chivalric games of the sixteenth-century tournament, which had become more about ritual than actual battle training.

Due to his new role attending and serving at court, a large part of a nobleman's distinction had to be his intelligence and thus preparedness to be of use to the court both in policy and in social relations. This new role meant that sons of the nobles and gentry must attend a university if they were to rise to any degree of influence in society. Gentlemen needed to be able to carry on a conversation with members of both sexes on a wide variety of subjects, as well as to be able to participate in a variety of sports and other diversions. Universities such as Cambridge and Oxford were geared to provide the classical education required of a gentleman, an education that served as the basis for Hobbes's social mobility. The universities were incorporating more and more scientific training, so that by the end of the seventeenth century, being well-educated scientifically was just as important as knowing Greek and Latin. But in Hobbes's day, the necessity of a scientific education was still an emerging idea and a subject of debate.

> The fact that under both Puritan and Anglican regimes most heads of colleges remained classical scholars or leading divines indicates that to a large extent science was not expected to oust these foci of the university but to take its place alongside them. The chief function of the university was to train clergymen and educate gentlemen.[40]

In sum, being a gentleman meant being educated and having good manners, usually as the result of proper breeding and upbringing by a respectable family. It also meant being honorable, courageous, magnanimous, and just. A gentleman was recognized as having an elevated status in society, because of these qualities. This new focus on education became a value to all who aspired to social advancement, including those who were neither noble nor members of the gentry.[41] During Hobbes's time, as we have seen, a class of men whose wealth came from their own enterprise and not through inheritance was increasingly influential. These men most often did not have noble titles, but they aspired to them; they married into them or purchased them, and strove to be considered gentlemen. For them, the balance was beginning to shift away from the mix of aristocratic and Christian ideals of the Middle Ages, toward a more singularly Christian understanding of the gentleman as a man of universal good will and charitable conduct toward all.[42] Martial notions were an ever-diminishing part of the mix, and admiration for productivity was making up a greater part of what it meant to be a gentleman. As an example of the latter emphasis, we see even the wife of Hobbes's patron, the aristocrat Margaret Cavendish, reflecting the new way of thinking in 1655, "Every man should, like a Bee, bring Hony to the Hive, and not, like the effeminat [*sic*] Drone, suck out the sweet, and idely live upon the Heroick labour of others."[43] For his own part, Hobbes echoes a disdain for those who are idle or do not take care to conserve and grow their wealth. "The damages which befall some particular subjects through misfortune, folly, negligence, sloth, or his own luxury, may very well be severed from those which concern the ruler."[44]

Thus the gentlemanly code still encompassed an older aristocratic meaning, which celebrated pursuits such as preparation for battle and hunting and other games, and would have chafed at the idea of any type of equality with the common people, even spiritual equality. But it was moving toward an understanding of the gentleman as equally charitable to all, kind, religious, and productive. Books about gentlemanly conduct at this time tended to reflect both the older and the newer sense of what it meant to be a gentleman, retaining much discussion of the aristocratic view, but sometimes employing the new focus on Christian responsibilities, and a growing idea that those other than the nobles and gentry could be gentlemen.

When Hobbes referred to the idea of the gentleman positively in his writings, his thoughts sometimes reflected the older aristocratic meaning and even its expression in the code of chivalry. Hobbes also sometimes seems to expound the newer notions of honest hard work, including the increasingly popular idea of the gentleman as a Christian of universal good will. It is possible to get an idea of what "gentleman" in the positive sense meant in its various nuances to Hobbes by looking at the way he wrote about related subjects such as shame, status, virtue, and vice.

Hobbes's commentaries on issues having to do with gentlemanly behavior reflected a mixture of the prevailing norms, as when he treats of shame in book 2, chapter 8 of *The Whole Art of Rhetoric*. There he lists several things of which men are ashamed. To throw down their arms and run away is considered cowardly. To have illicit sexual intercourse is shamefully intemperate. Not to help others with money when we should is shameful, as well as "to receive help from meaner men." He has a healthy sense of manliness which even comports somewhat with the emerging contemporary ideal of honest work. Again, in *The Whole Art of Rhetoric*, he distinguishes men in power from those who are simply rich. Men in power, he says, "have a greater sense of honour than the rich, and their manners are more manly. They are more industrious than the rich, for *power* is sustained by industry."[45] In the same work he says that it is a sign of effeminacy to be unable to do work that men who are older and weaker can do. Even in a work written late in his life, his views reflected an admiration for those who were industrous. "Work is good; it is truly a motive for life." "Idleness is torture. In all times and places, nature abhors a vacuum."[46] But Hobbes also reflects the older aristocratic notions about work and merit when he writes, "To want those things which one's equals, all or most of them, have attained to, is also a thing to be ashamed of. And to suffer things ignominious; as to serve about another's person, or to be employed in his base actions."[47]

At the very beginning of *Leviathan*, in his introduction, Hobbes expresses a decidedly aristocratic vision of the relationship between gentlemen and their inferiors. Speaking of human nature, the subject of the first part of *Leviathan*, he remarks that "there is a saying much usurped of late, that wisdom is acquired, not by reading of *books*, but of *men*."[48] He goes on to tell us that this usually leads men to look at other people's actions as proof of the unattractive side of human nature. But Hobbes discourages this arrogance with the recommendation:

> *read thyself*: which was not meant, as it is now used, to countenance, either the barbarous state of men in power, toward their inferiors; or to encourage men of low degree, to a saucy behaviour toward their betters; but to teach us, that for the similitude of the thoughts and passions of one man, to the thoughts and passions of another, whosoever looketh into himself, and considereth what he doth, when he does *think, opine, reason, hope, fear*, &c. and upon what grounds; he shall thereby read and know, what are the thoughts and passions of all other men upon the like occasions.[49]

In the middle of his attempt to establish a sort of universal notion of human nature—that we can know everyone else's nature by simply knowing our own—Hobbes inserts rather traditional aristocratic notions about the existence of superiors and inferiors. His comments reflect the idea, and probably his personal belief, that men in power should not abuse that power, and also that men of unclear status should act respectfully toward their superiors. What he says expresses very neatly the idea of mutual obligation between superior and inferior characteristics of feudal, even chivalric ideals. Here it appears in a statement whose overall purpose would seem to make both types of men equal in their very nature—the opposite of the aristocratic view that men are *unequal* in their very nature. In a way, Hobbes is attempting his own equalization of the high and low born, not through Christianity, but rather through his political philosophy, which also universalizes human nature.

In *De Homine*, Hobbes makes a distinction between the old and the new
nobility, somewhat like the contemporary distinction between the old wealth
and the "nouveau riche." "Ancient nobility," he writes,

> makes the disposition affable, because in bestowing honour on someone, they
> can be bountiful and kind to all, since under all circumstances they are secure
> enough about honour due to themselves. The disposition of new nobility is more
> suspicious, like those who, not yet certain enough of how much honour ought to
> be bestowed on themselves, often become excessively harsh toward inferiors
> and excessively diffident toward equals.[50]

As we will see in the next section, Hobbes still retained gentlemanly ideals
such as those described above even in one of his last works, *Behemoth*. In this
book we get a sense that Hobbes is deeply disappointed and disgusted with
the gentlemen who actively fomented rebellion in the Civil War. He uses
terms which lead the reader to believe that Hobbes measures actors' character by this ideal standard, but also that Hobbes has lost hope in that standard
precisely because of the behavior of these actors during the war. Stephen
Holmes writes:

> Throughout *Behemoth*, Hobbes invoked norms rhetorically. He spoke in favor
> of honesty, oath keeping, debt repayment, fair play, gallantry, civility, decency,
> and loyalty. With palpable sincerity, he denounced not only "wicked Parlia-
> ments" but, more generally, "impudence and villainy," flattery, "drunkenness,
> wantonness, gaming," and even "lewd women." More seriously, he lashed out
> repeatedly against cruelty and tyranny.[51]

Holmes argues that all of these references are merely rhetorical, and that it
is impossible to say if Hobbes actually took any of them seriously. Indeed, he
argues that Hobbes did *not* take them seriously, because he thought all these
terms were relative, a matter of perspective and opinion. While I agree with
Holmes that Hobbes does argue that such terms and their corresponding values are relative, it also appears (as argued in chapter 1) that Hobbes treated
such terms in two ways—as genuine concepts *and* as mere rhetoric. As we
turn to Hobbes's treatment of the gentlemen of the Civil War, we get the same
dynamic—Hobbes himself still holding genuine convictions about good and
bad character, noble and base actions, and so on, but also believing the most
important actors in the Civil War had lost their bearings and were using the
languages of honor and religion cynically and rhetorically. It is possible for
Hobbes to hold both positions simultaneously, and for there to be no contradiction between the two. Because Hobbes was trying to build a political theory on a firm foundation, he may have realized that the old-fashioned values
that he himself still respected were no longer generally shared, or, at the very

least, that they broke down in exactly the situations Hobbes hoped his theory would help men avoid, situations of political uncertainty and conflict.

GENTLEMEN IN THE CIVIL WAR

Behemoth, a book written late in his life, is Hobbes's account of the events of the English Civil War, coupled with his analysis of the war's causes. It is also Hobbes's account of how gentlemen conducted themselves during the war. As such, it promises to teach us much about what Hobbes really thought of the gentlemen of his own times. It is a story of widespread folly. The nobles and the gentry are depicted very much as they were, divided on whether to support the king or not, as well as whether popular government was desirable or not. Indeed, the army of the Parliament was led by a nobleman, the Earl of Essex, until he was replaced by another nobleman, Sir Thomas Fairfax. Hobbes wrote of the opposition to the king, "Most of them were members of the House of Commons; some few also, of the Lords."[52] As noted above, Hobbes tends to focus more on the division between city and country, especially the influence of London, more than the division between nobles and gentry. Nobles who were closest to court tended to side with the monarchy; nobles who were not so close or who were unpopular at court were more likely to side with the rebels.

Hardly any among the nobles or gentry who supported the rebellion appear to be, in Hobbes's analysis, motivated primarily by steadfast principle. And, indeed, supporters of the king (many of whom were unreliable supporters), are not put in a much better light.[53] Instead, almost all are depicted as being driven by pride and ambition, and as disguising these low motivations with principled rhetoric. Others are portrayed as morally confused, persuaded by lawyers and rhetoricians of the rightness of mixed monarchy.[54] Stephen Holmes points out that it is easy to get the impression that all actors involved were motivated by calculating self-interest, but this is not true.[55] Indeed, Hobbes thought the problem was that there was not enough rational self-interest among the principle actors, but rather too much pride and desire for status. As Robert Kraynak so aptly puts it, "Hobbes's history shows that the civil war was caused by opinions and doctrines of right, which were created and exploited by ambitious intellectuals solely for the purpose of displaying their wisdom and learning."[56] This competition for status or recognition brought about much self-destructive behavior:

> In most cases, the irrationality of behavior has its origins in the irrationality of an individual's motives—notably, in an unreasonable skittishness about insult and public humiliation. If people were rational, they would (for they easily

could) develop thick skins against gratuitous signs of undervaluing. But they do not do this. They do not do it because they are *ir*rational fools.[57]

There is a great deal of deceit, cowardice, and unmanliness displayed by all parties in Hobbes's *Behemoth*. Even the king, whom the character "A" in the dialogue calls "the best King perhaps that ever was,"[58] comes across as overly mild, weak-headed, and cowardly. Perhaps this is one reason why Charles II refused to allow the publication of *Leviathan* when asked to do so by Hobbes, along with a more practical reason: "Charles agreed with what Hobbes had written but knew that it would cause an unhelpful stir if it went into print."[59] Below we will examine the influential groups and individuals in the Civil War with the goal of understanding Hobbes's assessment of these various gentlemen, and how the experience of the Civil War might have influenced his rejection of the manly ideal of the gentleman as an independent source of restraint in the political world.

The Clergy

One of the most prominent themes in *Behemoth* is the fickle nature of the clergy. Hobbes does not single one particular sect out for special criticism; he finds fault with them all. All men of the cloth share the same flaw, in his view: they think too little of their religious principles and too much of their own position and status. Many times he treats them simply as cynical manipulators who use religion as a mere rhetorical cover for their own ambition.

Catholics

It should be no surprise that Hobbes devotes much attention to the Catholics in *Behemoth*, even though they were not a real threat during the war itself. The queen was a Catholic, and this was used by the Presbyterian ministers and leaders to accuse the king of designs to allow the old religion to come back.[60] But while this motivated some of the Catholic nobles and gentry to sympathize with the queen, they were not in any position in this conflict to affect change. The best Hobbes could do is to blame the Catholics for their inaction—they did not actively support the king as much as they could have. They did not see a clear way to gain advantage for themselves in the conflict, and so they remained fairly quiescent, thus hastening the destruction of the kingdom. Indeed, Hobbes puts an extra twist of consciousness on their quiescence:

the Papists of England have been looked upon as men that would not be sorry for any disorders here that might possibly make way to the restoring of the

Pope's authority. And therefore I named them for one of the distempers of the state of England in the time of our late King Charles.[61]

Presbyterians and Independents

There is another reason besides Catholics being easy targets why Hobbes dwells so much on them in *Behemoth*. He uses criticism of the Catholics to show how much other religious leaders, who would claim to be diametrically opposed to the Catholic Church in every way, actually mirrored much of the Catholic way of thinking as Hobbes saw it. The Presbyterian ministers are depicted by Hobbes as uniformly self-interested. They are not sincere in their religious convictions, but rather want the same power for themselves that formerly the pope had: to rule over the secular authorities and to make their own church completely supreme. Because the Presbyterians now predominated in the House of Commons, it was no wonder that they wanted to use their political power to fulfill their ambitions for themselves and their religion. Likewise, the Independents (the radical break-away Protestant sects that supported Cromwell when he took power from the Rump Parliament)[62] sought their own superiority. Hobbes dismisses them as unreasoning fanatics who looked for an opportunity to gain control for their own interests. As A says baldly toward the end of *Behemoth*, the Protestant ministers wanted a popular form of government so that religion would dominate politics, and so that "they might govern, and thereby satisfy not only their covetous humour with riches, but also their malice with power to undo all men that admired not their wisdom."[63]

Presbyterians dominated the House of Commons during that critical time in which Charles called Parliament in the hopes of raising money to fight the Scots. What drove the Scots into rebellion was the decision by the king to impose on them the Anglican Book of Common Prayer. Hobbes depicts it as a grave miscalculation to think that his now largely Presbyterian Parliament would back a war against the Presbyterian Scots. Instead, armed with the intellectual independence fostered by their theology, the Presbyterians in Parliament took the occasion to foment dissent and rebellion.

Hobbes shows that the ideas fostered by Protestantism of all kinds exacerbated political problems even more than had Catholic teachings. Whereas the Catholic Church retained control of the scripture by not allowing it to be translated into vernacular languages, the Protestants translated it and encouraged Bible reading. This, of course, led to a profusion of authorities on God's very thoughts, and that led to a general spirit of rebelliousness. "For after the Bible was translated into English, every man, nay, every boy and wench, that could read English, thought that they spoke with God Almighty, and understood what he said, when by a certain number of chapters a day they had read the Scriptures once or twice over."[64] This freedom to read the Bible was responsible for the critical attitude of the Christian sects that caused so much trouble in the war. Hobbes also takes aim at the sheer chicanery of Presbyterian and Independent ministers, in particular how they used dramatic rhetoric to awe their congregants into thinking them godly and above reproach. Typically sardonic, Hobbes notes that they could quote and use Biblical passages "as that no tragedian in the world could have acted the part of a right godly man better than these did; insomuch as a man unacquainted with such art, could never suspect any ambitious plot in them to raise sedition against the state, as they then had designed."[65]

Anglicans

One would expect that the established Church of England would be treated by Hobbes less harshly than the rest. But the Anglican ministers are shown to be little better than Catholics or Presbyterians and Independents when it comes to their motivation. Describing Hobbes's point of view, Kraynak writes, "When the power of the Popes was broken in England, the Bishops arrogated to themselves the right to define orthodoxy and employed the old methods of excommunication, disputation, and rhetoric to become the established Church of England."[66] Though they did not preach rebellion, their own desires for supremacy over the government made them lukewarm in their support for the king, and thus of very little help. They did not so much disapprove of the supremacy of the Catholic Church in principle as they wanted that supremacy for themselves. All men, it seems, were tempted by power, no matter their sect, as A points out by questioning:

> Do the clergy in England pretend, as the Pope does, or as the Presbyterians do, to have a right from God immediately, to govern the King and his subjects in all points of religion and manners? If they do, you cannot doubt but that if they had number and strength, which they are never like to have, they would attempt to obtain that power, as the others have done.[67]

This question is not immediately or directly answered, but the question itself gives away Hobbes's opinion. A then answers his own question by setting forth in very brief form what the duty of man is regarding religious beliefs. This duty amounts to acknowledging the truths of natural religion: God's omnipotence, omniscience, and so on, but which must also include obedience to the king in all matters. The clergy should serve at the pleasure of the king, who is the only sure source of knowledge about God's intentions.[68] Even though the Anglican ministers did not preach disobedience to the king as the Presbyterians and Independents did, Hobbes thinks that they were part of the problem, that they had not been teaching their flocks the duty of obedience to the sovereign power because they themselves were uncomfortable with this duty.

Gentry and Nobles

As for the gentry and the nobility, those who supported the rebellion did so out of self-interest. They are depicted by Hobbes as having no principles, of lying, scheming, and double crossing when it suits their purposes. "[C]ertainly the chief leaders were ambitious ministers and ambitious gentlemen; the ministers envying the authority of bishops, whom they thought less learned; and the gentlemen envying the privy-council and principal courtiers, whom they thought less wise than themselves."[69] Most of the nobility and gentry tended to side with monarchy, Hobbes writes, but because of their own ambitions, they did not want to think of the king's power as absolute. Instead, because of their classical education, they liked the idea of mixed monarchy, in which the king would truly have to share his power with them. This is the reason, in Hobbes's view, why so many of them at first acquiesced to the demands of their democratically minded brethren in the House of Commons, and some ended up accused by the king of treason.[70] Time and again Hobbes claims that they simply did not understand how much their own fate was wrapped up with the fate of the king's sovereignty, until it was too late and the rebels were out of control.[71] As A tells how the Rump Parliament (that excluded the Lords) was born, he comments, "Nor was it a little folly in the Lords, not to see that by the taking away of the King's power they lost withal their own privileges; or to think themselves, either for number or judgment, any way a considerable assistance to the House of Commons."[72] Holmes argues "They did not understand that weakening the king would expose their own order to an attack by the Commons."[73] But as we will see, this folly was driven by certain elites' resentment of the king's favoritism and disloyalty.

Individuals in the Civil War

Hobbes singles out certain figures for sustained analysis in *Behemoth*. He does so because they are so important to the course of events, of course. But the length and level of detail he provides, especially in the case of Thomas Wentworth and Oliver Cromwell, lends credence to the idea that he is providing his readers with object lessons in good and bad character. So much of Hobbes's criticism is about these men's characters that it is hard to deny his interest in this aspect of the conflict. Scholars have a tendency to think that Hobbes rejects personal character as a factor out of hand, that he argues that all are equally motivated by self-interest and cannot be otherwise—therefore there is no reason for him to discuss character issues. But we see it here in *Behemoth* on every page. Hobbes, in fact, uses his analysis of these gentlemen's faulty characters to once again justify his turn to a more sure means of keeping order. Hobbes does not think character is an intangible thing that does not exist, or that it is not important in understanding why things happen. But he does seem to think that the Civil War proved that gentlemen cannot be relied upon to actually have good characters, at least not enough of the time to warrant entrusting them with government.

Charles I

One would expect that the hero of Hobbes's story would be Charles I, and indeed, in part, he is. Hobbes praises him early in *Behemoth* as a man who "wanted no virtue, either of body or mind, nor endeavoured anything more than to discharge his duty toward God, in the well governing of his subjects."[74] He also depicts Charles as a fairly able commander, as when he holds his own in the face of a determined and skillful enemy such as Lord Essex. On the other hand, the impression of Charles that Hobbes ultimately gives us is of a man who is not quite up to the job, sometimes fatally indecisive, too quick to compromise, and fickle toward his own friends and supporters. Hobbes points out, also early in *Behemoth*, that if the king had only had enough money, he would have found enough soldiers to fight off all his enemies, but this was because the people of England did not care "much for either of the causes, but would have taken any side for pay or plunder."[75] This statement leads us to wonder what has gone wrong with Charles's leadership, and we find out quite soon that the king's mismanagement of his own affairs in fact set the stage for the crisis. Hobbes believed that the king had been made the victim of an elaborate plot to drag him into a war with Scotland. The plotters wanted to force him to call a Parliament (he had refrained from doing so for ten years) in order to raise taxes to pay for the war. Hobbes speculates that it was the archbishop of Canterbury who persuaded the king to impose the Book of Common Prayer on the Scots. When the Scots resisted, the plotters thought they had succeeded, but Charles initially managed to raise an army from willing nobles and gentry, thus bypassing Parliament.

But the Scots asked to negotiate, "and the King, willing to avoid the destruction of his own subjects, condescended to it."[76] He then backed down on the imposition of the Book of Common Prayer. In this way, the plotters of Parliament were thwarted momentarily, but at a high price. Not too much later, the Scots decided to try to invade England, and the king was finally forced to call Parliament in 1640. As could have been predicted, the members, the majority of them Presbyterians, sided with the Scottish Presbyterians and were of no help in raising an army. Instead they used the time they had to list grievances against the king, especially for having raised extra-parliamentary taxes while they had not been in session. Having gained nothing, and lost considerable political capital, the king dissolved the Parliament, and went back for a second time to his supporters in the nobility and gentry to prepare an army to fight back the Scots.[77] Hobbes points out with irony that, due to the insistence of members of Parliament, which he was soon forced to convene again, "both the armies were maintained at the King's charge, and the whole controversy to be decided by a Parliament almost wholly Presbyterian."[78]

Hobbes continues to draw the readers' attention to times in which Charles backed away from a decision, compromised when he should have stood firm, and walked away from those who had supported him. Charles did not protect some ministers and writers who defended him. They were imprisoned by Parliament, which caused other of his supporters to flee the country.[79] When Charles was accused of being secretly a Catholic (and even being governed by his wife), because the queen was a Catholic, he did not vigorously defend either the queen or himself from these aspersions,[80] a failure which certainly made him seem cowardly and unmanly.

Instead of imprisoning one of his chief detractors, Sir Thomas Wentworth, he made him a baron, "and not long after he made him of the Council, and after that again Lieutenant of Ireland, which place he discharged with great satisfaction and benefit to his Majesty, and continued in that office, till, by the envy and violence of the Lords and Commons of that unlucky Parliament of 1640, he died," unprotected by Charles.[81] In this case, the king obtained some useful service from a former detractor, but his way of handling the problem, and his inability to save Wentworth from the consequences of the Parliament's charge of high treason, is emblematic of Charles's lack of spine. Baumgold observes that in his political theory, "Hobbes warned repeatedly [in *De Cive* and *Leviathan*] about the dangers of favoritism and leniency toward grandees."[82] Hobbes clearly thought this episode displayed something about the character of both Charles and Wentworth worth spending several pages on (more on Wentworth, who was eventually made Earl of Strafford by Charles for his about-face, below). Hobbes belabors what can only be described as Charles's cowardice in the face of Parliament. He writes that the king publicly disagreed with the sentence against Wentworth, but in the end was too afraid of Parliament to stop it.

> [H]e would have pardoned him, if that could have preserved him against the tumult raised and countenanced by the Parliament itself, for the terrifying of those they thought might favour him. And yet the King himself did not stick to confess afterwards, that he had done amiss, in that he did not rescue him.[83]

Charles gave in to Parliament's demand that they have the power to levy soldiers without his consent, "which is in effect the whole sovereign power," in order to hopefully get their help against the Scots' rebellion, "because the present time was unseasonable to dispute it in."[84] He attempted to arrest some rebellious members of the Parliament, but when he arrived they had already fled. Upon being castigated by Parliament for coming there with too much force, he later waived his charges against the rebels.[85] Not long later, Parliament sent ten of the king's supporters in the House of Lords to the Tower and passed a bill depriving them of their right to vote in Parliament, "and to this bill they got the King's assent."[86] Then they passed a bill excluding all the bishops from voting in the upper house, but the king did not agree to this. The reader cannot help but feel that this refusal is far too little, too late, and that a large part of the cause of the war was the king's prior lack of courage in standing up to his enemies.

Hobbes is very careful in his treatment of this delicate subject, trying not to cross the line into all-out criticism of the sovereign, but his criticism is sometimes very thinly veiled. He recognizes that rebellious members of parliament wanted "to stick upon his Majesty the dishonour of deserting his friends, and betraying them to his enemies."[87] They asked the king to turn over the men who supposedly advised him to come armed to Parliament, which he refused to do in this case. But one of the men whom they accused himself was forced to flee the country. Again, the king could not or did not adequately protect his friends.[88] Martinich sums up Hobbes's opinion of Charles I as expressed in *Behemoth* in this way: "To his sorrow and to the sorrow of the nation, Charles I was too accommodating to Parliament, allowed the universities to teach doctrines that subverted his authority, and acted too moderately when factions challenged first his policies and later his very legitimacy."[89] Conrad Russell describes Charles's problem as "the phenomenon of diminished majesty." "The sort of pressure Charles was put under in 1641–2 is the sort to which only a king esteemed weak could have been subjected: not even the most rabid Presbyterian would have thought it worth telling Queen Elizabeth she could not have Tonnage and Poundage until she agreed to abolish bishops."[90] Russell writes that commentators then and now swiftly agree that Charles was an ineffectual monarch, but they never succeed in ascertaining what it was that made him so. He admits that much of this is a matter of personality or what amounts to style, and that Charles's "ability to rub people up the wrong way," whatever that means, had a lot to do with his failure.[91] It is not surprising, then, that Hobbes also did not put his finger on it, but gave a sense of it through his description of how Charles behaved. After all this, Hobbes's praise of the king's courage as he faced his execution seems kind. But attributing to him "courage, patience, wisdom, and goodness"[92] does not erase the impression of the king already made by the previous narrative.

Essex

Both great Parliamentary generals before Cromwell were nobles. Robert Devereaux, the third Earl of Essex, was first asked by Parliament to provide an armed guard for them to secure their travel to and from the House, on the pretence that otherwise the king and his men would threaten them. Then, when they had raised an army, they asked Essex to be the general of their forces in England and Ireland. Hobbes depicts Essex as an able and experienced military man who exuded judgment and courage. He attributes his alliance with Parliament to the fact that he was not "so great a favourite at court, as that they might not trust him with their army against the King."[93] Hence, Hobbes attributes a selfish motive to Essex's choice to aid Parliament—he had not been treated well by the king and court, and had potentially much more to gain with the Parliament. Why was Essex unpopular at court? Hobbes goes on to analyze Essex's reasons for turning against the king by explaining this unpopularity:

> I believe verily, that the unfortunateness of his marriages had so discountenanced his conversation with ladies, that the court could not be his proper element, unless he had had some extraordinary favour there, to balance that calamity. But for particular discontent from the King, or intention of revenge for any supposed disgrace, I think he had none, nor that he was any ways addicted to Presbyterian doctrines, or other fanatic tenets in Church or State; saving only, that he was carried away with the stream (in a manner) of the whole nation, to think that England was not an absolute, but a mixed monarchy; not considering that the supreme power must always be absolute, whether it be in the King or in the Parliament.[94]

Holmes states the problem of the divorced Essex more bluntly: "Essex agreed to lead the parliamentary army because his wife's too-public dalliance had humiliated him at court, calling his manliness into question and exposing him to the disagreeable reputation of a cuckold."[95] But in 1644, Essex resigned his commission because the Parliament no longer had confidence in him, "suspecting the Earl of Essex, though I think wrongfully, to be too much a royalist, for not having done so much as they looked for, in this second battle at Newbury."[96] The king had offered Essex pardon in exchange for his loyalty (as he had done with others, but Essex did not accept),[97] and as J. S. A. Adamson explains, Parliament's suspicion had its origin in an offer Charles had made to Essex in 1644 "to join forces with him to impose a settlement that guaranteed Essex dominance of the future government."[98] Essex had also been known to disobey the Committee of Both Kingdoms'[99] military orders and act independently. "Misgivings as to Essex's military objectives were now heightened by the prospect that he might accept Charles's offer and turn against the Scots."[100] At this point Sir Thomas Fairfax was made general.

In Hobbes's description of Essex, one can clearly see an opportunist. Here is a man who made his decisions based upon what he could gain, and perhaps also upon personal resentment, but never because of principle. The one principle discussed, that of admiration for mixed monarchy, seems more like an excuse than a reason. Essex is someone who is "carried away" by this latest way of thinking, and carried away also by his popularity with the people. Ironically, he was treated by the Parliament with the same degree of respect as he had paid the king. As soon as they no longer found him useful, they discarded him without apologies, accusing him of being too friendly with the king, but really being fearful of his personal ambition.

Essex died in the same year the king was arrested, 1646, and Hobbes takes pains to point out these two events in the same paragraph, perhaps to show the connection between the two men, which Essex insisted upon denying.[101] That connection, in Hobbes's view, was—or should have been—one of mutual safety. The nobles could not be safe without a strong monarch, and the monarchy could not be safe without an obedient and supportive upper class. But neither side acted as if they truly knew that, until it was too late to change the course of events.

Strafford

Hobbes singles out Sir Thomas Wentworth (later Earl of Strafford) as an example of a man with a particularly waffling character. Wentworth was a member of the upper gentry, "by birth and estate very considerable in his own county, which was Yorkshire,"[102] and often chosen to serve in Parliament. He was well thought of by the common people. Hobbes describes his political leanings as fairly popular—he respected the precedents from previous Parliaments, objected to extra-parliamentary taxes, tried to keep parliamentary taxes low, and resisted the arbitrary exercise of the king's power against the people. He often sought redress of grievances against the king, such as when the king was too generous with one favorite, or gave too much power to one of his officers, and of course, when the king decided to tax the people without consent of Parliament. A notes in *Behemoth* that he was among those who often refused to give the king money when asked.[103]

Then, Wentworth changed his mind, and allied himself with the king against the Parliament. A explains that the cause of this change of heart was entirely selfish. When the Parliament was called by the king in desperation to raise money for the war against the Scots, Sir Thomas Wentworth was in effect bribed:

During that Parliament the King made Sir Thomas Wentworth a baron, recommending to him for his great ability, which was generally taken notice of by the disservice he had done the King in former Parliaments, but which might be useful for him in the times that came on: and not long after he made him of the Council, and after that again Lieutenant of Ireland, which place he discharged with great satisfaction and benefit to his Majesty, and continued in that office, till, by the envy and violence of the Lords and Commons of that unlucky Parliament of 1640, he died. In which year he was made general of the King's forces against the Scots that then entered into England, and the year before, Earl of Strafford.[104]

The Earl of Strafford's sad tale shows how freely members of the gentry and nobility disrespected the king, not realizing that by doing so they were ultimately undermining their own position in society.[105] The earl was no doubt motivated by envy and resentment to side with those who were critical of the king and wanted a mixed form of government. At least this is what Hobbes wishes his readers to believe. Then, having finally been given what he always wanted, high title and the seeming respect of the king, he turned his back on his previous "principles" and, not surprisingly, was looked upon as a traitor by his fellow Parliamentarians. Clearly, Hobbes thinks Wentworth was never motivated by high principles to begin with. Richard Cust agrees with this assessment in his analysis of Wentworth's political maneuvering. He, too, concludes that Wentworth was a supreme opportunist with no moral core.[106] This type of character surely must be one reason why Hobbes and others of his time became so cynical about the claims of gentlemen to be better than those beneath them.

Hobbes describes how the House of Lords condemned Strafford for treason, partly out of envy for the high status he had attained and partly out of fear of the House of Commons.[107] In a strangely unselfish act, Strafford urged the king to sign his condemnation in the hopes that the people could be placated and the danger pass. As noted above, the king acquiesced, but Hobbes notes that he felt regret and even guilt over not protecting his man. Indeed, as Robert Ashton notes, he did vow never to employ Strafford's murderers, which does not seem much consolation.[108] Archbishop Laud, who was imprisoned in the Tower along with Strafford, "wrote apropos the death of Strafford that the King 'knew not how to be or be made great.'"[109] The Earl of Strafford was beheaded 12 May 1640. Hobbes spends eight pages on Strafford's story, from its inglorious beginning to its equally inglorious end. It would seem to be an important study in the character of certain gentlemen, and a cautionary tale, perhaps, for those who do not think strategically enough about the identity of their true benefactors.[110]

Cromwell

The figure of Oliver Cromwell, who is most often treated as a hero in literature old and new, is not surprisingly treated by Hobbes as the ultimate cynical manipulator. As Jeffrey R. Collins points out, Hobbes was not alone in this view: "Posterity remembers Cromwell as a true believer, the ringleader of the saints, and such zealotry hardly seems likely to have seduced Hobbes's hard-nosed political loyalties. But contemporaries were far more prone to portray Cromwell as a strongman, an ambitious practitioner of statecraft. From 1648 on, he was relentlessly characterized as a 'Machiavellian.'"[111] In *Behemoth*, we watch as Cromwell works this way and that, rising in the ranks as a military man for the Parliament, always with one eye on eventually taking advantage of the growing political vacuum. Religious principles mean nothing to Hobbes's Cromwell. He seems to be attuned to Presbyterianism until it turns out that in order to gain control for himself he needs those Hobbes calls "fanatics," men who adhered to the various independent Protestant sects, such as Anabaptists and Quakers. "These were Cromwell's best cards," Hobbes writes, as though Cromwell is playing poker, "whereof he had a very great number in the army, and some in the House, whereof he himself was thought one; though he were nothing certain, but applying himself always to the faction which was strongest, and was of a colour like it."[112] This chameleon-like character had no other motivation than raw power, and Cromwell had a great deal of military and political acumen to serve his ambition. Hobbes argues that Cromwell even held out the possibility of allying with the king at one point, using him to rid himself of Parliament, but "it seems he meant first to try what he could do without the King; and if that proved enough, to rid his hands of him," which he eventually did.[113] Indeed, Hobbes writes that Cromwell's real goal was none other than to set himself up in the place of the king.[114] After the Charles's execution, the main obstacle to Cromwell was the Rump Parliament.[115] His ultimate aim was complete supremacy, in Hobbes's view, not democracy or mixed monarchy. Cromwell's control of the military forces eventually guaranteed that he would get his way, and he was named Protector of England, Ireland, and Scotland in 1653.

Cromwell did not take the title of king only because he was afraid of his army officers who wished to succeed him, and would not have countenanced the idea of Cromwell's son inheriting his throne. Cromwell's fear of "mutiny" was the only thing that prevented him from taking the coveted title.[116] Nevertheless, he obtained the legal right to name his successor, and he proceeded to name his son, Richard, who became protector upon Oliver's death in 1658.[117] But Richard was not the man his father was, and was unable to retain his hold on power. He resigned—to no one in particular, since the Parliament had been barred from sitting.[118]

Collins points out the possibility that Hobbes might have at a certain point admired Cromwell, at least for understanding the necessity to take charge in an atmosphere of weakness and chaos. He might have especially understood the benefit of crushing the power of the old church and placing the new firmly under the control of the government.[119] Nevertheless, Hobbes certainly wanted to leave his readers with the impression that it was also understandable, after all this self-inflicted chaos, and after seeing another and less-desirable man almost become king, that the English people should restore Charles's son, Charles II, to the throne in 1660. In the end, Cromwell's ambition and oppression is treated by Hobbes as his downfall.

DIAGNOSIS

In chapter 1, I argued that Hobbes had one foot planted in the traditional view of honor as based upon character and ability, associated with the moral virtues and separable from power. He had the other foot firmly planted in power politics, in which the very term honor was empty of content, and entirely relative to power, however that power was attained. We can still see his nostalgia for honor in *Behemoth*, when A identifies as wise "he that knows how to bring his business to pass (without the assistance of knavery and ignoble shifts) by the sole strength of his good contrivance." He states that a fool can beat a more skilled man by cheating, but this does not make him wise. Then B replies: "According to your definition, there be few wise men now-a-days. Such wisdom is a kind of gallantry, that few are brought up to, and most think folly. Fine clothes, great feathers, civility toward men that will not swallow injuries, and injury toward them that will, is the present gallantry."[120] Just as Thucydides had noted the inversion of traditional values in the Corcyrean Civil War with great dismay, so we get the sense here that Hobbes does not admire the radical departure from the traditional notion of gentlemanly character that took a powerful hold during the years surrounding the English Civil War. A true gentleman was still someone who believed in doing things openly and honestly, not by any means necessary. A true gentleman did not overly value the trappings of wealth and power, but lived by a code closer to the old chivalric/gentleman's code. As he argues in *De Cive*, a just man does things because they are right, not simply because he is afraid of the law, indicating that a true gentleman is inwardly motivated to do right.[121] Later in the same text, he writes, "They who sin only through infirmity, are good men even when they sin; but these, even when they do not sin, are wicked."[122] If nothing else, this comment shows that Hobbes, in his mature work, still believed in the possibility of good moral character. Even in *Leviathan*, Hobbes warned the aristocrats of his day that instead of taking advantage of their position, they were under a special obligation not to take advantage, just because of their privileged rank. This argument underscores his admiration for good character, which is more than simple obedience to the law:

> The honour of great persons, is to be valued for their beneficence and the aids they give to men of inferior rank, or not at all. And the violences, oppressions, and injuries they do, are not extenuated, but aggravated by the greatness of their persons; because they have the least need to commit them.[123]

The impression of Hobbes these passages leave us (as well as those discussed in chapter 1 concerning honorable conduct on the battlefield) is of someone who very much respected at least some of the gentlemanly values, especially self-restraint and magnanimity. As Keith Thomas puts it, Hobbes was "in no way opposed to an aristocracy as such," but wanted to "eliminate all the more offensive forms of aristocratic behaviour" that he thought started most conflicts, namely that code of honor that was "concerned with personal and family matters" and not with the state as a whole.[124] But, as we have seen from his treatment of the civil war in *Behemoth*, Hobbes found so few of the aristocratic qualities he admired in the leading men of his time that he had to admit that, for most of them, "gentleman" had become an empty term. It was an old-fashioned ideal which could no longer be relied upon, as it had been in the past.[125] Oakeshott points out that Hobbes's friend Sidney Godolphin was emblematic of this character driven by noble pride or honor, which could produce peace and civilization on its own if there were enough of it, but he states Hobbes's view that "it is not because pride does not provide an adequate motive for a successful endeavour for peace, but because of the dearth of noble characters. . . . In short, Hobbes perceived that men lack passion rather than reason, and lack, above all, *this* passion. But where it is present, it is to be recognized as capable of generating an endeavour for peace more firmly based than any other and therefore . . . the surest motive for just conduct."[126] Thomas, who also notes Hobbes's great admiration for Godolphin, explains that Hobbes was not rejecting all notions of honour and courage. On the contrary, he was prescribing a course of action which only the truly "gallant" could follow, and inveighing only against the latest fashion, the "'fine clothes, great feathers, civility toward men that will not swallow injuries, and injuriy toward them that will,' which constituted 'the present gallantry in love and duel.'"[127]

The common people who disrespected their "superiors" were quite right, though the consequences of forgetting their place were regrettable. Their "superiors" had proven that there was nothing intrinsically better about them. What could have set these gentlemen apart was their knowledge, attitude, and behavior, not their bloodlines, as many of them believed. When placed in an environment in which power was disputed, any higher motivations they might have had slipped away and were replaced by ignoble motivations that were all too apparent (at least to Hobbes).

At the end of chapter 4 of *Leviathan*, echoing Thucydides' description of the overturning of all traditional values that took place during the Corcyrean civil war, Hobbes begins to question whether gentlemanly terms such as wisdom and courage mean anything at all, "for one man calleth wisdom what another calleth fear; and one cruelty, what another justice; one prodigality, what another magnanimity; and one gravity, what another stupidity, &c." In Hobbes's view, these are *essentially disputable words*, depending on the speaker's perspective, and therefore "can never be true grounds of any ratiocination."[128] Hobbes goes on to define good and evil in relative terms, always referring back to the individual's perspective, driven by self-interest. And we know that in chapter 10 of *Leviathan*, Hobbes makes the virtues associated with honor relative to power. His agenda is to discourage people from making moral judgments about the government and its laws. If "good" and "evil" are in a practical sense subjective, then the only way out of the conflict they cause is to artificially impose their definitions and enforce obedience. As we know, this is the job of the great artificial man, the *Leviathan*.

In *De Homine*, written after *Leviathan*, Hobbes treats the virtue of courage in a way that may help explain why he must cast doubt upon the universality of the virtues associated with honor. There, he groups courage with prudence and temperance and calls them all cardinal virtues. He says that they are not the virtues of citizens, but of men. This sounds pleasant. However, his point is that they are virtues useful to individual men, but of dubious use to the state. "For just as the state is not preserved save by the courage, prudence, and temperance of good citizens, so it is not destroyed save by the courage, prudence, and temperance of its enemies."[129] In other words, there is such thing as true virtue in the individual, but it can either be helpful or harmful to the commonwealth, depending upon the situation. We know already that Hobbes thinks these virtues can become corrupted in a political setting, surely when coupled with excessive zeal, ambition, and pride. It is not a good idea to demand that the state recognize and elevate men who display these virtues, because they may be turned against the state.

When we think of Hobbes's undermining of aristocratic virtue in the context of his discussion of the history of titles of nobility in *Behemoth* (and his similar discussion in *Leviathan*), we can see clearly that Hobbes believes gentlemen no longer can serve as the source of societal values and ideals. Rather, "gentlemen" must be creatures of the state, their titles accorded not because of character or even bloodlines, but because of their cooperation and obedience. First, he must show that such titles and honors originated not in honorable actions or good birth, but on the much baser foundation of conquest. With

disillusionment will come a more practical approach to the distribution of influence and status in society. He points out that the Angles and the Saxons originated the system of titles of honor used in the England of his day. Chieftains,
chosen by their own peoples to lead conquests, doled out privileges to their followers based on their loyalty and bravery, making some rulers of particular ter-
ritories, and others their chief advisors and officers. The kings of England before the Norman Conquest had certain people who, based upon their loyalty and
service, where chosen to advise and serve their king. The Normans did likewise, replacing the current nobles with men who were loyal to them. And so the
practice continued until Hobbes's own time, always under the same rule—titles
of honor and nobility were given at the pleasure of the sovereign for the value
of the service rendered by those who were loyal to him.[130]

Hobbes's brief history of titles of nobility serves as a reminder, first, that
such status originated from and should continue to be established by the sovereign at the time. There is no intrinsic value in heritage—the value of these
men comes from their service to the king. Secondly, and related to the first
point: currently, the nobles and gentry must remember that they have no independent power—they are creatures of the sovereign, serving at his pleasure. It is wrongheaded for them to use their position to criticize him or undermine him because they would not exist without him. Hobbes points out
repeatedly that the ultimate design of the Presbyterians in particular was to
eliminate the monarchy and the lords entirely, thus making noble titles politically irrelevant. Some of the nobles went along with the Presbyterians' plans
anyway, showing that they did not understand who and what was ultimately
responsible for their privileged position.

Given that Hobbes still seems to believe in a gentlemanly ideal, and yet he
rejects that ideal when it comes to making his political proposals, we have to
wonder, is Hobbes simply of two minds? Is he a political realist unable to
completely discard his old-fashioned gentlemanly sensibilities? Or is there a
way to reconcile these two aspects of Hobbes's teaching? Could it be that true
gentlemanly qualities are only possible in an environment in which the power
structure is well defined, where the parameters are fixed, known, and pre-
dictable? Is this why Hobbes argues in *Leviathan* and elsewhere that the sovereign must define honor and establish what qualifies as honorable? In *Behemoth*, Hobbes discusses three "royal virtues," that is, virtues that the *sovereign*
should have: fortitude, frugality, and liberality. Of fortitude, Hobbes says,
"though it be necessary in such private men as shall be soldiers, yet, for other
men, the less they dare, the better it is both for the commonwealth and for
themselves."[131] The other two are royal virtues inasmuch as they are used for
the betterment of the commonwealth. Frugality preserves and "increases the
public stock," and liberality rewards those who do good things for the com-

monwealth, especially in wars. It is for the sovereign to display virtue and to define it for others. Clearly, the sovereign should define it in such a way to encourage the good of the commonwealth. Without this strong guidance in virtues, "several men praise several customs, and that which is virtue with one, is blamed by others; and, contrarily, what one calls vice, another calls virtue, as their present affections lead them."[132] It is not that there is no such thing as virtue, or that there are not some absolutely good qualities in a man which can be identified and should be encouraged (witness Hobbes's natural laws), but that in a chaotic environment there can be no agreement on what these virtues and qualities are, and no way to guarantee that those who practice them will not be victimized. Because of this, the sovereign's absolute power is Hobbes's first priority. But once this is accomplished, how the sovereign governs, what virtues he displays and encourages, are important to Hobbes as well. The commonwealth will be most successful when the sovereign displays appropriate virtues, and when his laws foster appropriate virtues and discourage those virtues that are not conducive to peace and good order.

Strauss finds that even in *Leviathan*, Hobbes is still capable of saying that magnanimity is or has been considered the *origin* of honor and justice, thus reflecting the traditional view. At the same time, "Precisely because magnanimity is a form of pride, even though it be the most 'honourable' form, it cannot be accepted by Hobbes as the origin of justice. As it rests on a sense of superiority, it runs counter to the recognition of the natural equality of all men, and in the last analysis it is only the recognition of this equality which Hobbes allows to stand as just self-estimation. The theory that magnanimity is the origin of all virtue is thus directly opposed to Hobbes's real intention."[133] While Hobbes continued to admire aristocratic morality personally as an ideal, he had rejected it as not only unusable as a foundation for his political theory, but also as actually dangerous to peace and good order. Thus it was not necessarily a radical doubt about moral truth that led Hobbes to insist that the sovereign define what is virtuous for others. Rather, it might have been instead a doubt about whether or not members of the commonwealth could abide by what they knew was right in a situation (such as a civil war, or another state of nature), where what was right competed with what was in their individual self-interest as they defined it. With the opportunity to gain the sovereignty for themselves firmly out of reach, such men could channel their natural ambition into positive ways of proving their worth as gentlemen through proving their worth to the commonwealth. But when the opportunity to gain sovereignty for themselves was present, the lower aspects of human nature would come to the fore, and the civilized aspects would be forgotten. For this reason, Hobbes must have felt that he had no choice but to insist on

absolute sovereignty above all else as the solution to the problem of competing values and clashing egos.

HOBBES'S SOLUTION

Hobbes returned again and again to the universities in his writing, because it
was at the universities that gentlemen learned their place in the larger
scheme of things. Would they learn that obedience to the sovereign power
was the chief virtue of a gentleman, or would they be taught that the learned
man must exercise personal freedom in pursuing the good and true, even at
the expense of public order? As George MacDonald Ross points out, for the
most part, Hobbes thought that they learned "that they themselves have
greater authority than the sovereign on matters related to governance,
whether through divine inspiration, superior reasoning, or past authority."[134]
In *Behemoth*, Hobbes opined that the universities were the pope's tool during that time when the Catholics dominated England, infusing the upper
classes with Catholic theology and superstition.[135] At that time, the universities were employed, in his view, to keep the people in awe of the church's
authority. But these institutions had now become the "Trojan horse" of the
rebels, because of their teaching of seditious doctrine through the classics, as
well as new interpretations of the Bible. Hobbes blamed the Catholic Church
for bringing knowledge of the Greek and Roman classics to university-educated
gentlemen. This encouraged in them a love for reading in the original. As
they rejected Catholic authority, and turned toward Protestantism, they did
not reject their pursuit of classical knowledge. As Michael Krom explains,
"The schools and universities of Hobbes's own day, while no longer under
the power of the Roman Catholic Church, still continued the tradition of
spreading the Aristotelian-based opinions inimical to peace."[136] And as Hobbes
himself puts it, they:

> became acquainted with the democratical principles of Aristotle and Cicero, and
> from the love of their eloquence fell in love with their politics, and that more
> and more, till it grew into the rebellion we now talk of, without any other ad-
> vantage to the Roman Church but that it was a weakening to us, whom, since we
> broke out of their net in the time of Henry VIII, they have continually endeav-
> oured to recover.[137]

Hobbes was particularly critical of the universities for emphasizing the
teachings of Aristotle, and critical more generally of the ancient position on
issues like the best regime and the good life. For instance, when dealing with
regime types, Hobbes argued against the ancient classification, insisting that

there were only three forms of government, rule by the one, the few, and the many. Other names for government really just expressed the *opinions* of some people:

> There be other names of government, in the histories, and books of policy; as *tyranny*, and *oligarchy*: but they are not the names of other forms of government, but of the same forms misliked. For they that are discontented under *monarchy*, call it *tyranny*; and they that are displeased with *aristocracy*, call it *oligarchy*: so also, they which find themselves grieved under a *democracy*, call it *anarchy*.[138]

For the ancients, in order for government to be good, it needed to aim at producing morally good people. Thus ancient philosophy provided standards by which to judge governments, praising some forms and criticizing others. Likewise, ancient philosophy identified the rightly ordered soul, and thus what justice and virtue were in the individual. Laws that tended to encourage the rightly ordered soul were good, and those that encouraged vice were bad. For Hobbes, this way of thinking made it possible for people to justify rebellion against their governments, always in his view a more dangerous proposition than simply accepting tyranny. Indeed, he makes the second cause of the dissolution of governments (after lack of an absolute power) "*Private judgment of good and evil*,"[139] and even more directly, one of the most frequent causes of rebellion is "*Imitation of the Greeks and Romans.*"[140]

> From the reading, I say, of such books, men have undertaken to kill their kings, because the Greek and Latin writers, in their books, and discourses of policy, make it lawful, and laudable, for any man so to do; provided, before he do it, he call him tyrant. For they say not *regicide*, that is, killing a king, but *tyrannicide*, that is killing of a tyrant is lawful. From the same books, they that live under a monarch conceive an opinion, that the subjects in a popular commonwealth enjoy liberty; but that in a monarchy they are all slaves. I say, they that live under a monarchy conceive such an opinion; not that they live under popular government: for they find no such matter. In sum, I cannot imagine, how any thing can be more prejudicial to a monarchy, than the allowing of such books to be publicly read.[141]

Now the laity, as well as the clergy, were steeped in the tradition of popular government and individual moral choice. The independence of the Protestant frame of mind appropriated the ancient teachings as well as Biblical teachings, and applied them directly to the rebels' own political situation. Hobbes observes that in the House of Commons, the "greatest part" were men who had received a classical education and had learned to admire the histories of the Greeks and Romans.[142] Thus, the very education which the gentry and nobility required in order to maintain their status, also the very education that opened the door to Hobbes's own path to gentlemanly status, which had provided all of the gentlemen of Hobbes's day with their polish and acceptability, was primarily responsible, in his view, for the eventual rebellion of some of them.

> He shows that the idea of distinguishing between just and unjust regimes, like the idea of distinguishing between orthodoxy and heresy, was invented by men for the purpose of domination. In particular, it was invented by Socrates and other philosophers of ancient Greece and Rome, who sought to diminish the power of kings and to defend the republics of their time, while making themselves the arbiters of justice.[143]

Hobbes knew that lasting peace would only come about when "the nobility and gentry know that the liberty of a state is not an exemption from the laws of their own country, whether made by an assembly or by a monarch, but an exemption from the constraint and insolence of their neighbors."[144] That is, these elites must realize that they cannot truly be free as long as they demand to be exempt from the laws or above them, as long as they claim some right to judge and oppose the commands of the sovereign because of their supposedly elevated status. They cannot be free, because through such attitudes they will inevitably create conflict, which produces the fear and insecurity that circumscribe everyone's choices. Peter Hayes points out that for Hobbes "the natural equality between men means that honorable positions have a conventional rather than a naturalistic basis. The only claim to superiority by those at the head of society lies in acts of benevolence to those beneath them."[145] True freedom, in Hobbes's view, comes from equal obedience to the sovereign will on the part of every member of society, regardless of social or economic status. They must stifle their ambition to enlarge their freedom.

Hobbes's answer to the problem of university education has already been alluded to, and is basically the same in *Behemoth* as it appears in *De Cive*[146] and *Leviathan*: the universities must be brought firmly under the control of the sovereign power; their teachings must be in line with the interests of the commonwealth. The universities, A says, are "nevertheless . . . not to be cast away, but to be better disciplined: that is to say, that the politics there taught be made to be (as true politics should be) such as are fit to make men know, that it is their duty to obey all laws whatsoever that shall by the authority of the King be enacted."[147] Whereas the laity is now being taught a Christianity of conflict by prideful ministers (who themselves are taught by "vain philosophers" in the universities)[148] whose own honor- and glory-seeking wreaks havoc upon the commonwealth, the religion they should teach should emphasize the meekness of the Christian personality. This is the part of the Christian teaching that is edifying in Hobbes's view, the part that is compatible with obedience to the king and can only be helpful to our fellow human beings. Writing of the inherent dangers Hobbes saw in a religion based upon a book which all could read and interpret, and sensing the implications Hobbes's preferred Christian teaching of meekness and obedience had for manly ideals, Holmes comments, "So valuable is this unmanning or dis-couragement to the state that the appalling risks of a book-based religion must be run."[149]

As an example of this "unmanning" or "dis-couragement," A says that universities and the preachers they train should teach a version of Christianity which emphasizes

> a quiet waiting for the coming again of our blessed Saviour, and in the mean time a resolution to obey the King's laws (which also are God's laws); to injure no man, to be in charity with all men, to cherish the poor and sick, and to live soberly and free from scandal; without mingling our religion with points of natural philosophy, as freedom of will, incorporeal substance, everlasting nows, ubiquities, hypostases, which the people understand not, nor will ever care for.[150]

Hobbes's preferred meek Christian virtues certainly depart from the previous emphasis on martial valor in the code of chivalry, but they also depart from the gentlemanly ideal of Hobbes's own day: the man as an independent thinker, someone who acts on his own principles and is willing to argue and to take up arms if necessary for the right cause. They call not for independence of thought, courage, and strength, but rather "humility, equity, justice, mercy, and other moral virtues befriending peace, which pertain to the discharge of the duties of men one toward the other."[151] In fact, most of Hobbes's laws of nature, which are to be used as the basis for teaching the moral law, encompass the peaceful Christian virtues. He summarizes his intent in *De Cive*:

> Reason declaring peace to be good, it follows by the same reason, that all the necessary means to peace be good also; and therefore that modesty, equity, trust, humanity, mercy, (which we have demonstrated to be necessary to peace), are good manners or habits, that is, virtues. The law therefore, in the means to peace, commands also good manners, or the practice of virtue: and therefore it is called moral.[152]

To put this teaching into the context of Hobbes's observations in *Behemoth*, the upper-class men of Hobbes's day had, in his view, already departed from the traditional gentlemanly character with their disregard for others, their selfishness, irresponsibility, and cowardice. They had abused religion, manipulating it in an attempt to grab power. Instead of providing a higher purpose and source of genuine principles, a means of thinking beyond themselves about the common good, religion had become a mere tool for the destruction of that good. In this context, it becomes understandable why Hobbes would want to remind his fellow citizens of what might be considered the feminine side of Christianity—the soft, charitable, obedient side. The gentlemen of his society, in particular, had displayed a great arrogance, and they especially needed to be taught in the universities that a good Christian is an obedient soul who must give up the desire to lord over others, for the sake of peace.[153] Thus, Hobbes takes up the cause of the newer idea of the gentleman as a man of Christian virtue, and wishes to shape that idea further in the direction of humility and weakness. Hobbes takes great care in both *De Cive* and *Leviathan* to show that all of the meeker virtues are enjoined by the Bible, through multiple citations for each one. He calls the laws of nature not only the whole moral law, but the "whole law of Christ."[154] We can see his joining of natural law with the law of Christ and his own political teaching of sovereignty and obedience in his words:

> But because they who love God cannot but desire to obey the divine law, and they who love their neighbours cannot but desire to obey the moral law, which consists as hath been showed above in chap. III in the prohibition of pride, ingratitude, contumely, inhumanity, cruelty, injury, and the like offences, whereby our neighbours are prejudiced, therefore also love or charity is equivalent to obedience.[155]

In place of the universities' current emphasis on the classics, and in addition to his particular version of Christian theology, Hobbes would have introduced more science and mathematics into the universities, and not only natural science and mathematics,[156] both of which he highly praised as much more concrete and useful, but also and most importantly his own science of politics. Hobbes called for his political science to be taught instead of Aristotle's. "Therefore I think it may be profitably printed, and more profitably taught in the Universities" as conducive to "the public tranquillity," he wrote.[157] A solid education in Hobbes's political science, coupled with his theology, would produce the gentleman ready to obey his sovereign and contribute positively to his society. As Jeremy Anderson points out, changing education is essential to the sovereign because he literally cannot rely solely on the use of force and the threat of force to maintain the peace: "So the more menacing—and hence effective—the sovereign's threat of punishment is, the more expensive it is to maintain it, and the greater the tendency for subjects to see the sovereign not as the protector of their prosperity but as the obstacle to it."[158] "In other words, if the people are not 'diligently and truly taught' the reasons for the sovereign's right to rule, they will not see the sovereign's penalties as legitimate exercises of power but as acts of aggression which they will oppose in self-defense."[159] Thus, only by fundamentally changing the way the elites, and then the common people, think, will lasting obedience and peace be obtained.

ABSOLUTE OBEDIENCE AND THE MARTYR

Given the solution discussed above, which involves learning a new Christian theology that demands absolute obedience to the sovereign will, and given Hobbes's own references to martyrs, it is appropriate to focus on this figure for a moment. The martyrs of the Old and New Testament were the heroes of the Christian religion, willing to die for their faith rather than obey their pagan sovereigns, and they were certainly a source of great admiration for the Christian knighthood. The emulation of such religious conviction seems to be encouraged by the biblical authors (and by Catholic and early Protestant churches alike through the lives of the saints), and this fact is particularly challenging to Hobbes's insistence that, in effect, there is no principle, religious or otherwise, worth dying for. "Hobbes," writes John Seaman concerning Hobbes entire approach to Christianity, "that great philosopher of civil peace, found religion deeply problematical. In the *Leviathan*, he claimed that it was an unresolved religious issue, the problem of how to obey both God and human authority, which had provided thus far the 'most frequent praetext of Sedition, and Civille Warre, in Christian Commonwealths, and, apparently, the difficulty was specifically Christianity, not religion as such, for Hobbes suggested that outside Christendom there were no civil wars about religion.'"[160] Seaman convincingly argues that Hobbes was not a Christian writer per se, and also did not have as his purpose the destruction of Christianity, but had in view, instead, the religion's liberalization. "It is the secular concern for preserving a this-worldly civil peace, with its essentially liberal emphasis on securing rights-respecting relationships between people, that overshadows in the public sphere the biblical concern for a righteous relationship between people and God."[161] Ronald Beiner writes that while Machiavelli attempted to paganize Christianity to try to subdue its tendency toward meekness and humility, Hobbes sought to "Judaicize" it. "What it means to Judaicize Christianity is that the Christian religion ceases to assert any otherworldly claims whatsoever, and limits itself to this-worldly claims on behalf of Christ's eventual reclamation of temporal power."[162]

Perhaps there can be no better example of Hobbes's rejection of otherworldly claims than his treatment of martyrdom. Through it, we can perhaps see most clearly how deeply Hobbes rejects previous definitions of the good Christian, which he believed caused men of his own time to seek war instead of peace. As we have seen, Hobbes repeatedly insists that the only rational, and even Christian, position for a subject is complete obedience to the sovereign, even in those areas having to do with religious conscience. In *De Cive*, he writes that citizens must think of themselves as transferring "their right of judging the manner of God's worship on him or them who have the sovereign power. Nay, they must do it; for else all manner of absurd opinions concerning the nature of God, and all ridiculous ceremonies which have been used by any nations, will be seen at once in the same city."[163] Hobbes describes a situation in which a citizen is commanded to do something that directly affronts God. In this instance, Hobbes seems at first to stand with the martyr, writing "it does not follow, neither must we obey."[164] He also argues that if a sovereign should ask men to worship him as a God (in the sense of praying for him to do things only God can do, like making it rain), the subject should not obey.[165] But he argues that anything short of this direct denial of God or His powers should be obeyed, including worshipping of idols or calling God by a different name. He makes a distinction between worship of God (divine worship) and "civil worship." Most of the actions that a sovereign would actually demand of his subjects are included under this category, such as "genuflection, prostration, or any other act of the body whatsoever."[166] These things demonstrate obedience to the civil power and therefore are not a sin.

Again, Hobbes separates those laws which cannot be obeyed from those that can. If the sovereign orders atheism, or idolatry, or apostasy, he must not be obeyed. But we have already seen that worshiping the sovereign himself with "civil worship" is not idolatry for Hobbes, and that we must obey the sovereign even when he asks us to worship idols, if it is an attempt to honor God (which we must assume it is, even if misguided). Hobbes distinguishes between natural and conventional worship, and argues that what is natural is honoring God, while what is conventional is the way we do it. Therefore, many actions can honor God, and as long as the intent of the citizen is to do so, there is no sin, regardless of what the action may be.[167]

When it comes to apostasy, Hobbes argues that there is only one article of faith which one must believe to be saved, "that Jesus is Christ," and this need only be "believed with an inward faith."[168] Therefore, there is really no way the sovereign can make us commit apostasy, since nothing he does can affect our inward dispositions, and "with Christ, the will to obey is obedience."[169] Hobbes works very hard to make this seemingly blasphemous obedience a Christian imperative:

> But then what shall we answer to our Saviour's saying, (Matt. 10:33) *Whosoever denieth me before men, I will deny him before my Father which is in heaven.* This we may say, that whatsoever a subject, as Naaman was, is compelled to do in obedience to his sovereign, and doth it not in order to his own mind, but in order to the laws of his country, that action is not his, but his sovereign's; nor is it he that in this case denieth Christ before men, but his governor, and the law of his country.[170]

The entire responsibility remains with the sovereign and not with the subject, so that people with sensitive consciences need not be worried about their spiritual future if they obey what they consider a sinful law or order. The only real sin the citizen can commit is treason.[171]

As Strauss points out, in *Elements*, *De Cive*, and *Leviathan*, Hobbes "denies the obligation and even the right of martyrdom to the ordinary Christian who has not the special vocation of preaching the Gospel."[172] Thus it appears that only a minister has any obligation to resist a sacrilegious order. But then in *Leviathan*, in an attempt to bolster this position, Hobbes reinterprets the very word "martyr" so that it does not mean what countless generations thought it had. It is impossible for a modern man to be a martyr, "since 'martyr' means 'witness'; since Saint Peter considered only witnesses to the resurrection of Christ to be Christian martyrs; and since no one today fits this category, it follows that no one today can claim the distinction of being a martyr."[173] Through this argument, Hobbes eliminates the possibility of obligating anyone, even the most holy or most prominent, to resist a sacrilegious order.

Hobbes circumvents any objection, including, as we have seen, the seemingly absolute commandment against idolatry.[174] He meticulously reinterprets the Bible so that Christians are morally obligated to abject obedience and have no moral responsibility of their own *except for that obedience*. The subject can literally never go wrong by obeying, even to the point of what conscientious Christians of his day would think of as committing mortal sin deserving eternal punishment. Hobbes reassures Christians that the only thing they need to do in order to receive salvation is to believe in their hearts (without any outward appearance whatsoever) that Jesus is the Christ.[175] Hobbes goes so far as to wryly mock martyrdom as a form of hypocrisy:

> But what? Must we resist princes, when we cannot obey them? Truly, no; for this is contrary to our civil covenant. What must we do then? Go to Christ by martyrdom; which if it seem to any man to be a hard saying, most certain it is that he believes not with his whole heart, that Jesus is the Christ, the Son of the living God (for he would then desire to be dissolved, and to be with Christ) but he would by a feigned Christian faith elude that obedience which he hath contracted to yield unto the city.[176]

Hobbes comments with an obvious smile in *Leviathan* that "To die for every tenet that serveth the ambition, or profit of the clergy, is not required."[177] He writes something very similar on the very last page of *De Cive*, implying that most cases of martyrdom are the result of misguided followers of some ambitious individual or institution.[178] He links his doubt about the motivation of martyrs directly with the Christian saints:

> To this end also tends the canonization of saints, which the heathen called apotheosis; for he that can allure foreign subjects with so great a reward, may bring

those who are greedy of such glory, to dare and do anything. For what was it but an honourable name with posterity, which the Decii and other Romans sought after, and a thousand others, who cast themselves upon incredible perils?[179]

Hobbes's reference to the Decii is particularly striking, because the Decii were not Christian martyrs of Rome, but members of a prominent Roman family, of which three members, all named Publius Decius Mus, had died in battle for their country. By using this reference, he equates the motivation of Christian martyrs who became saints with the motivation he imparts to the Decii, which is the dangerous pursuit of honor and glory (though they were faithful subjects of Rome).

While we can certainly sympathize with his motivations, a strong argument can be made that Hobbes's teaching runs counter to any sound understanding of Christian obligation. Perhaps this is the main reason why his theology failed to convince his contemporaries. As A. P. Martinich has concluded, "his critics were correct, to a large extent, in sensing that his attempt to salvage religion would not work. Rather than supplying an adequate conceptual foundation for religion, on the whole his views fit into a long tradition that tended to undermine it, often contrary to the intentions of the authors."[180] In effect, Martinich thinks that Hobbes destroyed a great deal of the essence of his religion in order to save it, but that he was making a sincere effort and was not simply an atheist.

One can make the case that Hobbes's theology also failed because his advocacy of absolute obedience takes aim at any reasonable notion of manliness. As F. C. Hood put it, "He did not believe that Christian faith was necessarily accompanied by fortitude, or that fortitude was required of all Christians. Lack of fortitude is dishonourable, but is not a breach of any of God's laws."[181] And as we have seen, dishonor is in the eye of the beholder, in a practical sense. But a gentleman is independent-minded, principled, and courageous. While a gentleman might avoid tilting at windmills, the idea that he would give up all judgment, and in a servile manner obey every command in order to survive, would certainly make him less than a gentleman. Especially in the area of religious beliefs and practice, an area that was becoming more and not less important to the manly ideal in Hobbes's day, a gentleman would not be willing to voluntarily submit to such subjection. But of course, stubborn pride like this was a great deal of the problem, in Hobbes's view. There were a great many gentlemen who were too fixated on high principles because of their pride, especially in matters of religion, and too willing to take up the sword rather than be subjected to a change in their outward religious beliefs and practices. For them it was not enough, as Hobbes advocated, to believe what you wanted to in the silence of your heart, while outwardly bowing to the prevailing power. That would have violated their consciences and their pride.

But here we get to the heart of the matter—for Hobbes, pride is always a bad thing, leading men into conflict. For the gentleman, pride is the ultimate motivation, and conflict is far from the worst outcome. Loss of pride, loss of a sense of self is a far worse fate than even the loss of one's life. We simply have two diametrically opposed views of what is important—life or dignity—and hence two different judgments placed upon pride. When one chooses life as the most important aim no matter what the cost, one of necessity loses one's dignity, but for Hobbes, dignity is equated with sinful pride, and is a concept that merely gets in the way of survival and comfort. If one puts dignity first, it can come at the cost of one's life. This is a conflict that cannot ultimately be resolved to the satisfaction of the community, perhaps, but is resolved every day in the lives of individuals, through the choices they make.

CONCLUSION

Hobbes's criticism of actual gentlemen during the civil war, as well as his treatment of gentlemanly virtues in his political philosophy, tends to destroy the previous meaning of the word "gentleman" as an independent-minded man of superior quality and wisdom. "Gentleman" comes to mean simply a member of the upper class, a status obtained through the will of the sovereign. While the ancient philosophers preferred that power be assigned to men on the basis of their attainment of the virtues they admired, in Hobbes's world men were called virtuous if they were recognized by others as having power, regardless of their actual merits. The meaning of such words as wise, courageous, good, and charitable were in a practical sense relative—and this argument eliminates the independent usefulness of any of the manly virtues, at least when it comes to the building of the political regime that Hobbes desires.

In his political philosophy, Hobbes develops themes that aim at the very existence of true gentlemen. He destroys the ideals of physical courage and martial valor by making self-preservation the absolute and inviolable imperative upon which the social system must rest. He makes it impossible to see the risking of one's life for a greater good as anything but a foolish presumption. He criticizes the education of the gentleman for doing precisely what it was designed to do: creating a moral, principled man who is intellectually strong and independent-minded. Such a man is too much of a threat to absolute sovereignty. Hobbes encourages abject obedience to the sovereign for the sake of peace, obedience so total—even to the point of delegitimizing martyrdom—as to seem servile and thus inappropriate for a true gentleman.

Hobbes's primary mission, of course, was not the destruction of the ideal of the gentleman, but rather the establishment of a new type of political system which he hoped would provide more stability, peace, and prosperity.

This system would be constructed not on ideals, but on basic facts of experience such as fear of death and desire to survive. But in the process of constructing the new political science, Hobbes rather directly and consciously attacked many of the virtues and qualities of the gentleman of his day. It is reasonable to conclude that Hobbes thought that even the true gentleman was an obstacle to peace and had to be a necessary casualty of political progress. Many of the virtues of the gentleman were relics of an ancient and medieval past whose romantic reputation was an unacceptable cause of conflict. Hobbes concluded that the ideal of the gentleman had to be given up for the sake of peace.

NOTES

1. John Aubrey, *Aubrey's Brief Lives*, ed. Oliver Lawson Dick (London: Secker and Warburg, 1950), 148.

2. A. P. Martinich, *Hobbes: A Biography* (Cambridge: Cambridge University Press, 1999), 5.

3. Miriam M. Reik, *The Golden Lands of Thomas Hobbes* (Detroit: Wayne State University Press, 1977), 25.

4. Martinich, *Hobbes: A Biography*, 19.

5. Lisa T. Sarasohn, "Thomas Hobbes and the Duke of Newcastle: A Study in the Mutuality of Patronage before the Establishment of the Royal Society," *Isis* 90, no. 4 (December 1999): 718. She states on the same page that Hobbes "was, to some extent, a dependent of Devonshire's and, as such, a kind of servant rather than a gentleman."

6. Hobbes was excluded from membership in the Royal Society. Most scholars seem to attribute this more to the perception of Hobbes among nonadmirers as boorish, or the popular perception of Hobbes as an atheist. As Quentin Skinner ably points out, however, Hobbes's problems with intellectuals seemed to be much more severe in England than on the continent, and even in England he was well respected by many scholars. See his "The Ideological Context of Hobbes's Political Thought," *The Historical Journal* 9, no. 3 (1966): 286–317.

7. See Noel Malcolm, *Aspects of Hobbes* (New York: Oxford University Press, 2003), 318.

8. Sarasohn, "Thomas Hobbes and the Duke of Newcastle," 718–19.

9. Gabriella Slomp, *Thomas Hobbes and the Political Philosophy of Glory* (London: Macmillan Press Ltd., 2000), 22.

10. See Sara Hutton, "In Dialogue with Thomas Hobbes: Margaret Cavendish's Natural Philosophy," *Women's Writing* 4, no. 3 (1997).

11. Sarasohn writes, "Newcastle wrote poems and prefaces to her scientific works, defending her right to publish her audacious ideas on the grounds that her philosophy was better than any written before." Sarasohn, "Thomas Hobbes and the Duke of Newcastle," 735.

12. Vickie B. Sullivan, *Machiavelli, Hobbes, and the Formation of Liberal Republicanism in England* (Cambridge: Cambridge University Press, 2004), 82.

13. Lawrence Stone, *The Crisis of the Aristocracy: 1558–1641* (Oxford: Clarendon Press, 1965).

14. Thomas Hobbes, *Behemoth or the Long Parliament*, ed. Ferdinand Tönnies (Chicago: University of Chicago Press, 1990), part 1, pp. 39–40.

15. Hobbes, *Behemoth*, part 1, p. 4.

16. Stone, *The Crisis of the Aristocracy,* 51.

17. Hobbes recognizes this as a problem. He lists it as such in *Behemoth*, as "The selling of titles of honour, of judges, and serjeants' places, and other offices." *Behemoth*, part 2, p. 84.

18. For instance, Hobbes depicts the Parliament's army as financed by "the great purse of the City of London," *Behemoth*, part 2, p. 110. In part 3, p. 142, A criticizes the merchants as "men that never look upon anything but their present profit; . . . If they had understood what virtue there is to preserve their wealth in obedience to their lawful sovereign, they would never have sided with the Parliament; and so we had had no need of arming." Deborah Baumgold, while arguing that a "concept of class is absent from the theory," observes that "some readers have seen an analysis in terms of material causes in his remarks concerning the role in the rebellion of merchants and the city of London." Baumgold, "Hobbes's Political Sensibility: The Menace of Political Ambition," in *Thomas Hobbes and Political Theory*, ed. Mary G. Dietz (Lawrence: University Press of Kansas, 1990), 82.

19. Hobbes, *Behemoth*, part 1, p. 22.

20. Stone, *The Crisis of the Aristocracy*, 51.

21. Stone, *The Crisis of the Aristocracy*, 23.

22. Stone, *The Crisis of the Aristocracy*, 9.

23. Stone, *The Crisis of the Aristocracy*, 35.

24. Alison Wall, "Patterns of Politics in England, 1558–1625," *The Historical Journal* 31, no. 4 (December 1988): 955.

25. C. B. Macpherson, *The Political Theory of Possessive Individualism: Hobbes to Locke* (Oxford: Clarendon Press, 1962), 62–63.

26. Macpherson, *The Political Theory of Possessive Individualism*, 65.

27. Thomas Hobbes, *De Cive*, ed. Sterling P. Lamprecht (Westport, Conn.: Greenwood Press, 1982), part 2, ch. 6, sect. 15, p. 80.

28. Keith Thomas, "The Social Origins of Hobbes's Political Thought," in *Hobbes Studies*, ed. K. C. Brown (Oxford: Basil Blackwell, 1965), 188.

29. Leo Strauss, *Natural Right and History* (Chicago: University of Chicago Press, 1953); *The Political Philosophy of Hobbes: Its Basis and Its Genesis*, trans. Elsa M. Sinclair (Chicago: University of Chicago Press, Midway reprint, 1963).

30. Baumgold, "Hobbes's Political Sensibility," 82.

31. Thomas, "The Social Origins of Hobbes's Political Thought," 191.

32. Norbert Elias, *The Civilizing Process: The History of Manners*, trans. Edmund Jephcott (New York: Urizon Books, 1978), 212.

33. Diane Bornstein, *Mirrors of Courtesy* (Hamden, Conn.: Archon Books, 1975), 9.

34. Bornstein, *Mirrors of Courtesy*, 107.

35. David Burchell, "The Disciplined Citizen: Thomas Hobbes, Neostoicism and the Critique of Classical Citizenship," *The Australian Journal of Politics and History* 45, no. 4 (1999): 506.

36. Richard Barber, *The Reign of Chivalry* (London: David & Charles, 1980), 50.

37. Elias, *The Civilizing Process*, 53.

38. Barber, *The Reign of Chivalry*, 184.

39. Barber, *The Reign of Chivalry*, 183–84.

40. Barbara J. Shapiro, "The Universities and Science in Seventeenth-Century England," *The Journal of British Studies* 10, no. 2 (May 1971): 72.

41. See Bornstein, *Mirrors of Courtesy*, especially pp. 112–17, for a good discussion of the transition from the warlike chivalric values to the more peaceful values of a gentleman through a discussion of popular courtesy books.

42. W. Lee Ustick wrote: "Not only is religion respectable, in the late seventeenth century, as well as necessary for the salvation of the soul; the obligation to be of service to mankind—a trait connected with the Christian spirit rather than the age-old concept of *noblesse oblige*—finds frequent expression in conduct books late in the century." *Modern Philology* 30, no. 2 (November 1932): 161.

43. Margaret Cavendish, *The World's Olio* (London: J. Martin and J. Allestrye, 1655), 663. Obtained through *EEBO: Early English Books Online*, eebo.chadwyck .com. Hobbes of course resided in the Cavendish household, and yet Margaret denied any direct contact with him, a denial that may or may not have been totally accurate. Margaret apparently commented upon Hobbes's work, for the most part negatively.

44. Hobbes, *De Cive*, part 2, ch. 10, sect. 2, p. 115.

45. Thomas Hobbes, *The Whole Art of Rhetoric*, book 2, ch. 8, p. 459, and ch. 19, p. 471, in *The English Works of Thomas Hobbes*, ed., Sir William Molesworth, vol. 7 (Ger.: Scientia Verlag Aalen, 1962).

46. Thomas Hobbes, "De Homine," in *Man and Citizen [De Homine and De Cive]*, ed. Bernard Gert (Indianapolis: Hackett Publishing Company, 1991), ch. 11, para. 11, p. 51.

47. Hobbes, *The Whole Art of Rhetoric*, book 2, ch. 8, p. 459.

48. Thomas Hobbes, *Leviathan*, ed. Michael Oakeshott (New York: Macmillan Publishing Co., 1962), author's introduction, para. 7, pp. 19–20.

49. Thomas Hobbes, *Leviathan*, author's introduction, para. 7, p. 20.

50. Hobbes, "De Homine," in *Man and Citizen*, ch. 13, para. 5, p. 66.

51. Stephen Holmes, "Political Psychology in Hobbes's *Behemoth*," in *Thomas Hobbes and Political Theory*, ed. Mary G. Dietz (Lawrence: University Press of Kansas, 1990), 125–26. I have omitted Holmes's reference numbers after the quotation of certain terms for clarity. The reader is encouraged to check Holmes's citations, which are very thorough, concerning these terms and ideas in *Behemoth*.

52. Hobbes, *Behemoth*, part 1, p. 27. A says of cities: "those great capital cities, when rebellion is upon pretence of grievances, must needs be of the rebel party: because the grievances are but taxes, to which citizens, that is, merchants, whose profession is their private gain, are naturally mortal enemies; their only glory being to grow excessively rich by the wisdom of buying and selling" (part 3, p. 126).

53. Hobbes even complains that the numbers that actually supported the king with contributions of horse and arms were very few. *Behemoth*, part 3, p. 112. An exception to this lukewarm response would be Hobbes's own patron, the Earl of Newcastle, who is depicted as steadfastly behind the king, and serving ably as commander of the king's troops in the north. See *Behemoth*, part 2, pp. 103, 122–24, for mentions of Newcastle.

54. Hobbes, *Behemoth*, part 3, p. 119.

55. Holmes, "Political Psychology," 122.

56. Robert P. Kraynak, "Hobbes's Behemoth and the Argument for Absolutism," *The American Political Science Review* 76, no. 4 (December 1982): 838.

57. Holmes, "Political Psychology," 123.

58. Hobbes, *Behemoth*, part 2, p. 95.

59. Martinich, *Hobbes: A Biography*, 323.

60. A says, for instance, that the Parliament "to increase their disaffection to his Majesty, they accused him of a purpose to introduce and authorize the Roman religion in this kingdom: than which nothing was more hateful to the people; not because it was erroneous (which they had neither learning nor judgment enough to examine), but because they had been used to hear it inveighed against in the sermons and discourses of the preachers whom they trusted to" (*Behemoth*, part 2, p. 60).

61. Hobbes, *Behemoth*, part 2, p. 20. One of the pieces of legislation passed by the Long Parliament showed what position the Catholic Lords were in: "7. That the votes of Popish lords in the House of Peers be taken away, and that a bill be passed for the education of the children of Papists in the Protestant religion" (*Behemoth*, part 2, p. 106).

62. Hobbes lists "Brownists, Anabaptists, Independents, Fifth-monarchy-men, Quakers, and divers others, all commonly called by the name of fanatics: insomuch as there was no so dangerous an enemy to the Presbyterians, as this brood of their own hatching" (*Behemoth*, part 3, p. 136).

63. Hobbes, *Behemoth*, part 4, p. 159. Again he compares them with Catholics: "What have we then gotten by our deliverance from the Pope's tyranny, if these petty men succeed in the place of it, that have nothing in them that can be beneficial to the public, except their silence?" (*Behemoth*, part 4, p. 172).

64. Hobbes, *Behemoth*, part 1, p. 21.

65. Hobbes, *Behemoth*, part 1, p. 24. Hobbes's artful slams on these ministers continue with great ire through page 26.

66. Kraynak, "Hobbes's Behemoth," 839.

67. Hobbes, *Behemoth*, part 1, p. 47. See also pp. 56–57, where Hobbes makes the same connection with the pope, implying that the Anglican clergy were no better in assuming that "their spiritual power did depend not upon the authority of the King, but of Christ himself, derived to them by a successive imposition of hands from bishop to bishop." Indeed, Hobbes even characterizes the Anglican clergy as believing that they had "divine right (not depending on the King's leave), to the government of the Church" (*Behemoth*, part 2, p. 95).

68. See for instance Hobbes, *Behemoth*, part 1, pp. 51–52, where Hobbes repeats the teaching from *Leviathan*: "And because men do, for the most part, rather draw the

Scripture to their own sense, than follow the true sense of the Scripture, there is no other way to know, certainly, and in all cases, what God commands, or forbids us to do, but by the sentence of him or them that are constituted by the King to determine the sense of the Scripture, upon hearing of the particular case of conscience which is in question."

69. Hobbes, *Behemoth*, part 1, p. 23.

70. A says "the King had accused the Lord Kimbolton, a member of the Lords' house; and Hollis, Haslerigg, Hampden, Pym, and Stroud, five members of the Lower House, of high-treason," causing more of a stir when he visited the House of Commons with an armed guard to arrest the latter five. Hobbes, *Behemoth*, part 2, p. 96.

71. See for instance Hobbes, *Behemoth*, part 1, p. 33.

72. Hobbes, *Behemoth*, part 3, p. 155.

73. Holmes, "Political Psychology," 125.

74. Hobbes, *Behemoth*, part 1, p. 2.

75. Hobbes, *Behemoth*, part 1, p. 2.

76. Hobbes, *Behemoth*, part 1, p. 29.

77. Hobbes, *Behemoth*, part 1, pp. 32–33.

78. Hobbes, *Behemoth*, part 1, p. 35.

79. Hobbes, *Behemoth*, part 1, p. 36.

80. Hobbes, *Behemoth*, part 1, pp. 60–61.

81. Hobbes, *Behemoth*, part 1, p. 66.

82. Baumgold, "Hobbes's Political Sensibility," 77–78.

83. Hobbes, *Behemoth*, part 2, p. 71.

84. Hobbes, *Behemoth*, part 2, p. 80.

85. Hobbes, *Behemoth*, part 2, p. 87.

86. Hobbes, *Behemoth*, part 2, p. 88.

87. Hobbes, *Behemoth*, part 2, p. 96.

88. Hobbes, *Behemoth*, part 2, p. 97.

89. Martinich, *Hobbes: A Biography*, 323.

90. Conrad Russell, *The Causes of the English Civil War: The Ford Lectures Delivered in the University of Oxford, 1987–1988* (Oxford: Clarendon Press, 1990), 162.

91. Russell, *The Causes of the English Civil War*, 185.

92. Hobbes, *Behemoth*, part 3, p. 154.

93. Hobbes, *Behemoth*, part 3, p. 111.

94. Hobbes, *Behemoth*, part 3, p. 112.

95. Holmes, "Political Psychology," 134.

96. Hobbes, *Behemoth*, part 3, p. 130.

97. Robert Ashton, *The English Civil War: Conservatism and Revolution 1603–1649*, 2nd ed. (London: Weidenfeld and Nicolson, 1989), 171.

98. J. S. A. Adamson, "The Baronial Context of the English Civil War," in *The English Civil War*, ed. Richard Cust and Ann Hughes (London: Arnold, 1997), 94.

99. The Committee of Both Kingdoms was created by Parliament when the Scots entered the war as an agency for directing its military efforts. See Robert Ashton, *The English Civil War*, 277–78.

100. Adamson, "The Baronial Context," 94.

101. Hobbes, *Behemoth*, part 3, p. 332.

102. Hobbes, *Behemoth*, part 2, p. 65.

103. Hobbes, *Behemoth*, part 2, p. 65.

104. Hobbes, *Behemoth*, part 2, p. 66.

105. B notes, "It is a strange thing the whole House of Lords should not perceive that the ruin of the King's power, and the weakening of it, was the ruin or weakening of themselves" (Hobbes, *Behemoth*, part 2, p. 70).

106. Richard Cust, "Wentworth's 'change of sides' in the 1620s," in *The Political World of Thomas Wentworth, Earl of Strafford: 1621–1641*, ed. J. F. Merritt (Cambridge: Cambridge University Press, 2003), 63–80.

107. Hobbes, *Behemoth*, part 2, p. 69.

108. Ashton, *The English Civil War*, 143.

109. Maurice Ashley, *The English Civil War: A Concise History* (London: Thames and Hudson, 1974), 51.

110. As to why the nobles did not clearly see where their self-interest lay, A says "For the Lords, very few of them did perceive the intentions of the Presbyterians; and, besides that, they durst not (I believe) oppose the Lower House." He continues, "For indeed the most of them so carried themselves, as if they owed their greatness not to the King's favour and to his letters patent, which gives them their authority, but to the merit of their conceived learning (and had?) no less care of the praises of each other than they showed irritability to defend the dignity of their jurisdiction and of their office, being ever highly offended with those that dissented from their spirit or their ideas" (*Behemoth*, part 2, p. 89). Some material in parentheses which does not change the meaning has been omitted for clarity by the author.

111. Jeffrey R. Collins, *The Allegiance of Thomas Hobbes* (Oxford: Oxford University Press, 2005), 156.

112. Hobbes, *Behemoth*, part 3, p. 136.

113. Hobbes, *Behemoth*, part 3, p. 139.

114. Hobbes, *Behemoth*, part 3, p. 143.

115. Hobbes, *Behemoth*, part 4, p. 179.

116. Hobbes, *Behemoth*, part 4, p. 189.

117. Hobbes, *Behemoth*, part 4, p. 191.

118. Hobbes, *Behemoth*, part 4, p. 194. After his resignation the Rump reemerged, but Hobbes records that period of time in which it seemed that the sovereignty was nowhere with particular irony. He summarizes the many shifts of power on pp. 195–96, for emphasis. One cannot help but see the folly in the English people's inability to agree or focus on any larger goal than their own immediate and narrow self-interest.

119. Collins, *The Allegiance of Thomas Hobbes*, 158.

120. Hobbes, *Behemoth*, part 1, p. 38.

121. Hobbes, *De Cive*, part 1, ch. 3, sect. 5, pp. 45–46.

122. Hobbes, *De Cive*, part 2, ch. 14, sect. 18, p. 167.

123. Hobbes, *Leviathan*, ch. 30, para. 16, p. 254.

124. Thomas, "The Social Origins of Hobbes's Political Thought," 199.

125. And Hobbes's knowledge of Thucydides' *History* would have argued that it was always unreliable.

126. Oakeshott, *Hobbes on Civil Association*, 132.
127. Thomas, "The Social Origins of Hobbes's Political Thought," 196.
128. Hobbes, *Leviathan*, ch. 4, para. 23, p. 40.
129. Hobbes, "De Homine," in *Man and Citizen*, ch. 13, para. 9, p. 69.
130. Hobbes, *Behemoth*, part 2, pp. 76–77.
131. Hobbes, *Behemoth*, part 1, p. 45.
132. Hobbes, *Behemoth*, part 1, p. 45.
133. Strauss, *The Political Philosophy of Hobbes*, 55–56.
134. Ross, "Hobbes and the Authority of the Universities," 69.
135. Hobbes, *Behemoth*, part 1, p. 40.
136. Krom, "Vain Philosophy, the Schools and Civil Philosophy," 118.
137. Hobbes, *Behemoth*, part 1, pp. 43–44.
138. Hobbes, *Leviathan*, part 2, ch. 19, para. 2, p. 142.
139. Hobbes, *Leviathan*, part 2, ch. 29, para. 6, p. 238.
140. Hobbes, *Leviathan*, part 2, ch. 29, para. 14, p. 241.
141. Hobbes, *Leviathan*, part 2, ch. 29, para. 14, pp. 241–42. See also, Hobbes, *De Cive*, part 2, ch. 12, sect. 13, p. 139.
142. Hobbes, *Behemoth*, part 1, p. 3.
143. Kraynak, "Hobbes's Behemoth," 839–40.
144. Hobbes, *Behemoth*, part 1, p. 59.
145. Peter Hayes, "Hobbes's Bourgeois Moderation," *Polity* 31, no. 1 (Autumn 1998): 57.
146. Hobbes writes in *De Cive*, "Wherefore also, on the other side, if any man would introduce sound doctrine, he must begin from the academies. There the true and truly demonstrated foundations of civil doctrine are to be laid; wherewith young men, being once endued, they may afterward, both in private and in public, instruct the vulgar." Hobbes, *De Cive*, part 2, ch. 13, sect. 9, p. 146.
147. Hobbes, *Behemoth*, part 1, p. 58.
148. See Krom, "Vain Philosophy, the Schools and Civil Philosophy," 108.
149. Holmes, "Political Psychology," 142.
150. Hobbes, *Behemoth*, part 1, p. 58.
151. Hobbes, *De Cive*, part 3, ch. 15, sect. 8, p. 180.
152. Hobbes, *De Cive*, part 1, ch. 3, sect. 31, p. 58.
153. See Hobbes, *Behemoth*, part 1, p. 59: "I am therefore of your opinion, both that men may be brought to a love of obedience by preachers and gentlemen that imbibe good principles in their youth at the Universities, and also that we never shall have a lasting peace, till the Universities themselves be in such manner, as you have said, reformed; and the ministers know they have no authority but what the supreme civil power gives them; and the nobility and gentry know that the liberty of a state is not an exemption from the laws of their own country, whether made by an assembly or by a monarch, but an exemption from the constraint and insolence of their neighbors."
154. Hobbes, *Man and Citizen* [*De Homine and De Cive*], ed. Bernard Gert (Indianapolis: Hackett Publishing Company, 1991), part 1, ch. 4, sect. 24, p. 163.
155. Hobbes, *De Cive*, part 3, ch. 18, sect. 3, p. 196

156. As George MacDonald Ross points out, "Hobbes is amply justified in his further criticism that universities neglected mathematics and science based on experiment and reason, in favour of Aristotelian metaphysics, divinity, and law." "Hobbes and the Authority of the Universities," 75.

157. Hobbes, *Leviathan*, "A Review, and Conclusion," para. 16, p. 510.

158. Anderson, "The Role of Education in Political Stability," 100.

159. Anderson, "The Role of Education in Political Stability," 101.

160. John W. Seaman, "Hobbes and the Liberalization of Christianity," *Canadian Journal of Political Science* 32, no. 2 (June, 1999): 227.

161. Seaman, "Hobbes and the Liberalization of Christianity," 245–46.

162. Ronald Beiner, "Machiavelli, Hobbes, and Rousseau on Civil Religion," *The Review of Politics* 55, no. 4 (Autumn 1993): 628.

163. Hobbes, *De Cive*, part 3, ch. 15, sect. 17, p. 190.

164. Hobbes, *De Cive*, part 3, ch. 15, sect. 18, p. 190.

165. Hobbes, *De Cive*, part 3, ch. 15, sect. 18, p. 192.

166. Hobbes, *De Cive*, part 3, ch. 15, sect. 18, p. 192.

167. Hobbes, *De Cive*, part 3, ch. 15, sect. 18.

168. Hobbes, *De Cive*, part 3, ch. 18, sect. 11, p. 207.

169. Hobbes, *De Cive*, part 3, ch. 18, sect. 12, p. 207.

170. Hobbes, *Leviathan*, part 3, ch. 42, para 11, p. 364.

171. See for instance *De Cive*, part 2, ch. 14, p. 155.

172. Strauss, *The Political Philosophy of Thomas Hobbes*, 72.

173. A. P. Martinich, *The Two Gods of Leviathan: Thomas Hobbes on Religion and Politics* (Cambridge: Cambridge University Press, 1992), 304.

174. See Hobbes, *Leviathan*, part 4, ch. 45, para. 23, p. 471.

175. See *De Cive*, part 3, ch. 18, sect. 10, p. 205. For a treatment of the minimal obligation of the subject to believe in Christ, and the absolute obligation to obey his sovereign, see Richard E. Flathman, *Thomas Hobbes: Skepticism, Individuality and Chastened Politics* (London: Sage Publications, 1993), 153–54.

176. Hobbes, *De Cive*, part 3, ch. 18, sect. 13, p. 208. See also *Leviathan*, part 3, ch. 43, para. 15, pp. 430–31.

177. Hobbes, *Leviathan*, part 3, ch. 42, para. 13, pp. 365–66.

178. Hobbes, *De Cive*, part 3, ch. 18, sect. 14, p. 211.

179. Hobbes, *De Cive*, part 3, ch. 18, sect. 14, p. 210.

180. Martinich, *The Two Gods of Leviathan*, 8.

181. F. C. Hood, *The Divine Politics of Thomas Hobbes: An Interpretation of Leviathan* (Oxford: Clarendon Press, 1964), 249.

Chapter Three

Fear and Self-Preservation

It was useful first to explore Hobbes's use of the term honor itself in some detail, and next to take that idea out of the purely abstract realm by looking at Hobbes's own life and times and what he did with the idea of honor in his treatment of the real-life men of his day, especially those prominent in the English Civil War. We have seen that precisely because Hobbes cannot count on gentlemen to be honorable and to maintain order for themselves or for others he must offer a new political science based upon fear and self-interest. We should expect, then, that the core elements of his theory would reflect his rejection of honor as a standard, indeed his condemnation of honor or pride as the main source of unnecessary conflict and suffering. We would expect that his state of nature and social contract would show most clearly what must replace, in his view, the old-fashioned reliance upon honor in the maintenance of *salus populi*.

In this chapter, I will begin with a review of the most familiar parts of Hobbes's theory, the state of nature and social contract, with the aim of reflecting on my previous observations concerning honor and the gentleman. Hobbes's theory relies upon his readers rejecting honor and accepting the primacy of fear. The state of nature is a place in which each human being is motivated to kill or be killed. Hobbes does not present any hope that some will be so much better at this game than others that they can preserve themselves for long. He wants his readers to accept that all are equally vulnerable, that the thing most to be avoided, the reason for submitting to an all-powerful sovereign, is fear of violent death. His entire reason for depicting the state of nature in this way is to contradict the most prevalent political disease of his day: disregard for safety, too little fear of pain and death, in fact, a dearth of "timorousness" caused by a sort of mental intoxication brought on by the arguments of intellectuals and theologians. Hence, the origin of the social contract

99

must be fear, and fear must be seen as a legitimate source of agreement, instead of a factor that mitigates a person's obligation.

Next I will examine some key ideas that emerge from this discussion of the state of nature and social contract. By looking at them more closely, I hope to be able to explore their implications for honor. Hobbes's state of nature supposes a sort of radical equality. I will explore the idea of equality that Hobbes establishes by looking more closely at what he thinks about human differences. Hobbes rejects the Aristotelian notion that there are important differences in quality among different types of people: free and slave, high and low born, male and female. Here I will deal specifically with two important elements of the aristocratic or honor society—the idea of inherent differences among classes and the idea of inequality between the sexes. The idea of inherent differences among classes served as intellectual backing for the feudal notion (still in existence but being eroded in Hobbes's time) that some men are fitter to rule than others because of their superior quality. The feudal notion of nobility, not only of actual status, but of character, is radically challenged by Hobbes. So is the traditional acceptance of women as naturally inferior to men. Hobbes seems to claim that women are men's equals in the state of nature, and that any inequality between the sexes is the result of conscious agreement, not nature. I will investigate Hobbes's reasoning on the relationship between men and women and between parents and children at length, in order to determine just how deeply Hobbes disagrees with the idea of inherent gender differences that matter politically. At the conclusion to this chapter and in the conclusion to this book, I will explore the question of whether assumptions of inequality must preexist certain types of moral responsibility or duty, and whether these types of responsibilities and duties are beneficial to society or not.

Hobbes's social contract obviously poses difficulties for any idea of moral duty that is not grounded in fear and the desire for self-preservation. This becomes particularly evident in his treatment of military service. So next, I will turn to this issue, in the hopes of exploring the ultimate limits of a political philosophy built upon individual self-preservation. Hobbes cannot tell a man who has entered into the social contract to preserve his life that he should sacrifice that life for the greater good of his community. Or, to put it more accurately, he does in a roundabout way tell him that, but he contradicts himself so glaringly that, in doing so, his argument does not seem to hold up. Hobbes's confusing treatment of the obligation to fight in defense of one's country demonstrates, perhaps more than in any other area, the problems posed for a society which rejects honor as an inadequate, and indeed dangerous, restraint upon men, and thus sees the life of the gentleman as a quaint but unreliable and even harmful ideal.

THE STATE OF NATURE AND THE SOCIAL CONTRACT

Hobbes famously believes there is no *summum bonum* or greatest good for all men.[1] He expresses this view, contradicting Aristotle, in an effort to explain why the ancient solution of morally good government is not good enough. For Plato and Aristotle, the truth about the good life was not arrived at through perspective and opinion, but through reason. It was a permanent truth that did not change, regardless if people understood it or acknowledged its existence. But in Hobbes's view, men determine what they think is good based upon their individual passions, and there can be no higher standard. They will never achieve agreement on what way of life is best, but they can agree that power is a good, because through power they can achieve whatever they define as their own personal goods. Their desire for power is what makes the state of nature a continual state of war.

Exactly what assumptions and arguments about human nature and the state of nature does Hobbes make in order to come to this seemingly extreme conclusion, a conclusion which precipitates the necessity for absolute sovereignty? Through attempting to answer this question in this section, and by focusing on certain assumptions and arguments of Hobbes in greater detail in later sections of this chapter, I hope to show that some of his most fundamental premises and arguments run counter to the very existence of honor. An honorable man still believes in the existence of the Good apart from his individual good, and that it should guide his decisions and actions, and he therefore rejects the view that power is a good thing to have regardless of its ends.

Why does Hobbes think that people can never agree on what is good? He posits that people are the products both of their bodily existence and their educations (broadly conceived): "The causes of this difference of wits, are in the passions; and the difference of passions proceedeth, partly from the different constitution of the body, and partly from different education."[2] Human beings cannot control their physical differences at all, and most can only affect the environment in which they grow up and in which they live to a limited degree.[3] Their imaginations and dreams are caused by their internal and external circumstances. Something as seemingly insignificant as indigestion can determine a man's dreams.[4] Speech is used with great inconsistency because of the tendency of men's thoughts to be determined by their own individual circumstances and the passions they produce. "The names of such things as affect us, that is, which please and displease us, because all men be not alike affected with the same thing, nor the same man at all times, are in the common discourses of men of *inconstant* signification."[5] This inconsistency in language has produced even more confusion and animosity. How human beings sense and see the world is, quite literally, different. Thus, the variations that exist in intelligence, personalities, and opinions are deep, natural, and inevitable, and because of this, conflict among people is also natural and inevitable, unless it is stopped by the greater force of a sovereign power.

In chapter 8 of *Leviathan*, Hobbes deals with many human differences that cannot be controlled or changed in any meaningful sense, including variations in areas like intelligence (some are smart, some are stupid, and some are "idiots"), judgment, fancy or imagination, prudence, and even character (some are prone to craft, a sort of "crooked wisdom").[6] Differences in wit, as he calls these, are caused by differences in underlying passions or desires, which in turn are, again, caused by our physical makeup and education. But, though we differ in passions, we are the same in knowing the means to obtain what we want: "The passions that most of all cause the difference of wit, are principally, the more or less desire of power, of riches, of knowledge, and of honour. All which may be reduced to the first, that is, desire of power."[7]

If people differ in levels of strength, intelligence, and character, certainly they will differ in levels of desire for power, a fact which would seem to point toward the formation of natural hierarchies, and might conceivably even lead toward the old-fashioned idea that those who are better qualified have an obligation to rule benevolently over their natural inferiors. But the differences in the levels of desire for power have a curiously equalizing effect when discussed within the context of Hobbes's state of nature. As he formulates it, the state of nature is a state in which there is no overarching authority, no government, to check people's actions. The consequences of putting people, with all their differences and various levels of desire for power, into this anarchic situation are that everyone must share the same concern: survival. This is how he begins chapter 13 of *Leviathan*, which introduces the natural condition of mankind, or the state of nature:

> Nature hath made men so equal, in the faculties of the body, and mind; as that though there be found one man sometimes manifestly stronger in body, or of quicker mind than another; yet when all is reckoned together, the difference between man, and man, is not so considerable, as that one man can thereupon claim to himself any benefit, to which another may not pretend, as well as he. For as to the strength of body, the weakest has strength enough to kill the strongest, either by secret machination, or by confederacy with others, that are in the same danger with himself.[8]

In *De Cive*, Hobbes addresses the objection that there are moral differences or differences in character among men which might make some feel an obligation not to attack and even to protect others: "[F]or though the wicked were fewer than the righteous, yet because we cannot distinguish them, there is a necessity of suspecting, heeding, anticipating, subjugating, self-defending, ever incident to the most honest and fairest conditioned."[9] That is, in the state of nature, there *will* be those who are "righteous" and those who are "wicked," those who desire less and those who desire more power. But everyone must be *suspected* by everyone else of an equal desire for power and designs to obtain it, because there is no sure way to know the true intentions of our fellow human beings. The situation is tragic: many would prefer to live in relative peace with each other, but they cannot, because their circumstances prevent them from doing so: "And the cause of this," writes Hobbes, "is not always that a man hopes for a more intensive delight, than he has already attained to; or that he cannot be content with a moderate power: but because he cannot assure the power and means to live well, which he hath present, without the acquisition of more."[10]

This tragic situation is what makes the state of nature a perpetual state of war from which everyone wishes to escape, and it is this state of war which forces everyone to a fairly equal level of both hostility and desire for power. This is why Hobbes can make such a universal statement as this about humanity: "So that in the first place, I put for a general inclination of all mankind, a perpetual and restless desire of power after power, that ceaseth only in death."[11] Suddenly, those who might be motivated, given assumptions more like Aristotle's or De Charny's, to assume the duty of ruling and protecting the weak find themselves in the same humbling predicament as everyone else, and they cannot afford to think of anyone but themselves.

Thus, Hobbes has in mind a particular, very important, type of equality which does not entail sameness in areas such as strength, intelligence, beauty, and so on, which he is willing to acknowledge do exist. But even this type of limited equality cannot be completely absolute. Hobbes has to know that there will be those who are feeble minded. And of course there will be children in the state of nature. At the very least, neither of them would be intellectually equipped to devise the stratagems necessary to kill those stronger or more intelligent than themselves. However, Hobbes ignores these instances of significant inequality in the devising of his theory, and does not even mention them when he is establishing the conditions in the state of nature. It is not that there are no exceptions to his rule, but that his premise of equality holds true enough of the time to be a determining factor in what happens in the state of nature. Significantly, he does not think that gender produces enough inequality of strength, fortitude, or intelligence to exclude women from the equality he describes in the state of nature. He concentrates on what type of environment is created for all adult individuals of normal ability, an environment really created by those who are the most bellicose. Because no one can read another's mind, he or she must assume that each other person is capable of murder, and must act to preempt accordingly. Equality is established on the equal threat that each normal adult individual poses to every other normal adult individual.

Hobbes proceeds to list the three principle causes of conflict in the state of nature as competition, diffidence, and glory: "The first, maketh men invade for gain; the second, for safety; and the third, for reputation."[12] It is easy to understand how self-interest and fear could become predominant in the state of nature, at least given Hobbes's assumptions about human nature. But he repeatedly emphasizes the particularly problematic nature of the third cause of quarrel. Concern with reputation, or what he often calls vainglory and pride, seems like a social passion and not the type that one would expect in the primitive state of nature. The existence of pride in the state of nature has been puzzling to many of Hobbes's readers.[13] As a consequence, scholars have argued endlessly about whether his state of nature is meant to be a depiction of some past reality (or current reality in "savage" societies), or is really just an intellectual construct for showing his readers the consequences of their destructive attitudes and behaviors.

Rousseau pointed out that Hobbes's natural men were actually social men, because pride, a very social passion, had already grown so strong in them. Hobbes, wrote Rousseau, "wrongly injected into the savage man's concern for self-preservation the need to satisfy a multitude of passions which are the product of society and which have made laws necessary."[14] Of course, Rousseau wanted to argue that a true natural man was more like an animal, devoid of any social passions, certainly devoid of prideful concerns. Clearly, Hobbes did not see natural man in this way, as truly primitive or as completely pre-social. As we will see, families can and do form in Hobbes's state of nature. They seem to be established on the basis of one party being able to subdue another, rather than on bonds of love, but they are social units nonetheless. Not only does Hobbes account for families in the state of nature, but also small confederacies that might be likened to gangs or tribes. So it is perhaps more useful to think of Hobbes's state of nature as a depiction of how human beings living in civil society would act if government could no longer keep them in awe. Indeed, among other situations, it is an image of civil war, as Hobbes himself acknowledges.[15] It should not surprise us, then, that pride—a thoroughly social passion—is one of the three causes of conflict in the state of nature.

Hobbes argues that it is inherent in human nature for every man to "looketh that his companion should value him, at the same rate he sets upon himself: and upon all signs of contempt, or undervaluing, naturally endeavours, as far as he dares . . . to extort a greater value from his contemners, by damage; and from others, by the example."[16] He repeatedly suggests that pride is also the least legitimate cause of quarrel. It makes men harm others for "trifles, as a word, a smile, a different opinion, and any other sign of undervalue, either direct in their persons, or by reflection in their kindred, their friends, their nation, their profession, or their name."[17]

In chapter 2 of this book, I referred to pride as a sort of intellectual intoxication, or drunkenness, which took over so many leading figures in the English Civil War. Hobbes blamed pride as the source of a great many of the errors of his day. Pride and love of honor blurred in his analysis. Honor-seekers became vainglorious and dangerous men. The reference to drunkenness is not a gloss on Hobbes's opinion. Rather, this is exactly the way he describes the nature of pride. In *Leviathan*, speaking specifically of the madness or excess of passions called "inspiration," which was driven by pride (and thinking no doubt of Oliver Cromwell, who claimed to know and speak on behalf of God's true intentions), he compares the actions of those who boast of inspiration with "the variety of behaviour in men that have drunk too much."[18] Pride caused them to act like madmen, and through their leadership, caused all of England to lack the healthy inhibitions that would have prevented conflict. Though he states the problem more abstractly in *Leviathan* than in *Behemoth*, the point is the same:

> For example, though the effect of folly, in them that are possessed of an opinion of being inspired, be not visible always in one man, by any very extravagant action, that proceedeth from such passion; yet, when many of them conspire together, the rage of the whole multitude is visible enough. For what argument of madness can there be greater, than to clamour, strike, and throw stones at our best friends? Yet this is somewhat less than such a multitude will do. For they will clamour, fight against, and destroy those, by whom all their lifetime before, they have been protected, and secured from injury.[19]

What causes men to become like this, able to attack their friends and defenders, and literally ruin their own lives? Hobbes writes, "The passion, whose violence, or continuance, maketh madness, is either great *vain-glory*: which is commonly called *pride*, and *self-conceit*; or great *dejection* of mind."[20]

By including pride in the three principle causes of quarrel in the state of nature, and highlighting it as the most troublesome cause of quarrel, Hobbes necessitates its complete elimination, leaving no room for any distinction between healthy pride, or love of honor, and destructive pride, or vainglory. Pride in all its aspects is to be squashed with the social contract, which will institute an absolute sovereign under whom all will be equally humble. Fear and self-interest alone are salvageable sources of quarrel, because they can also lead to peace.

At the end of *Leviathan*'s chapter 13, as opposed to the beginning, Hobbes lists fear of death *before* desire for commodious living as the chief of the "articles of peace." It is precisely the lack of fear, the drunkenness of valor and self-righteousness, that Hobbes thinks most plagues mankind, continuing to produce unnecessary wars. Hobbes wants to turn men's heads in a different direction. It is not that he thinks that human beings are by nature always fearful, *but that by nature they are not fearful enough.* Yet, the basic experience of fear is overriding when it is upon us, or so Hobbes thinks. How to get people to understand this when they are not yet in a situation of dire threat? This is Hobbes's task, and to that end he must continue to remind us of the hazards of civil war through his description of the state of nature and its consequences. This is the reason for his perhaps most famous paragraph in *Leviathan*, and it is a warning that he repeats again and again, aimed squarely at those who would start or support civil conflict:

> In such condition, there is no place for industry; because the fruit thereof is uncertain: and consequently no culture of the earth; no navigation, nor use of the commodities that may be imported by sea; no commodious building; no instruments of moving, and removing, such things as require much force; no knowledge of the face of the earth; no account of time; no arts; no letters; no society; and which is worst of all, continual fear, and danger of violent death; and the life of man, solitary, poor, nasty, brutish, and short.[21]

But more than simply describing the dire consequences of civil conflict in this way, Hobbes must undermine our admiration for those who would lead us down the path to self-destruction for some higher, supposedly more noble purpose than mere survival. It is this zeal for the cause that such men evoke that makes people forget the consequences of civil conflict. In his day, as we know, such men were the theologians, university dons, and members of the gentry and nobility, who were educated and inspired by theologians and professors. To teach his readers how they should think about the origins and purposes of government, as opposed to what they are often taught by such men, Hobbes moves into a discussion of the rights and laws of nature as the means of obtaining the good things peace can bring, especially the escape from the constant fear of violent death. The sole right of nature, of course, is the liberty of each man to do whatever it takes in the state of nature, including killing others, in order to ensure his safety: the right of self-preservation.[22] The liberty to act on this right is without any limits, because limits can only be set by some higher power, which is absent in the state of nature. The first law of nature (Hobbes defines a law of nature as a "precept, or general rule of reason,"[23]) is that every man has a right to every thing he thinks necessary in order to preserve himself. The second law is to seek peace if at all possible. Every man should be willing to lay down his right to all things if every other man is also willing. But Hobbes cautions that if this is done unilaterally, it is like committing suicide.[24]

The difficulty of thinking about Hobbes's state of nature as an actual historical situation is most acute in the seeming impossibility of getting the individuals in the state of nature, so radically mistrustful and full of pride, to agree all at the same moment to contract for peace. This problem is so insurmountable that the whole scenario Hobbes devises seems incredibly unlikely and false. This is another reason for seeing his state of nature and social contract teachings more as constructs than descriptions or blueprints.[25] Hobbes spends the rest of chapter 13 in *Leviathan* discussing covenants and how they are formed. His discussion here is not so much about how a government was actually formed at some point in the past, but how citizens are to think of the formation of their government now. Hobbes wants the citizens of his England, as well as those of other countries, to imagine what life would be like if civil order broke down and no one was in charge, and to see the origins of their own civil societies in a social contract in which each citizen as an individual has a stake, acknowledging the foundation of his government in his own informed consent.

After thoroughly discussing the laws which establish the social contract, Hobbes goes on to treat of other laws of nature. These read like rules for how to get along with others in society, and generally reflect the meek Christian virtues discussed in the previous chapter, virtues designed to check the sin of pride. The laws of nature are known to all in the state of nature as rules of right reason about obtaining peace, but they cannot be acted upon at all until people are safe within civil society. The third law of nature is justice itself, which Hobbes defines as *"that men perform their covenants made."*[26] Without the willingness to abide by their contracts and agreements, which they can do in the security of civil society, they would immediately slide back into the state of nature. The rest of the natural laws resemble moral rules that are good to follow in society (and procedural rules built upon these moral rules), including: gratitude, complaisance or accommodation, ability to pardon others or forgiveness, a law against unlimited revenge and against contumely or hatred.

The ninth natural law, against pride, seems redundant when we think about what must be the main cause of all the other things Hobbes wishes to prevent, including ingratitude, irascibility, an unforgiving nature, revenge, and hatred or contempt. For Hobbes, pride amounts to believing that one is better than others, and expressing that belief with the demand to be treated differently than others. We know already that this was the main problem, from his perspective, that brought about the English Civil War. It seems clear that Hobbes's purpose was, as Strauss suggested, to substitute aristocratic warrior pride for bourgeois fear and desire for ease, or what Peter Hayes terms the "fearful bourgeois civic spirit."[27] With the aim of knocking down pride, Hobbes reminds his readers—obviously aiming at the nobility and gentry—of their natural equality once again: "The inequality that now is, has been introduced by the laws civil," he writes.[28] Contrary to people's beliefs, what we all have in common, our vulnerability in the midst of social anarchy, is far more important than our differences:

> If nature therefore have made men equal, that equality is to be acknowledged: or if nature have made men unequal; yet because men that think themselves equal, will not enter into conditions of peace, but upon equal terms, such equality must be admitted.[29]

Hobbes adds the natural law against arrogance, which is pride in action, or demanding more than others have, due to a presumed superior quality. He then moves into the laws of nature that concern procedure. All these have to do with treating people fairly and equally in business and before the law. In a bow toward the upper class, Hobbes does allow for primogeniture and right of first seizing, conceiving these as the result of a sort of lottery for things that cannot be held in common.[30] But by reminding the aristocrats that their property and status ultimately derived from something as base as first seizing, or—so to speak—winning life's lottery, as well as the direct gift of the sovereign, he is attempting to instill in them a healthy humility.

Of course, the laws of nature are binding only on the conscience in the state of nature. They cannot be acted upon safely, and therefore cannot be obligatory, until civil society has been established. Contrary to older notions of the obligation to do justice even in the face of danger and possible death, Hobbes makes it clear that there is no obligation until civil laws are made by the sovereign and can be enforced. If men could act on moral obligations without the backing of force, there would be no need for government at all, he reasons.[31] "For the laws of nature, as *justice, equity, modesty, mercy,* and, in sum, *doing to others, as we would be done to,* of themselves, without the terror of some power, to cause them to be observed, are contrary to our natural passions, that carry us to partiality, pride, revenge, and the like. And covenants, without the sword, are but words, and of no strength to secure a man at all."[32] Even within civil society, the laws of nature are not binding on the people unless the sovereign's laws reflect them, and they cannot be said to be binding on the sovereign at any time, because he is the source of the law. The sovereign's laws may or may not reflect the laws of nature. Hobbes is quick to point out that the sovereign's laws are not to be judged on whether or not they adhere to the laws of nature. For the sake of peace, citizens must obey even those laws which contradict natural laws. As he writes in his chapter dealing with the rights of sovereigns, "he that complaineth of injury from his sovereign, complaineth of that whereof he himself is author; and therefore ought not to accuse any man but himself; no nor himself of injury; because to do injury to one's self, is impossible. It is true that they that have sovereign power may commit iniquity; but not injustice, or injury in the proper signification."[33] That is, the sovereign can violate the moral rules of reason that are the laws of nature (and the laws of God), and this Hobbes calls iniquity, but that does not matter to the citizens, who must not use the laws of nature as their guide once in civil society, but only the sovereign's law. The right to self-preservation and the consequent imperative to seek peace through mutual agreement to establish a sovereign trump the moral authority of the laws of nature. However, these natural laws were surely Hobbes's attempt to give citizens sound guidance, and to give sovereigns sound political advice.

In contrast to the theoretical social contract he constructed, Hobbes knew that conquest was the starting point for most actual regimes, and that this unattractive fact could pose a problem for any government's legitimacy. Indeed, not much later, in Locke's social contract theory, we find an argument for revolution on the basis of past unjust conquest, even if that conquest happened many generations earlier.[34] Hobbes knew he had to eliminate this source of argument against the legitimacy of current regimes. For this reason he argued that covenants made under duress, in which people agree to submit in order to spare their lives, were just as valid as covenants made without coercion. He argued against the distinction which Locke would make, between free and forced agreement.[35] In *The Elements of Law* he argued that "there appeareth no reason, why that which we do upon fear, should be less firm than that which we do for covetousness. For both the one and the other maketh the action voluntary."[36] He stated, fairly convincingly, that if this were not so, no truces among enemies would be valid, "nor any laws could be of force; which are all consented to from that fear."[37] By saying this, Hobbes linked the legitimacy of his theoretical social contract, justified from the compelling nature of the fear of violent death in the state of nature, with the contract as it is frequently made, at the hands of a conqueror, whose compelling argument is also fear. Both contracts are equally legitimate, in his view. Since fear is the very foundation of government itself, how can contracts made out of fear be void?

To explain how legitimate covenants can come from situations in which one party is coerced, in *The Elements of Law*, *De Cive*, and *Leviathan*, Hobbes employs the example of the robber, who demands money be paid the next day in exchange for sparing his victim's life. While such agreements may be made void, he argues (as when the police intervene and arrest the thief), they are not made void because they are extorted through fear of death. Unless the law intervenes, the victim is obligated to follow through on his promise to pay the thief.[38] His examples are most complete and vivid in *Leviathan*:

Therefore prisoners of war, if trusted with the payment of their ransom, are obliged to pay it: and if a weaker prince, make a disadvantageous peace with a stronger, for fear; he is bound to keep it; unless, as hath been said before, there ariseth some new, and just cause of fear, to renew the war. And even in commonwealths, if I be forced to redeem myself from a thief by promising him money, I am bound to pay it, till the civil law discharge me. For whatsoever I may lawfully do without obligation, the same may I lawfully covenant to do through fear: and what I lawfully covenant, I cannot lawfully break.[39]

Hobbes has to make this argument if the edifice of his social contract is to stand in the face of historical fact. Yet in doing so, the small vestige of the idea of duty which remains, the argument that somehow a man is bound to keep his promise because he has once made it, even under conditions of fear, rings hollow. If fear overrides all other reasons for action, a victim of crime or conquest could very reasonably renege on his agreement out of fear, not simply out of a sense of justice. The thief and the victim agree and both are, according to Hobbes, bound by their agreement. Of course, the thief performs his part immediately by not killing his victim. But the victim would have to put himself into another potentially dangerous situation—putting himself into the hands of the thief again in order to repay him. What if he would be safer simply fleeing and never coming back? As we will see later in this chapter, Hobbes himself will argue that in a war, a soldier is not obliged to continue to fight if he thinks his life is in danger, and can even surrender to the other side, if he thinks it will save his life. If fear can justify disregarding the obligation to fight in direct violation of the sovereign's orders, how can fear, whether of the chaos of the state of nature or of the conquering power, also be a solid foundation for government?

Hobbes's theory of the state of nature and social contract poses a challenge for a society that values honor. It raises fear to the level of supreme importance, and as we have seen, it completely overcomes pride as a positive motivating factor. Pride, which Hobbes comes to associate with those who seek "honor," becomes entirely negative, a source of intellectual intoxication and irrational bellicosity. The rationale for equality in the state of nature which Hobbes devises rules out any positive role for an honorable attitude toward natural inequalities—each man and woman is compelled to think only of self-interest and survival. It is this supremacy of self-preservation, the supremacy of fear as the most useful motivator, which represents the most lethal challenge to any positive notion of honor. The idea that there is nothing worth dying for is an idea whose time has come in Hobbes's thought. As we will see, his overriding emphasis on fear and individual survival seems to turn on itself when it comes to obtaining any degree of unity and loyalty in the state if it is under attack. Yet it is this compelling fear which he hopes will be much more durable and convincing to his readers than the traditional notions of honor, duty, and moral obligation. Is this really so? As we explore in more depth Hobbes's thoughts on human differences in class or quality and gender, and his thoughts on military service, I will also attempt to provide more food for thought concerning this larger question.

DO NATURAL INEQUALITIES MATTER?

By insisting on the principle of equality in the forming of the social contract and, to a great but not absolute extent, within civil society, Hobbes provides a conscious, profound, and challenging answer to Aristotle.[40] As we have seen, he consciously contrasts his ideas on equality to Aristotle's ideas on natural inequality. For Aristotle, the differences among human beings are naturally translated into different roles in the household and in the political community. But because his focus is the great equality which fear of violent death can produce, and which leads to the humility necessary to allow men to submit to an all-powerful *Leviathan*, Hobbes must reject any claim to significant natural inequality. He takes aim at that way of thinking which insists that inequality is socially and politically relevant. Whereas the ancient and medieval writers distinguished between deserved and undeserved pride (the magnanimous man displayed deserved pride through his graciousness, because of his superior abilities, for instance), and we have seen that to a certain extent Hobbes still personally acknowledges this distinction, we also know that he turns away from it as relevant for his political theory. Martin Bertman is able to discern what this modern turn of thought in Hobbes means for the traditional ideas of heroism, chivalry, and gentlemanly conduct:

> The aristocratic classical tradition, exemplifying what E. R. Dodds called a "shame-culture," and other sources more contemporaneous with Hobbes, applauds heroic, honor-seeking and coveting behavior: Homer, Aristotle, Tasso, Castiglione, Clarendon. Heroic men are seen to have important and attractive social traits just because of devotion to personal honor; even Hobbes points out, in concert with Aristotle, that such individuals do not cheat, lie, or fail in magnanimity. Nevertheless, and especially, their disposition to seek honor cannot be the basis for the state. Honor is too unstable for the end of peace.[41]

Hobbes's thought represents a complete rejection for political purposes of the "Homeric hero" and "the aristocratic warrior society."[42] These ideals formed the assumptions that underlay previous notions about government: that rank mattered, that responsibility lay with those who were in some way naturally better, and that obedience was due to those who were one's superiors. For Aristotle, each type of regime represented some ideal way of life, embodied by a certain type or class of people. William Mathie writes that Aristotle thought

"Every city is informed by one or another regime; every city is characterized both by some authoritative way of life and by some particular arrangement of offices."[43] Aristocracy's claim was that those who were wiser should rule, that "in an aristocracy the life and doings of the gentlemen are viewed as the best kind of human activity and the franchise and arrangement of offices are such as to ensure rule by men of this kind."[44] The better regimes were those in "which citizenship and political honors are granted in proportion to ethical-political virtue, and not on the basis of mere freedom, wealth, or force,"[45] writes Thomas Lindsay, who argues that Aristotle anticipated Hobbes's understanding of government as being founded upon selfishness, especially in his treatment of democracy and oligarchy, but refused to accept the idea that all government was or must be so established.[46]

Contrasting with Aristotle's assumption that there are better and worse regimes, ways of life, and examples of leadership, Hobbes argues that there can be no justification for obedience based upon moral or other superiority. While Plato and Aristotle could judge regimes largely on whether or not those in charge were selfless or selfish, whether they made decisions based upon the common interest or solely their own, Hobbes rejects this type of comparison, and "his rejection of the possibility of distinguishing, as Aristotle does in classifying the regimes, between rule in the common interest and rule in the ruler's own private interest, and his denial that there can ever be true instances of mixed government, would indicate the existence and character of this change."[47] For Hobbes, any regime is a good regime if it keeps its citizens safe. Though he does argue that monarchy is most likely to do this successfully, he does not argue that monarchy and the accompanying system of aristocracy are or should be *morally* superior in any way, only that because of the way that self-interest works, they should be more stable and rational.

For Hobbes, there are only three possible types of government: democracy, aristocracy, and monarchy—that is, government by one, few, or many. He famously disputes the other forms of government considered distinct by the ancients—tyranny, oligarchy, and mob rule—arguing that they are simply monarchy, aristocracy, and democracy disliked.[48] He argues in favor of monarchy for many reasons, but most of those reasons can be reduced to the fact that all human beings are basically the same, motivated by self-interest, assumed to be ambitious, and in these ways quite equal. Aristocracy still appears somewhat better than democracy, not because the members of it are of a higher quality, and thus more likely to possess wisdom and patience, but simply because there are fewer of them to cause trouble. Still, there are enough to cause many of the problems of democracies on a smaller scale—such as factional strife, demagoguery, cronyism of leaders, lack of decisive-

ness, and most importantly, an inability to see the interest of the people coin-
ciding with their own. Through this line of reasoning, Hobbes links aristocracy (along with democracy) to the type of ambition which can lead to treason and civil war.[49]

In chapter 30 of *Leviathan*, Hobbes takes a fairly rare direct swipe at the
nobility's pretensions of superior wisdom, labeling them instead as a source
of strife. First, he separates wisdom neatly from social standing:

> But the best signs of knowledge of any art, are, much conversing in it, and con-
> stant good effects of it. Good counsel comes not by lot, nor by inheritance; and
> therefore there is no more reason to expect good advice from the rich or noble,
> in matter of state, than in delineating the dimensions of a fortress; unless we
> shall think there needs no method in the study of the politics, as there does in
> the study of geometry, but only to be lookers on; which is not so.[50]

Next, Hobbes briefly traces the historical origins of the aristocracy back to
conquest. He makes it clear that the noble class, which he treats as artificial
or conventional and dependent upon the pleasure of the sovereign, can be a
source of stability, or a source of turmoil. Hobbes states that if it becomes a
source of turmoil, the sovereign should strip it of its influence:

> Whereas in these parts of Europe, it hath been taken for a right of certain per-
> sons, to have place in the highest council of state by inheritance; it is derived
> from the conquests of the ancient Germans; wherein many absolute lords join-
> ing together to conquer other nations, would not enter into the confederacy,
> without such privileges, as might be marks of difference in time following, be-
> tween their posterity, and the posterity of their subjects; which privileges being
> inconsistent with the sovereign power, by the favour of the sovereign, they may
> seem to keep; but contending for them as their right, they must needs by degrees
> let them go, and have at last no further honour, than adhereth naturally to their
> abilities.[51]

Hobbes repeatedly gives the same motives and passions to the aristocracy
as he does to every other member of society. If we think that monarchs can
spend too much money enriching their family, friends, and other hangers-on,

> yet is the same both greater in an aristocracy, and also more likely to come to
> pass; for there not one only, but many have children, kindred, and friends to
> raise; and in that point they are as twenty monarchs for one, and likely to set for-
> ward one another's designs mutually, to the oppression of all the rest.[52]

Moreover, aristocracy is shown in Hobbes's political theory as originating
from majority consent, the same as any other form of government the people

might choose out of the social contract, and thus as artificial as any other kind of government. For instance, in *De Cive* he writes:

> An aristocracy or council of nobles endowed with supreme authority, receives its original from a democracy, which gives up its right unto it, where we must understand that certain men distinguished from others, either by eminence of title, blood, or some other character, are propounded to the people, and by plurality of voices are elected, and being elected, the whole right of the people or city is conveyed on them, insomuch as whatsoever the people might do before, the same by right may this court of elected nobles now do. Which being done, it is clear that the people, considering as one person, (its supreme authority being already transferred on these) is no longer now in being.[53]

Since all government is *to be seen* as originally the choice of the people for their own well-being, aristocracy must be seen in this way too. If the nobles rule, it is not because of their inherent superiority of quality or wisdom, but rather because of their practical utility for keeping the peace. In this context, Hobbes again disagrees with Aristotle on the issue of inherent inferiority and superiority as the basis for all government:

> I know that Aristotle, in his first book of Politics, affirms as a foundation of the whole political science, that some men by nature are made worthy to command, others only to serve; as if lord and servant were distinguished not by consent of men, but by an aptness, that is, a certain kind of natural knowledge or ignorance. Which foundation is not only against reason (as but now hath been showed) but also against experience. For neither almost is any man so dull of understanding as not to judge it better to be ruled by himself, than to yield himself to the government of another; neither if the wiser and stronger do contest, have these ever or after the upper hand of those.[54]

According to Hobbes, then, "inequality was introduced by a general consent," and so any claims by the aristocracy to superior breeding and natural worthiness, claims that used to provide justification for greater moral obligations on the part of those with more power, are simply false.[55] He makes it clear that property, the gentleman's main source of power, is also not naturally his. Those of the upper class enjoy their property at the pleasure of the sovereign, who is the source of all property—hence property is also founded on the original agreement.[56]

So there is nothing about the aristocracy which makes them actually better than the people. But because power is always exercised more rationally in the fewest hands; the government is "most able; which simply imitates the government of monarchs most, and the people least of all."[57] One's "superiors" are no better than anyone else, and they provide no better model for genuine morality, and yet they set the moral rules. The people should accept that they set these rules not because the aristocrats are their true moral superiors, but because, if they do not, there will be chaos and danger of violent death. They are not superiors in the traditional sense at all; they simply have more power, "for all government *is* based upon consent, not aptness to govern."[58]

DO GENDER DIFFERENCES MATTER?

Thomas Lindsay's article, "Aristotle's Appraisal of Manly Spirit," is perhaps the best treatment available on Aristotle's view of what Hobbes calls pride, which Lindsay rightly locates within the category of gender (because Aristotle and Hobbes both do). Lindsay argues that Aristotle knew very well the danger of manly spiritedness, in the ambition of some men to become tyrants, and in their tendency both to destroy themselves and to destroy good political order in the attempt to seek glory for themselves. Hobbes, for these very reasons, rejects what everyone in his time, including himself, identifies with manly or gentlemanly virtue, because of its tendency to produce disruption and rebellion. But Aristotle tries to avoid the "detestable male excesses"[59] while trying to obtain the great goods for humanity, particularly the political community, which he believes can only be derived from the same manly spiritedness. This is because, for Aristotle, the goal of the city is not just preservation, but the good life. The good life is not simply Hobbes's commodious living with its security and private comforts, but living in conformity with what is beautiful and good. Lindsay writes:

> That even the "strongest" can be overcome "either by secret machination, or by confederacy with others," as Hobbes states it, does not solve the political problem of spiritedness for Aristotle. Such a solution threatens also to assassinate— or, at the very least, to render publicly suspect—the winning bravery, frankness, and initiative or "pioneering spirit" that such individuals embody. If, for the sake of civic peace, Hobbes requires all men to renounce pride, for the sake of an ennobled politics, Aristotle will not.[60]

Instead of recommending this renunciation, Aristotle devises another way around the problem of manly *thumos*, the natural tendency of men to brook no limitations on their own ambitions. He teaches that, just as soldiers in the military must learn obedience, so the manly citizen must learn first to follow and obey and then to lead. Aristotle's polity, in which citizens take turns leading and being led, presents the opportunity for men to harness their ambition in ways which satisfy their longings while not bringing destruction to the city. In this way, Aristotle recognizes manly spirit as an essential ingredient in good leadership. Lindsay points out that, ultimately, this spiritedness is treated by Aristotle as a human trait, though it is a trait seen by him most predominantly in males.[61]

Even more important than providing the spiritedness necessary to handle a crisis, such as a war (courage in both leaders and those they lead is most required at this time), is the fact that for Aristotle, spiritedness is necessary for intellectual inquiry. While Hobbes has given up on the possibility that independent inquiry can be anything but a destructive force driven by pride, Aristotle sees it as little less than the soul of a good political order.

> Hobbes, no less than Aristotle, recognizes that spiritedness is essential to a vital political life. But, for Hobbes, spiritedness and therewith politics undermine peace and prosperity. As we have seen, Aristotle knows well the dangers of manly spirit. But for reasons both political and philosophic, he will not bend to the Hobbesian enterprise. If successful, Hobbes's war on spiritedness, Aristotle believes, must culminate in the death of philosophy, which, for Aristotle, is both the peak of human excellence and the highest happiness: the individual who truly has "something within him that is divine" will eschew rule, even political rule, in favor of solitary contemplation.[62]

Though we are not used to thinking in these terms, our discussion of how Hobbes compares with Aristotle, and why Hobbes ultimately rejects Aristotle on many key points, shows Hobbes's pursuit of peace at the expense of honor. Hobbes's theory is an undertaking that aims to eliminate (among other things) a certain type of manliness. We can understand why arguing that our political decisions ought to be driven by fear, that all our virtues (or the natural laws) should seek to instill humility, and that the timorous man is preferable to the courageous man, might seem anathema to the manly ideal or the true gentleman. But we can now see that the opposition between Hobbes's modern man and the traditional man runs deeper. Hobbes rejects any claim to superiority of ability or worth, including the claims of the gentleman, Lindsay's *anêr*, or manly man. In so doing, Hobbes denies that some, in having more virtue, ought to have more responsibility to guide their community through rule. He also utterly rejects the idea that there are those who are "wise," who, while preferring the private and contemplative life, might usefully speak "unpalatable truths" to the public.[63] Instead, in his experience, there are so many who just pretend to be wise, that we are better off not allowing *anyone* to make this claim or speak without sovereign authorization. As Lindsay argues, it is not that Aristotle and his teacher Plato did not understand that there are many pretenders and only few truly wise, but rather that these ancient philosophers did not think it necessary to apply Hobbes's extreme solution to the problem of pretenders. Instead they thought it better to *risk* the political turmoil he wanted to avoid at all costs, in the hopes that mankind could at least sometimes achieve actual good government, a political community capable of humanizing all.

The Price of Equality?

In our modern society, perhaps the most controversial and unresolved area of potential inequality resides in the relationship between men and women. Are men and women completely equal in every way? If not, are their inequalities of any social or political importance? Even if some of us answer the first question in the negative, we tend to be much more circumspect about the second question, tending to err on the side of gender differences being insignificant. Generally speaking, most of us have found the equality of men and women to be socially and economically satisfying. However, we do not often ask what if anything is lost when the natural inequalities that do exist are denied because of their incongruity with our desire for and reliance upon equality. In particular, it is not often we ask if we have lost any sense of moral obligation in the adoption of the egalitarian perspective on gender.

In the past, as we have seen, moral obligation was often associated with an acknowledgement of supposedly natural advantages and disadvantages: in this case, the natural advantages men supposedly had over women, which led to the moral obligation of men to protect women. While it is not for this book to fully explore how well the egalitarian, gender-neutral, basis of moral obligation has fared, we can see how well Hobbes is able to replace the old with a modern foundation for moral obligation partly through reassessing the importance of gender differences. We can do this by examining how and why Hobbes dismantles the traditional patriarchal theory so predominant in his day, and how and why he treats the family without regard to (in fact while denying) *natural* male leadership.

Hobbes bases equality in the state of nature, as we have seen, on "how easy a matter it is, even for the weakest man to kill the strongest. . . . All men therefore among themselves are by nature equal; the inequality we now discern, hath its spring from the civil law."[64] There is plenty of evidence to suggest that by "man" here, Hobbes meant humankind. Apparently, Hobbes did not exclude women from the equality of the state of nature, or even place qualifications on their equality. If men are equal because even the weakest can kill the strongest due to moments of vulnerability as well as the ability of the weaker to scheme against the stronger, then the same could be said for women: even the weakest women also pose a threat to each other and to men in the state of nature. Since all human beings are sometimes completely vulnerable, as when they sleep or when they are not on guard for some other reason, all are vulnerable to others who can plan and wait. Logically, also, if inequality among men ("from riches, power, nobility of kindred"[65]) springs from the civil law and not from nature, then the inequality between women and men has its origins in the civil law as well.

The above statements are presented as speculation about what would follow on the issue of women's status from what Hobbes has to say about men in the state of nature. But we do not have to presume Hobbes's views on the basis of what logically follows from his argument about mutual vulnerability in the state of nature, because he addresses the question of women's equality in nature directly. As Gabriella Slomp rightly cautions, all this is not to say that Hobbes was an early advocate of women's equality and rights. If he were, he would have "defended the status of women against patriarchal rules inside political states."[66] Instead, he seems to assume that men will almost always rule over women in civil society. However, dealing with women's place in the state of nature, and the origins of marriage as not natural but contractual, Hobbes presents a theory that challenges the old view, not only of male domination, but also (most importantly for our subject) of the moral obligations so-called superiors have to their inferiors.

In chapter 9 of *De Cive*, and chapter 20 of *Leviathan*,[67] Hobbes discusses the rights parents have over their children in nature, and the origins of these rights. The larger purpose of these chapters is most likely to critique the patriarchal theory of divine right, which Hobbes does not accept as a viable basis for absolute sovereignty. He believes that sovereignty has to be founded upon a social contract, upon the agreement of each and every individual who would be a citizen, and he wants his theory to explain to them that there are good reasons for accepting the old monarchy. In order to make this argument, Hobbes needs to show the flaws in the old patriarchal theory. To that end, he says that he must "inquire into the original of paternal government."[68] The first assumption he attacks is the idea of the father as the natural head of both the mother and the children. He quickly concludes:

> By the right therefore of nature, the dominion over the infant first belongs to him who first hath him in his power. But it is manifest that he who is newly born, is in the mother's power before any others; insomuch as she may rightly, and at her own will, either breed him up, or adventure him to fortune.[69]

In nature, the mother is the food source for the infant; the father simply cannot fulfill this role. The mother is naturally the infant's first line of survival and protection. Hobbes states that if the woman chooses to breed her child, her relationship to that child is conditional: "that being grown to full age he become not her enemy; which is, that he obey her."[70] Hobbes deals with the objection of those who say that the father should be lord because of the "pre-eminence of sex," by saying that this "signifies nothing." And here he provides the argument that allows us to accept the word "men" as humankind in his description of the equality of the state of nature:

> And whereas some have attributed the dominion to the man only, as being of the more excellent sex; they misreckon in it. For there is not always that difference of strength, or prudence between the man and the woman, as that the right can be determined without war. In commonwealths, this controversy is decided by the civil law; and for the most part, but not always, the sentence is in favour of the father; because for the most part commonwealths have been erected by the fathers, not by the mothers of families.[71]

Interestingly, Hobbes also points out in both *De Cive* and *Leviathan* that the Amazons, whom he depicts as a historical reality at least for the sake of argument, had a very different arrangement in their relationships with men than in most societies. In Amazon society, men were allowed to breed with women, but could not continue to live with them. Likewise, boy children were sent back to their fathers and only girl children allowed to stay, "so that the dominion of the females was in the mother."[72] He also mentions the case of women who are themselves sovereign leaders, who retain the leadership of their families within civil society because they are monarchs. In addition, he reminds his readers of an obvious fact: only the mother really knows who the father is. In the state of nature, the mother remains the sole authority on that subject, and so the children naturally belong to her to dispose of as she will.[73] In various places, Hobbes makes the point that the child owes allegiance to the mother, because she has nourished it, and argues that the child owes continuing loyalty even after it is grown and independent: "For else it would be wisdom in men, rather to let their children perish, while they are infants, than to live in their danger or subjection, when they are grown."[74]

Next, Hobbes explains how this natural sovereignty of the mother over her children can be dissolved. If the mother abandons her children, exposing them to whatever dangers come their way, anyone who chooses to protect the children obtains the dominion over them. If the mother is taken prisoner, the children come under the rule of the person who has power over her. Significantly, if the mother is the subject of a government, the children, along with all other individuals, come under the rule of the government.[75] Also significantly,

> if a woman for society's sake give herself to a man on this condition, that he shall bear the sway, he that receives his being from the contribution of both parties, is the father's in regard of the command he hath over the mother.[76]

Hobbes reminds his readers again that this type of agreement can go either way. Certainly the female predominates if she has become the head of state.

But this can also happen "universally," by agreement of both parties.[77] Hobbes tells us that marriage is a contract which can only be made in the civil state, and therefore its particulars are completely determined, not by nature or God, but by the sovereign.[78] He explains why it is that almost always the rule within civil society lies with the husband:

> But in a civil government, if there be a contract of marriage between a man and a woman, the children are the father's, because in all cities, to wit, constituted of fathers, not mothers governing their families, the domestical command belongs to the man; and such a contract, if it be made according to the civil laws, is called matrimony.[79]

While Hobbes does not explain here how cities come to almost universally be founded by fathers, and comes dangerously close to admitting some natural ability of fathers which makes them more capable or able to rule, he never anywhere explicitly contradicts his fundamental argument that gender relationships are based upon agreement of both men and women in civil society. If there is some natural ability which makes men more able to rule than women, it must not be so obvious that men's dominance can be forced on women in nature without, as Hobbes puts it, "war."[80] Even in dealing with hereditary succession in another place, Hobbes is equivocal about whether preference for the male is based upon anything natural:

> Among children the males carry the pre-eminence; in the beginning perhaps, because for the most part (although not always) they are fitter for the administration of greater matters, but specially of wars; but afterwards, when it was grown a custom, because that custom was not contradicted.[81]

And yet, several authors have pointed out that Hobbes can still be seen as an advocate of patriarchy. As Schochet points out, there are even places in Hobbes's writings when it appears that he assumed male leadership was natural after all, and also assumed that the male head of the family was the real actor in any agreement to leave the state of nature. For instance, Hobbes argues that "the parent ought to have the honour of a sovereign, though he surrendered his power to the civil law; because he had it originally by nature."[82] Schochet also cites this passage from *Leviathan*:

> originally the father of every man was also his sovereign lord, with power over him of life and death; and that the fathers of families, when by instituting a commonwealth, they resigned that absolute power, yet it was never intended, they should lose the honour due unto them for their education. For to relinquish such right, was not necessary to the institution of sovereign power.[83]

Richard Allen Chapman makes a good argument that Hobbes's model for the family was "the *patria potestas* of republican Rome," and that "[f]athers in Hobbes's state of nature had absolute power and could put their own children to death."[84] He shows, through numerous examples from *De Cive*, *Leviathan*, and other works, that Hobbes for the most part assumed male leadership in families, both in the state of nature and in civil society. For instance, in *Leviathan*, chapter 22, Hobbes writes, "For the father and master, being before the institution of commonwealth, absolute sovereigns in their own families, they lose afterward no more of their authority, than the law of the commonwealth taketh from them."[85] Critics of Hobbes such as Bishop Bramhall and Sir Robert Filmer accused him of not recognizing the existence of any natural order, not even that of the family in his state of nature. But they missed the references Hobbes made to the family in the state of nature as a "little kingdom"[86] and his reference to the real-life state of nature in America, where Native Americans lived without real government, except the government of their families[87]—a clear indication that for Hobbes, families did exist in the state of nature, and most often in the traditional mode of male leadership. As if to clear up misconceptions, Hobbes included this footnote in his English translation of *De Cive*:

What is objected by some, that the propriety of goods, even before the constitution of cities, was found in fathers of families, that objection is vain, because I have already declared, that a family is a little city.[88]

In a striking passage from *Leviathan*, Hobbes writes:

a great family, if it be not part of some commonwealth, is of itself, as to the rights of sovereignty, a little monarchy: whether that family consist of a man and his children; or of a man and his servants; or of a man, and his children, and servants together: wherein the father or master is the sovereign. But yet a family is not properly a commonwealth; unless it be that power by its own number, or by other opportunities, as not to be subdued without hazard of war.[89]

The critics also miss the fact that Hobbes did not deny that historical states were mostly founded by families or dynasties, which would have been headed almost always by males. For instance, Germany and all other countries, "in their beginnings, divided amongst an infinite number of little lords, or masters of families, that continually had wars one with another. . . ."[90] We have seen that Hobbes makes this point about the existence of families and typically male leadership in nature openly when he explains that governments have been for the most part established by fathers and not by mothers.

But notice in the passage quoted above that Hobbes does not include women or mothers when he cites those whom the man has a right to absolute sovereignty over. While it is unclear here why he excludes women from those over whom the man has sovereignty (at least automatically), it does perhaps point up that for Hobbes, the dominion of men over women was far from being automatically assumed. In the final analysis, Chapman argues, "Hobbes's view of the family subverts patriarchal attitudes,"[91] because the father leadership in the state of nature and civil society are not depicted as resulting from some natural quality of men that women do not have, or the idea that God ordained male leadership, but on the agreement of wives, and even the tacit agreement of children. In fact, even Hobbes's advice, that in civil society people are to be taught that male leadership has historical roots, seems more like a noble lie, based upon our knowledge of Hobbes's overall theory.[92] This and Hobbes's occasional comparison of kings with fathers of families suggests more that Hobbes thought the old patriarchal theory might still have rhetorical value for some people, rather than suggesting that Hobbes was a patriarchal philosopher.[93] Indeed, Hobbes's reliance on consent is continuous, and in striking contrast to traditional patriarchal theory. In chapter 20 of *Leviathan*, for instance, Hobbes argues that the parent's dominion over his or her children comes "from the child's consent, either express, or by other sufficient arguments declared."[94] Chapman concludes, "Indeed, the point about Hobbes's unique view of the family is that he saw it strictly in rational terms, as an artificial institution rather than a natural one."[95]

Gordon Schochet also notices the ways in which Hobbes's argument is similar to but in other ways radically different from the arguments of his contemporaries who advocated patriarchy. "Hobbes' denial of the generative origins of the governmental authority of fathers allowed him to rest his political doctrine on the proposition that no status among men was natural. The subordination of men was due to convention and human consent, not to nature."[96] If fathers entered into the social contract as lords of their families, then, it was not because they were placed there by nature—as implied in a few statements made by Hobbes—but because their families consented to their leadership. As Schochet points out, Hobbes was unique in arguing that the father's authority over his children was derived from their consent.[97] The preponderance of Hobbes's statements, and the thrust of his argument, points overwhelmingly to the position that the family both in nature and in civil society is an artificial thing, based upon consent, just as Hobbes depicts the larger family of a kingdom as resting on the consent of the citizens. For Hobbes, "all status is conventional."[98]

Carole Pateman argues that Hobbes is not a patriarchal theorist in the seventeenth-century sense, but rather provides a thoroughly modern patriarchal theory.[99] Unlike Sir Robert Filmer, who believed that masculine rule in families and in governments was based on men's generative power (the ancient belief that the male provided the essential material for the making of children, while the female merely provided a receptacle), Hobbes claimed that the female in nature is the sole owner and lord of her children. Mother-right is the original right over the children, in Hobbes's view, and this is simply logical. However, Pateman reconciles Hobbes's argument for male/female equality in the state of nature with his many statements, detailed above, which seem to assume male leadership of the family, even in the state of nature. Pateman concludes that this leadership comes about through conquest, rightly reminding us that for Hobbes, submission based on fear is just as valid a reason for consent as that based upon some lesser imperative. Hobbes asserts time and again that all agreements are freely willed, even those which are coerced, because a person willingly submits to her or his conqueror in order to survive. If it is true that Hobbes assumes that all or most females in the state of nature would be conquered before the social contract, Hobbes's contract would then be among males only—the males having already subdued all the females by conquest.[100] However, Gabriella Slomp is representative of those who disagree.

> Contrary to Pateman, it seems to me that for Hobbes not only men and women are equal "by nature," but also they retain their equality as long as they live in natural conditions. Even the weakest woman, either alone or with the help of others, by deception or some other clever device can pose a lethal danger to the strongest man, because of the immense fragility of the "human frame."[101]

But Hobbes's view that all status, all right over others is conventional and based upon agreement would still apply, even if the entirety of Pateman's argument were true.[102] Slomp concedes that Pateman is correct that Hobbes "associates often civil society with patriarchal marriage and with the legally-sanctioned subordination of women."[103] Indeed she differs from Pateman only by arguing that the inequality in civil society which Hobbes prefers is thought by him to come with the social contract and not before. She argues that in this case Hobbes promotes what has become customary because he also thinks that "this particular custom is beneficial to the commonwealth"[104] in much the same way that the custom of hereditary succession of monarchs is beneficial. Slomp speculates that it had the benefit of directing men's natural ambition into the private sphere and away from the public sphere, but this is pure conjecture and cannot be proven.

Can Honor Be Derived from Complete Equality?

Hobbes's declaration that all status is conventional directly contradicted not only Aristotle's teachings about the different and natural virtues of various types: male and female, free and slave. More importantly perhaps, it contradicted the view inherited from his more recent past that nobility of family, refinement of blood, and masculine virtue, that is, social rank, all were natural and mattered a great deal. As we have seen, Medieval Europe believed that rank reflected quality and virtue, that the woman was not as good as the man, and the common man was not as good as the nobleman. It was for this reason that the chivalric literature asked the nobles and knights to live up to higher moral and more refined social expectations. They were the model for others to follow. They were also burdened with the responsibility for leadership, because they were assumed to be more wise, more courageous, more steady. Medieval Europe's code for the man of rank was that of chivalry, certainly not universally followed, but held up as a moral ideal and a source of shaming for those men who did not make an effort to comply. This code assumed the superiority of men over women, in strength, and even generally speaking in prudence and wisdom. It assumed different natures for male and female, different abilities, different virtues, all based upon God-given traits assumed to be inherent in the sexes. It asked those who were more blessed by God in some very important ways to behave with gentility, kindness, and moderation toward those who were their inferiors: women and all others who were assumed to be more vulnerable, including children and the elderly.

Hobbes's idea that all status is conventional, including the difference in status between a man and a woman, challenged very directly one of the central pillars of honor: greater responsibility based upon being blessed with superior attributes—that is, that honor was attached not only to social status but to gender, and could not be correctly understood unless one acknowledged that men and women were in fact not equal. This natural inequality provided the argument on behalf of moral obligation for those who wielded power. If natural inequality was not acknowledged, in the traditional view of moral obligation, there would be no reason to treat anyone more gently than anyone else. Could this source of obligation, whose source was natural inequality, be replaced by a universal source, based upon long-term self-interest as Hobbes defined it?

As argued in chapter 2, it was not Hobbes's goal to break down the idea of a proper gentleman and turn men into brutes in their relationships with others more vulnerable. Indeed, his writings seem at many points to reflect a nostalgic admiration of old-fashioned gentlemanly qualities. However, he noticed that most of the "gentlemen" around him were not living up to the ideals to which they continued to pay lip service. He needed a firmer foundation for obedience, loyalty, and goodness. In his view, this necessitated leveling everyone, at least in theory. If everyone, high born and low, male and female, adult and child, head of household and servant, could see that they were all equally vulnerable in a crisis, and that they should all be equally obedient to the laws, held to the same standards before the absolute sovereign, we would finally obtain certain peace. It is doubtful whether Hobbes foresaw the full ramifications of his argument. For, while he did not obtain assent to his conclusion for absolute sovereignty, his argument concerning natural equality and the social contract was powerfully attractive, turning as it did in short order into Locke's version, which urged the very thing Hobbes wished to avoid: rebellion. In the long run, this type of liberal theory became accepted by his society and spread throughout the Western world, and with it came the necessary rejection of the idea of responsibility based upon superiority of some kind—even superior strength (which is the last acknowledged inequality between the sexes), intelligence, aggressiveness, and so on. Those arguments which encouraged restraint in human beings with natural advantages over others ceased in the long run to operate effectively, and a real source of moral order was vanquished. If at least some of those natural differences are real (such as one might argue superior male strength is real, or superior intelligence in some human beings as opposed to others), and yet chivalry and/or noblesse oblige are no longer considered legitimate reasons for good behavior, will society have achieved more or less order and civility, both of which Hobbes hoped to accomplish through his political science? While a full exploration of this question would fill another book, with much more information about current conditions in society and in particular women's status, I will explore it further in the conclusion to this chapter as well as in the conclusion to the book, in the hopes that I and others will be able to build upon the philosophical foundation provided here.

MILITARY SERVICE: IS COURAGE IMPORTANT?

Perhaps the question that Hobbes has the most difficult time answering concerns another topic that bears on gender, in particular, the issue of what is expected of men: the necessity for military service, that is, the necessity of asking men to risk and even give their lives in battle for the protection of the commonwealth. On the one hand, Hobbes knows that no society can guarantee its survival without the ability to defend itself militarily. On the other hand, his theoretical commonwealth is based upon the individual's desire for self-preservation, and especially the avoidance of violent death. It should come as no surprise that Hobbes has a difficult time reconciling these two ideas. Recalling the discussion of how his thought changed in subtle ways from his early to his later works on the meaning and importance of honor in chapter 1, we find that this issue of military service, traditionally so connected with the ideal of masculine honor, changed its significance for Hobbes similarly. Hobbes's treatment of this issue over time tends to confirm Strauss's central argument that Hobbes rejected any traditional admiration for honor in his later works, and attempted to replace it with fear of violent death. However, it is not so much that Hobbes rejects true honor as a motivating force for good men to perform military service. Rather, he fully accepts the truth that there are few men of true honor to be found, and too many guided by false honor and false courage. While he admires the few truly honorable men who do not cause conflicts for their own personal glorification, he knows that he cannot base his political theory on their existence—he cannot rely upon them to set and enforce standards because there are too few of them. They are overwhelmed by the many for whom "honor" is really what Hobbes calls "vainglory." Instead of counting on the truly honorable, he must devise a theory that deals with the nature of most people, and taps into aspects of human nature that can hopefully overwhelm the tendency to overweening pride if explained and handled correctly: the passions of fear and self-interest.

In his early work, *The Elements of Law*, as we have seen, Hobbes seriously admires honor in warfare. He first says that in war, a man's safety is the rule of his actions. He goes on to argue that fear is the only legitimate motivation for taking someone's life. The law of nature allows this and also "rapine" or thievery, but he notices that in this case, in ancient times, thieves would leave enough for people to live on and recover, so that the common people caught up in warfare would not perish. Cruelty is violence that goes beyond necessity (fear for one's own life) and involves an enjoyment of destruction and killing. So while Hobbes says that there is no law in war in the strictest sense, he argues that honorable and dishonorable behavior are possible in battle, and the former is preferable to the latter.[105]

> For nothing but fear can justify the taking away of another's life. And because fear can hardly be made manifest, but by some action dishonourable, that bewrayeth the conscience of one's own weakness; all men in whom the passion of courage or magnanimity have been predominant, have abstained from cruelty; insomuch that though there be in war no law, the breach whereof is injury, yet there are those laws, the breach whereof is dishonour. In one word, therefore, the only law of actions in war is honour; and the right of war providence.[106]

Also in *The Elements of Law*, Hobbes mentions men of a "timorous" nature in a negative way, placing them in the same category as those who are "superstitious" in a discussion of how people's imagination can deceive them.[107] In contrast, he describes courage as "the absence of fear in the presence of any evil whatsoever; but in a stricter and more common meaning, it is contempt of wounds and death, when they oppose a man in the way to his end."[108] He also expresses a fairly balanced view of courage and fear in battle in *Elements of Law* when he writes, "Courage may be virtue, when the daring is extreme, if the cause be good; and extreme fear no vice when the danger is extreme."[109] This is particularly noteworthy, because Hobbes is willing to admire courage if it is expressed for a good cause, a position close to the old chivalric admiration of courage. He also qualifies the excuse for fear, only accepting it in extreme danger. The tone of these remarks indicates that Hobbes still admired courage and did not fully justify cowardice.

In *De Cive*, Hobbes speaks very forthrightly about the necessity of the sovereign to defend the commonwealth. In fact, he holds that it is "unlawful" (by which he must mean against the law of nature) not to take the necessary steps of maintaining and supplying a military force for national defense. He mentions money as the prime obstacle, not the fearfulness of soldiers. It is because it is difficult to "wring suddenly out of close-fisted men so vast a proportion of monies" necessary to suddenly raise an army, that Hobbes recommends that a sovereign always be prepared and in readiness to fight.[110] As we have seen, Hobbes's observations in *Behemoth* also show that he understands it is relatively easy to find men to volunteer to fight for a cause such as the king's or Parliament's, but it is less easy (especially for the king) to find the money to pay and equip the army.

In *De Cive*, Hobbes takes a large step toward condemnation of the military code of honor. Discussing how sedition is able to get a start, he notes that there must be a commander whom others will follow:

not as being engaged by their submission to his command (for we have already in this very chapter, supposed these kind of men not to understand, being obliged beyond that which seems right and good in their own eyes); but for some opinion they have of his virtue, or military skill, or resemblance of humours.[111]

Here Hobbes puts men who take honor seriously ("what seems right and good in their own eyes") in the category of those who will likely follow a seditious commander, such as an Essex or Cromwell. The man whose courage is good if he follows a good cause may still exist, but Hobbes does not mention him. Instead, he begins to emphasize the arrogance of courageous men. Such men respect their commander because of some inherent quality they think he possesses, such as virtue or military ability. They pass judgment on him based upon their individual opinions and preferences, instead of knowing whom they should obey based upon who holds the sovereignty. Cast in this light, individual courage seems bad and destructive, not admirable.

In *Leviathan*, Hobbes's tone changes even more, and it is here that we see most clearly the possible contradiction between his social contract theory and his remarks on military service. By the time *Leviathan* was written, Hobbes was very determined to remind his readers of the rational fear of violent death and the need for submission to an absolute sovereign to avoid it. Hobbes reminds us that he has established in chapter 14 that no one can transfer by covenant the right to defend his own body. He says there, "*Subjects have liberty to defend their own bodies, even against them that lawfully invade them.*" They are "*not bound to hurt themselves.*"[112] They have a right to resist even lawful punishment because of their natural fear of death. As Thomas Schrock points out, Hobbes first mentions the sovereign's right to punish in chapter 14 of *Leviathan*, but "this first mention in the *Leviathan* of the right to punish is made part and parcel with a claim that the right to punish is reconcilable with the right to resist punishment."[113] In the final analysis, Schrock does not think Hobbes can have an absolute sovereign with any teeth if his subjects retain this natural right to resistance, and he concludes that Hobbes himself had become infected with the seditious doctrine he warned others against.[114] As F. C. Hood remarked, Hobbes even argued that a man could justly refuse a dishonorable or dangerous duty under certain circumstances. "The interesting point," wrote Hood,

> is that he has a right to refuse to execute a dangerous or dishonourable office, where refusal to obey does not frustrate "the end for which the sovereignty was ordained." Hobbes does not indicate who is to judge whether disobedience would, or would not, frustrate the end. It is probably that he thought that both the sovereign and the subject concerned had a moral right to judge, and a moral duty to judge honestly.[115]

In chapter 21 of *Leviathan*, Hobbes applies his fundamental directive of self-preservation directly to the issue of military service. He argues that no man can be bound to fight against an enemy. A sovereign can punish his refusal even by death, but a man still has the right to refuse. Hobbes argues that refusal to do military duty is not injustice, though he softens this statement by suggesting that it is not injustice if, for instance, a man is able to hire a substitute. Not only can he get a substitute to fight for him, but he also is allowed to simply run away:

> And there is allowance to be made for natural timorousness; not only to women, of whom no such dangerous duty is expected, but also to men of feminine courage. When armies fight, there is on one side, or both, a running away; yet when they do it not out of treachery, but fear, they are not esteemed to do it unjustly, but dishonorably. For the same reason, to avoid battle, is not injustice, but cowardice.[116]

Hobbes argues that in battle, if a soldier's life is threatened, he can run away, and he is justified in doing so. The essence of his argument has remained the same, and the stigma of "dishonor" and "cowardice" seems minimized by his argument. Even in *The Elements of Law*, Hobbes argued that cowardice in nature or in battle was not unjust but dishonorable, likewise seeming to minimize the stigma of dishonor. Hobbes also makes the same equation of timorousness with the superstitious personality as he did in *The Elements of Law*.[117] However, the thrust of Hobbes's remarks, what he chooses to emphasize and elaborate upon, has changed. Because of *Leviathan's* strong endorsement of the legitimacy of fear as a motivator, Hobbes entangles himself on the issue of military service to the point where his argument seems self-contradictory. He tries to make a distinction, for instance, between a soldier who is drafted, and one who volunteers for pay.

> But he that enrolleth himself a soldier or taketh imprest money, taketh away the excuse of a timorous nature; and is obliged, not only to go to the battle, but also not to run from it, without his captain's leave. And when the defence of the commonwealth, requireth at once the help of all that are able to bear arms, every one is obliged; because otherwise the institution of the commonwealth, which they have not the purpose, or courage to preserve, was in vain.[118]

Working his way through the various circumstances of service, Hobbes is evidently struggling mightily with the duty to defend one's country. Why taking money or making an agreement should hold in the state of nature which is the battlefield, when no other agreement can do so in the state of nature, is a question Hobbes does not answer.[119] Fear, it would seem, must override any other motivation or previous agreement. As Orwin explains, for Hobbes:

> Fear alone holds the solution to the human problem, for only it and its ancillary passions provide a ground for that selfish moderation of selfishness which introduces the political order. Fear is the basis of the subjection of the subject, and it is in its name that subjection is unqualified, except where the fear requires its qualification.[120]

The chief and only reason people enter into the social contract in the first place is to protect their lives. How can they then be made to voluntarily risk giving up their lives for the sake of protecting the community as a whole? Hobbes does not appeal to a sense of nobility or self-sacrifice, because his argument will not allow it. And yet, this is the very center of the gentlemanly ideal—to be indifferent to one's own survival, to be willing to give up one's own life in the service of a greater good. But we can easily see in so much of Hobbes's thought that it is this idea of the hero, the man of honor, which he has concluded is too destructive, and which he wishes to knock down. In his view, pretensions to heroism and valor are most often born of pride; they are really the fruit of self-love, not the love of others. These pretensions simply get people killed. This conclusion agrees with Slomp's observations about how Hobbes changed his treatment of the concept of glory by the time he wrote *Leviathan*. She argues that for Hobbes, glory was always the main motivator for human conflict, but that by the time he wrote *Leviathan*, Hobbes separated people into the ambitious glory-seeking few, who were troublemakers, and the many, who simply wanted to live their lives. It would seem that by the time he wrote *Leviathan*, he often equated honor-seeking with glory-seeking—and he pointed his finger at the few troublemakers who, in pursuit of their own preeminence, were quite willing to cause war.[121]

Timorousness does not seem too bad in light of the destruction that can be caused by the courageous man, who in *Leviathan* is often identified as the "vainglorious" man: "And generally all vain-glorious men, unless they be withal timorous, are subject to anger; as being more prone than others to interpret for contempt, the ordinary liberty of conversation: and there are few crimes that may not be produced by anger."[122] Hence, the character of those who value honor is treated in *Leviathan* as the prideful or vainglorious character, whose passions are mostly self-centered despite the principled rhetoric, and inherently destructive, and who could benefit from timorousness. "Courage" and "virtue military" are the values of the "great and ancient gentry,"[123] which largely caused the English Civil War. In chapter 11 of *Leviathan*, Hobbes most clearly turns the tables on chivalric values in favor of bourgeois values:

> Desire of ease, and sensual delight, disposeth men to obey a common power: because by such desires, a man doth abandon the protection that might be hoped for from his own industry, and labour. Fear of death, and wounds, disposeth to the same; and for the same reason. On the contrary, needy men, and hardy, not contented with their present condition; as also, all men that are ambitious of military command, are inclined to continue the causes of war; and to stir up trouble and sedition: for there is no honour military but by war; nor any such hope to mend an ill game, as by causing a new shuffle.[124]

Here Hobbes clearly *prefers* the so-called timorous man, the man who fears death and pain, the man who cares more about his daily comforts, the soft man (whom he also calls the "effeminate" man). Those who are "hardy" or "needy," and those who are "ambitious" for military honor are the source of war itself. They are accused here of *creating* the circumstances in which they can display their honor, take revenge against those who have slighted them, and compete for command. These ambitious men are treated as objectively more dishonorable than those who run from danger and seek only their own personal safety and comfort. They are Hobbes's modern rhetoricians, combining eloquence and flattery with "military reputation," to gain adherents.[125] Their courage is caused by unrealistic self-love, and not by a true adherence to principle. For this reason Hobbes can say that "amongst the passions, *courage* (by which I mean the contempt of wounds, and violent death), inclineth men to private revenges, and sometimes to endeavour the unsettling of the public peace."[126] While he also says in this sentence that timorousness, "many times disposeth to the desertion of the public defence," we also know that Hobbes ultimately cannot condemn timorousness and indeed prefers it to its opposite, though he understands that this is problematic for national defense. This preference for timidity, and its converse refusal to promote courage, represents a complete overturning of chivalric or gentlemanly values, a complete rejection of them in favor of something new, something that will work for more people more of the time, that "fearful bourgeois civic spirit"[127] which makes people peaceful and productive and reconciled to submission.

Above all, Hobbes wants to remind us that it is fear of death, and acting upon that fear, that is rational. Risking one's life (and especially persuading others to risk theirs) is folly and vanity, not to be admired and romanticized. For instance, Hobbes in several places mentions dueling as an effect of men's irrational obsession with honor. He advises the sovereign to use his authority to make dueling shameful:

And at this day, in this part of the world, private duels are, and always will be honourable, though unlawful, till such time as there shall be honour ordained for them that refuse, and ignominy for them that make the challenge. For duels also are many times effects of courage; and the ground of courage is always strength or skill, which are power; though for the most part they be effects of rash speaking, and of the fear of dishonour, in one, or both the combatants; who engaged by rashness, are driven into the lists to avoid disgrace.[128]

On the other hand, Hobbes does try to justify mandatory military service in the case when the commonwealth itself is threatened with imminent destruction. Remember that he says:

And when the defence of the commonwealth, requireth at once the help of all that are able to bear arms, every one is obliged; because otherwise the institution of the commonwealth, which they have not the purpose, or courage to preserve, was in vain.[129]

The point here seems to be simply an extension of his reasoning above. If the existence of the commonwealth itself is imminently threatened it makes sense from the point of view of our own individual survival to cooperate and come to its aid. This is hardly the same as a chivalric sense of selfless duty to protect the commonwealth. As we have seen, in *Leviathan*'s chapter 10, Hobbes does observe that "Dominion, and victory is honourable; because acquired by power;

and servitude, for need, or fear, is dishonourable."[130] But I have argued that
Hobbes strips honor of its original meaning in this chapter, making it relative to
nothing but power. Submitting to another for fear, then, may be *called* dishonorable because it is a sign that the one submitting does not hold the power, but
such submission is perfectly understandable nonetheless. In Hobbes's view, it
is the rational thing to do, and in fact is the basis of that great good of peace
which benefits all men. Hobbes lists the reasons it would be acceptable to
change allegiance, to obey another power. These instances include cases of ban-
ishment and captivity. Whenever the sovereign is no longer able to protect the
subject's life, and when his life can be protected by another, it is permissible,
indeed the only rational thing to do, to switch allegiance. "The obligation of
subjects to the sovereign, is understood to last as long, and no longer, than the
power lasteth, by which he is able to protect them."[131] There certainly is no
sense of moral obligation, duty, or loyalty here that would befit a gentleman.
But for Hobbes there is no particular nobility in dying.

In general, it is hard to know if Hobbes would accept any notion of the
greater or common good, since the social contract is based solely on the self-
interest in self-preservation of each individual involved. In his view, self-
preservation is (or should be) such an instinct that nothing can or should possibly interfere with it. If this is cowardice, Hobbes has no real problem with
cowardice—the survival instinct is certainly not something that in his view
people should try to resist. Of course, Hobbes continues to argue that one
should not be cruel because cruelty is not conducive to survival even in the
state of nature—it is literally not necessary. In *Leviathan*, he points out that vi-
olations of the law of nature (in kings) come with "natural punishments." For
example, injustice is punished by the violence of enemies.[132] This is an argument that makes sense but has nothing to do with honor. Instead it has to do
with rational self-interest, or prudence. The standard of conduct of a gentleman
has to do with absolute moral obligation, even in the face of possible damage
to himself. This standard could not be supported by Hobbes's argument.

Again, as we found in chapter 2, it is not that Hobbes personally had no admiration for true courage and honor, but that he thought these were so rare
that they could not be relied upon. Even in *Leviathan*, he continues to make
a distinction between a man who is just because of fear and a man who is just
because he knows it is the right thing to do. He distinguishes between the
righteous man whose basic character is not changed, even if he occasionally
makes a moral mistake or is forced to agree with something he knows is not
right, and the unrighteous man who, even if he obeys the law because he has
to, is inclined to evil—his character is bad. In chapter 14 of *Leviathan*
Hobbes's language reveals nostalgia for those of truly noble character, but
also a belief that such nobility is in critically short supply:

The force of words, being, as I have formerly noted, too weak to hold men to the performance of their covenants; there are in man's nature, but two imaginable helps to strengthen it. And those are either a fear of the consequence of breaking their word; or a glory, or pride in appearing not to need to break it. This latter is a generosity too rarely found to be presumed on, especially in the pursuers of wealth, command, or sensual pleasure; which are the greatest part of mankind.[133]

In chapter 15 of *Leviathan*, Hobbes writes, "That which gives to human actions the relish of justice, is a certain nobleness or gallantness of courage, rarely found, by which a man scorns to be beholden for the contentment of his life, to fraud, or breach of promise."[134] And at the end of *Leviathan*, he gives a nod again to the true gentleman, this time embodied in a friend:

> I have known clearness of judgment, and largeness of fancy; strength of reason, and graceful elocution; a courage for the war, and a fear for the laws, and all eminently in one man, and that was my most noble and honoured friend, Mr. Sidney Godolphin; who hating no man, nor hated of any, was unfortunately slain in the beginning of the late civil war, in the public quarrel, by an undiscerned and an undiscerning hand.[135]

In Hobbes's view, truly "gallant men" like Mr. Godolphin are confident enough in their own worth that they do not engage in the type of behavior typical of the troublemakers of his day. If they must go to war, they do it for the right cause. If they are courageous, their courage is valuable because it is in the true service of their country and not themselves. Hobbes observes that there are too few such men, and many more who do not understand true honor or courage. He highlights for criticism men who seek revenge for some "words of disgrace" or "some little injuries," "for the hurt is not corporeal, but phantastical, and, though in this corner of the world, made sensible by a custom not many years since begun, amongst young and vain men, so light, as a gallant man, and one that is assured of his own courage, cannot take notice of."[136] Kenneth Minogue has pointed out that Hobbes did believe that a truly moral sense could develop in some people, and that it was entirely admirable and desirable when it did. He expected that any wise sovereign would try to encourage as many characters like Mr. Godolphin's to develop as possible. "Moral obligation can be taught," writes Minogue, "and Hobbes believes that it ought to be taught and disseminated by the sovereign. But being a realist, he feels that most obedience to the sovereign, most of the time, will be rational rather than moral."[137] It is precisely because the gallant type of character is, in Hobbes view, "rarely found," and the other type of character which takes notice of small slights abounds, that Hobbes rejects gallantry or chivalric virtue as a foundation for his political theory. This does not mean that true gentlemen do not exist, or that the world would not be a better place with more of them, only that there are so few of them that they make no political difference. Meanwhile the false gentlemen, far more numerous, must somehow be checked.

This disappointment with most men, combined with a latent and indignant insistence on actual standards for character, is apparent also in *Behemoth*. There he is not afraid to say that the king's men, such as Prince Rupert, were courageous,[138] or that the king's attackers were motivated by covetousness and cowardice.[139] We know that Hobbes did not simply attribute true courage to the right side, because he often subtly and occasionally openly criticized Charles's lack of courage as a part of what caused the conflict to come to a head. He says that his followers attributed valor to Oliver Cromwell, but mistakenly, from not really knowing his character (or perhaps from not knowing what valor was).[140] Indeed, Hobbes distinguishes with great interest between true and false gallantry of men in general, no matter what side they are on:

> According to your definition, there be few wise men now-a-days. Such wisdom is a kind of gallantry, that few are brought up to, and most think folly. Fine cloaths, great feathers, civility toward men that will not swallow injuries, and injury toward them that will, is the present gallantry.[141]

Perhaps Hobbes is thinking here of the overturning of traditional values that Thucydides described happening during the Corcyrean civil war, in which "inconsiderate boldness, was counted true-hearted manliness: provident deliberation, a handsome fear: modesty, the cloak of cowardice: to be wise in every thing, to be lazy in every thing."[142] True gallantry is born of wisdom, but most men do not value either wisdom or true gallantry. Instead, the gallantry of his day is equated, in his view, with pomposity—a sort of silliness of dress, manners, and attitude. This view is not so far from de Charny's opinion of men who love finery more than effectiveness, and make themselves ridiculous, only in Hobbes's view, such men have become the majority. In *Leviathan*, Hobbes observes that "Vain-glorious men, such as without being conscious to themselves of great sufficiency, delight in supposing themselves gallant men, are inclined only to ostentation."[143] They are most loath to actually act if called upon. It is because of the predominance of such men of poor character, so vainglorious and spiteful, that Hobbes finds it necessary to turn to a more solid, presumably more reliable basis for social and political order. Is he correct that there are so few good men that we cannot rely upon them to provide leadership and order? If he is correct, should we agree with him that any effective political theory must start with and build from what human character is predominant, not what is possible? What does his argument, which puts self-preservation above duty to defend one's country, say about any state's ability to adequately defend itself? Is national defense possible without many young men still believing that there is something worth risking their lives for? Again, this is a question that, if fully explored, would require another book, with much additional material about contemporary military service. However, I will attempt an answer in the conclusion to this chapter as well as the conclusion of this book, which I hope will provide myself and other writers more material for future scholarship.

CONCLUSION

Hobbes could see that the winds were blowing in his times in the direction of the common or "bourgeois" man, the man whose credentials came not from noble blood or from past military service but from intelligence and enterprise. He could observe the effects of the Protestant Reformation, in which Luther and others led the common man in rebellion against the idea of permanent and unquestionable authority embodied in the Catholic Church. He could see the power of the commons to cause conflict in the English Civil War, as various types of Protestants fought with each other for religious supremacy and political control. He knew that these newly powerful men would not accept the idea that government was legitimate, and to be obeyed abjectly, because it was occupied by their supposedly natural superiors. So, he devised a theory in which all could consider themselves the authors of their government, equally benefiting from its rule and equally consenting to its authority. Hobbes's thought can be seen as a precursor of the eighteenth-century Enlightenment because of his faith in the power of reason to take the place of long-standing notions of moral duty and obligation built into the premodern social fabric. He reaches out to all who can listen, in school or in church, to his new doctrine, the new political science of rational self-interest. He expects them to follow his argument, accept its sense, and overturn age-old prejudices and superstitions in the process. Why not call him an Enlightenment thinker before his time?

Hobbes is in some ways a tragic figure, because as I have tried to show in all three chapters, as an individual of good character, he had one foot (or at least a few toes) in the past, in an age when the man of honor, courage, and refinement was admired. He considered himself a true gentleman, and he continued to admire those men who acted like true gentlemen. But he had lost his faith in most men, and had reconciled himself to the fact that not these, but the baser sort of people predominated and would one way or the other prevail unless checked. So, the task was to harness their passions and selfishness somehow, to make them see why they should restrain themselves, not for the sake of others, but for their own sakes, and to create a consensus as to political order, so their passions could be checked by the sovereign power if necessary. But I have, through the way I have treated this topic, invited the reader to question whether this source of restraint and obligation is as effective as the previous honor system, however imperfect. While asking this question is relatively safe, making a case for the superiority of the former source of obligation (honor) is fraught with danger. But if we were to make such a case, what would it be based upon? Here I will make a few observations derived from the subject matter of this chapter, and I will reserve more general speculations for the conclusion to this book, and to future research.

We have seen that Hobbes posits a natural equality in which inequalities in areas such as strength, character, and intelligence do not matter from the point of view of survival. Perhaps they do not, logically speaking, given Hobbes's assumptions about the state of nature. But when we examine this issue from the point of view of motivation, that is, what will motivate a man or woman to morally obligate him or herself to others, there might be a difference. Is motivation supplied by rational self-interest, grounded upon awareness of the fear of violent death, sufficient? Is it stronger than motivation from duty, the idea that because one can, one should act to protect others, treat them fairly and generously, and not abuse them? Is fear stronger than a sense of pride and shame, and for how much of the time? Which motivation truly appeals to the human imagination more strongly in times of stress? Even Hobbes knew how strong these motivations should be—so convinced was he of their strength that he spent a great deal of his political theory in trying to defeat their appeal.

Why did Hobbes face such a formidable foe in the existence of such seemingly ephemeral motivations as honor, glory, and piety? Edmund Burke famously pointed out that what he called prejudice was of quick assistance in times of need, while rational calculation was rather unreliable. Prejudice, as he defined it, was that gut-level preference for certain attitudes and actions and a similar gut-level distaste for others, a clear sense of right and wrong that was automatic, not based upon cold logic. Burke believed that rational calculation was weaker because, given a chance, most people were capable of reasoning themselves out of just about any sense of obligation, especially in an emergency, when they and/or their possessions might be at risk. This is why Burke preferred the instinctual "prejudice" of duty and its consequent shame—because given proper prejudices, a person did not have to think before he acted, but would be ready to do what was required to preserve the community. Burke wrote in the *Reflections*:

> because prejudice, with its reason, has a motive to give action to that reason, and an affection which will give it permanence. Prejudice is of ready application in the emergency; it previously engages the mind in a steady course of wisdom and

virtue and does not leave the man hesitating in the moment of decision skepti-
cal, puzzled, and unresolved. Prejudice renders a man's virtue his habit, and not
a series of unconnected acts. Through just prejudice, his duty becomes a part of
his nature.[144]

Burke, of course, believed both in noblesse oblige and in chivalry, though
he bemoaned that chivalry was dead—killed by the French revolutionaries—
the "age of chivalry is gone," he wrote, and the age of "sophisters, econo-
mists; and calculators" had succeeded it.[145] He would no doubt see Hobbes as
an early example of these "calculators" who killed chivalry.

For Burke, one of the hallmarks of a civilized society was the way its men
treated women, which is why he had so much to say about the treatment of
Marie Antoinette by the revolutionaries.[146] We look back at his attitude as re-
markably antiquated, and yet, can we, through our discussion of Hobbes, question the absolute equality we now take for granted, if only for the sake of argument? If we were able to concede, if only for argument's sake, that women
are more vulnerable to abuse than men because they are not only physically
weaker on average but also perhaps less prone to physical aggression—and
truly absorb what that means for the lives of real women around the world—
would we be able to so blithely reject the idea of moral obligations that assume
inequalities as a starting point?

As we have seen, Pateman demonstrates that Hobbes's starting assumption
of male-female equality in the state of nature ends up sanctioning male domination in the family and in government. This is the case because Hobbes assumes that any social arrangements now in force must be considered the result of prior consent. At some point, women of his time must have consented
to their social and legal inferiority. But remember that submission to the sovereign, or the female's submission to the male in the state of nature or in civil
society, can be brought about by conquest. Hobbes's theory relies upon fear-
based contracts being just as valid as contracts made under less restrictive circumstances. Most likely, the reason why almost all families in the state of nature and in civil society were male dominated is, after all, because the males
were stronger than the females, and so won their "consent" through conquest.
The females, then, obtained protection in exchange for their obedience, in the
same way all citizens of the properly ordered commonwealth obtain their
safety in exchange for the same. Is this a solid foundation for humane and equitable treatment of women by men?

In our day, of course, the logic of natural female equality, foreseen if not
seriously proposed in Hobbes's depiction of the state of nature, has emerged
as a real social and political force. Perhaps aided by the softening of society
through the bourgeois lifestyle, which rewards behaviors conducive to ease of
living and not the display of crude force, women have earned legal equality

with men in civil society in a way Hobbes would never have imagined. As Karen Green puts it, women have reversed their situation of inferiority, "perhaps because changing technology has altered the importance of muscle in the distribution of power and diminished the disadvantages of pregnancy."[147]

But yet the underlying assumptions which caused Hobbesian men to be able to conquer women and get their "consent" remain, and so we live in a world where the greatest displays of female accomplishments exist side-by-side with the most horrible cases of abuse of women and girls (and children generally) imaginable at any time. Domestic abuse has far from disappeared, even in democratic countries where women are legally the equals of men in every way, and sexual abuse of children seems dramatically on the rise. One might ask, with this as a backdrop, if some of the older honor/shame ethic might not be more effective in restraining men so inclined from abusing those who are in fact more vulnerable, than the modern reliance on the morality of total equality and rational self-interest. Whether or not such an honor/shame ethic would have to bring back all the old and undesirable inequalities is a matter for speculation in the conclusion to this book. But would acknowledging that certain inequalities—physical strength and lower inclination to aggression at the very least—remain relevant to our lives and relationships with men today do away with all other equalities? Or, to put it another way, would obligating men *because they are men* to be restrained at least with regard to physical strength and aggression with women and children motivate more of them to conform to certain desirable standards of conduct? If men judged *each other* at least partly on the basis of how they treated their wives and children, and others around them who were less able or inclined to aggression, ostracizing those who acted in an unmanly and shameful fashion, labeling them cowards for shirking their responsibilities or being abusive, would it help shape the character of young men such that more of them would not go down the path of abuse and irresponsibility? Would it perhaps make these same men see themselves as more responsible in other areas of life as well? Although women are sadly making gains regarding participation in criminal activity, men are still by far the most common perpetrators of domestic abuse, child abuse, as well as violent and even nonviolent crimes. Many bring children into the world and walk away from their responsibilities, leaving single mothers in poverty, trying to be both father and mother to their children. More and more, both mothers and fathers walk away from the children they create, leaving the grandparents to do the job of raising them. Doesn't it make sense for us, under these circumstances, to ask whether the assumptions of rational self-interest and full equality which underlie our social contract are good enough—or perhaps even whether they are responsible for society's regress with regard to male (and female) responsibility?

One area of life which might remind men of their special role in the protection of those more vulnerable is military service. Yet we see that Hobbes's way of thinking, based upon the primacy of fear of death and rational self-interest, hollows out any sense of obligation a man might have to fight for his country. If they adopt Hobbes's view about the primacy of individual self-preservation, young men must ask why it is ever smart and admirable to be a soldier when doing so is voluntary. They will not feel guilty or ashamed to try to escape this obligation, at least through legal means, should they be called. If they adopt Hobbes's skepticism about the motivations of those who call for war, or attempt to lead in battle, they are likely to see war as a result of some men's outsized desire for glory or thirst for blood, rather than a sad necessity that sometimes falls upon us in order that we remain safe and free. Can men who have no sense of obligation to their community beyond the mentality of a business transaction accept any obligation to put their lives on the line for the larger society? What if they have been raised to see society as existing solely for their safety and comfort, with no corresponding obligations? As Michael Krom writes, "it may be that the incorporation of those who will not flee from impending danger is essential to peace."[148] But if it is, Hobbes's political philosophy may contain a fatal flaw that does not allow it to achieve its primary objective.

These are questions which, at least for now, I simply want to pose for the reader's consideration, questions of contemporary significance which Hobbes's theory helps us form. Hobbes's influence upon us is, after all, not that remote. While it may not bear sway in its particulars, its modern turn away from honor, duty, and shame, and its turn toward fear-based action and individual rational self-interest, it bears considering as a foundational source for the way people now think in liberal societies. While not wishing to reject liberalism, or turn back the clock on so many aspects of progress, we might reexamine whether honor has to be rejected in exchange for peace, or whether there might be some way to have both, for the sake of the good life. I will turn to these questions in the conclusion to this book.

NOTES

1. Thomas Hobbes, *Leviathan*, ed. Michael Oakeshott (New York: Macmillan Publishing Co., 1962), part 1, ch. 11, para 1, p. 80.

2. Hobbes, *Leviathan*, part 1, ch. 8, para. 14, p. 62.

3. See Jan H. Blits, "Hobbesian Fear," *Political Theory* 17, no. 3 (August 1989): 417–31, for an excellent treatment of the fear of the unknown which Hobbes thought lay at the root of fear and uncertainty toward fellow human beings and the inconstancy of language.

4. Hobbes, *Leviathan*, part 1, ch. 2, para. 5, p. 25.

5. Hobbes, *Leviathan*, part 1, ch. 4, para. 24, pp. 39–40.

6. Hobbes, *Leviathan*, part 1, ch. 8, para. 12, p. 62.

7. Hobbes, *Leviathan*, part 1, ch. 8, para. 14, p. 62.

8. Hobbes, *Leviathan*, part 1, ch. 13, para. 1, p. 98.

9. Hobbes, *De Cive*, ed. Sterling P. Lamprecht (Westport, Conn.: Greenwood Press, 1982), preface, sect. 3, p. 12.

10. Hobbes, *Leviathan*, part 1, ch. 11, para. 2, p. 80.

11. Hobbes, *Leviathan*, part 1, ch. 11, para. 2, p. 80.

12. Hobbes, *Leviathan*, part 1, ch. 13, para. 7, p. 99.

13. See Robert Grafstein, "The Significance of Modern State of Nature Theory," *Polity* 19, no. 4 (Summer 1987): 529–50. Grafstein argues that objections such as this, which argue that the state of nature contains implausible social elements or motivations, miss the point. The larger significance of the state of nature theory, argues Grafstein, is that it shows that effective political institutions plausibly could have been made using highly individualistic assumptions, bringing such institutions thoroughly within the domain of the human and not some transcendent force, whether religious or social.

14. Jean-Jacques Rousseau, "Discourse on the Origins of Inequality," in *The Basic Writings* (Indianapolis: Hackett Publishing Co., 1987), part 1, para. 35, p. 53. Rousseau believed that savage man had little self-awareness and did not experience pride, jealousy, and other social passions which Hobbes assumes are natural, but which Rousseau believed came along with the corruption of society.

15. Hobbes, *Leviathan*, part 1, ch. 13, para. 11, p. 101. In this area, Hobbes mentions as proof of the existence of the state of nature our attitudes of mistrust for each other in society, the situation of savage people in America, civil war, and the hostility of nations in international anarchy.

16. Hobbes, *Leviathan*, part 1, ch. 13, para. 5, p. 99.

17. Hobbes, *Leviathan*, part 1, ch. 13, para. 7, pp. 99–100.

18. Hobbes, *Leviathan*, part 1, ch. 8, para. 23, p. 64.

19. Hobbes, *Leviathan*, part 1, ch. 8, para. 21, p. 63.

20. Hobbes, *Leviathan*, part 1, ch. 8, para. 18, p. 63.

21. Hobbes, *Leviathan*, part 1, ch. 13, para. 9, p. 100.

22. Hobbes, *Leviathan*, part 1, ch. 14, para. 1, p. 103.

23. Hobbes, *Leviathan*, part 1, ch. 14, para. 3, p. 103.

24. Hobbes, *Leviathan*, part 1, ch. 14, para. 4, p. 104.

25. See for instance David Boucher and Paul Kelly, eds., *The Social Contract from Hobbes to Rawls* (New York: Routledge, 1994). "Clearly the Hobbesian state of nature is not the description of a particular historical development. Most commentators agree that it is also not an historical generalization of the type: 'this is how most states originate,' however closely it may resemble certain historical realities. The usual conclusion is therefore that it is an 'hypothesis,' in the sense of a mental construction that goes beyond a generalization" (45). The authors conclude that Hobbes's construct is best understood as a sort of hypothesis or analysis, "the taking apart conceptually of the phenomenon experienced to find its necessary causality," and "such hypothesis re-

quire to be confirmed by constant reference back to experience—the latter must always, so to speak, be retained and consulted in the mind of the analyst as he proceeds with his work" (47–48). See also Jean Hampton, *Hobbes and the Social Contract Tradition* (Cambridge: Cambridge University Press, 1986).

26. Hobbes, *Leviathan*, part 1, ch. 15, para. 1, p. 113.

27. Peter Hayes, "Hobbes's Bourgeois Moderation," *Polity* 31, no. 1 (Autumn 1998): 69.

28. Hobbes, *Leviathan*, part 1, ch. 15, para. 21, p. 119.

29. Hobbes, *Leviathan*, part 1, ch. 15, para. 21, p. 120.

30. Hobbes, *Leviathan*, part 1, ch. 15, para. 27, p. 121.

31. Hobbes, *Leviathan*, part 2, ch. 17, para. 4, p. 130.

32. Hobbes, *Leviathan*, part 2, ch. 17, para. 2, p. 129.

33. Hobbes, *Leviathan*, part 2, ch. 18, para. 6, p. 136.

34. Locke writes that the people "of any country, who are descended, and derive a title to their estates from those who are subdued, and had a government forced upon them against their free consents, retain a right to the possession of their ancestors, though they consent not freely to the government, whose hard conditions were by force imposed on the possessors of that country." *Second Treatise of Government*, ed. Richard H. Cox (Arlington Heights, Ill.: Harlan Davidson, Inc., 1982), ch. 16, sect. 192, pp. 117–18.

35. Locke repeatedly argues that agreements made by force are not valid. "To which I shall say, they bind not at all; because whatsoever another gets from me by force, I still retain the right of, and he is obliged presently to restore" (*Second Treatise*, ch. 16, sect. 186, p. 116).

36. Thomas Hobbes, *Elements of Law*, 2nd ed., ed. Ferdinand Tönnies (London: Frank Cass and Company Limited, 1969), part 1, ch. 15, para. 13, p. 79.

37. Hobbes, *Elements of Law*, part 1, ch. 15, para. 13, p. 79.

38. See Hobbes, *De Cive*, part 1, ch. 2, sect. 16, pp. 38–39.

39. Hobbes, *Leviathan*, part 1, ch. 14, para. 26, p. 110.

40. For a thorough treatment of the similarities and differences between Aristotle and Hobbes, see Thomas A. Spragens Jr., *The Politics of Motion: The World of Thomas Hobbes* (Lexington: University Press of Kentucky, 1973).

41. Martin A. Bertman, "Equality in Hobbes, with Reference to Aristotle," *The Review of Politics* 38, no. 4 (October 1976): 541.

42. Bertman, "Equality in Hobbes," 540.

43. William Mathie, "Justice and the Question of Regimes in Ancient and Modern Political Philosophy: Aristotle and Hobbes," *Canadian Journal of Political Science* 9, no. 3 (September 1976): 450.

44. Mathie, "Justice and the Question of Regimes," 450.

45. Thomas K. Lindsay, "Liberty, Equality, Power: Aristotle's Critique of the Democratic 'Presupposition,'" *American Journal of Political Science* 36, no. 3 (August 1992): 749.

46. Lindsay, "Liberty, Equality, Power," 743–61.

47. Mathie, "Justice and the Question of Regimes," 451.

48. See for instance *De Cive*, part 2, ch. 7, sect. 2, pp. 87–88.

49. "Now in monarchy, the private interest is the same with the public. The riches, power, and honour of a monarch arise only from the riches, strength, and reputation of his subjects. For no king can be rich, nor glorious, nor secure, whose subjects are either poor, or contemptible, or too weak through want or dissention, to maintain a war against their enemies: whereas in a democracy, or aristocracy, the public prosperity confers not so much to the private fortune of one that is corrupt, or ambitious, as doth many times a perfidious advice, a treacherous action, or a civil war" (Hobbes, *Leviathan*, part 2, ch. 19, para. 4, p. 144).

50. Hobbes, *Leviathan*, part 2, ch. 30, para. 25, p. 258.

51. Hobbes, *Leviathan*, part 2, ch. 30, para. 25, pp. 258–59.

52. Hobbes, *The Elements of Law*, part 2, ch. 5, para. 5, p. 142.

53. Hobbes, *De Cive*, part 2, ch. 7, sect. 8, p. 92.

54. Hobbes, *De Cive*, part 1, ch. 3, sect. 13, p. 50.

55. Hobbes, *De Cive*, part 2, ch. 10, sect. 4, pp. 116–17. See also *The Elements of Law*, part 2, ch. 2, para. 6, p. 121.

56. Hobbes, *The Elements of Law*, part 2, ch. 5, para. 2, pp. 138–40.

57. Hobbes, *De Cive*, part 2, ch. 10, sect. 19, p. 127.

58. Mathie, "Justice and the Question of Regimes," 458.

59. Thomas K. Lindsay, "Aristotle's Appraisal of Manly Spirit: Political and Philosophic Implications," *American Journal of Political Science* 44, no. 3 (July 2000): 435.

60. Lindsay, "Aristotle's Appraisal of Manly Spirit," 441. For flow, I have removed Lindsay's internal citations.

61. "It is not difficult to see why the *spoudaios* of the bulk of the *Ethics* is never described as an *anêr*: virtue at its peak is not male but human virtue," writes Lindsay, in "Aristotle's Appraisal of Manly Spirit," 444.

62. Lindsay, "Aristotle's Appraisal of Manly Spirit," 445.

63. Lindsay, "Aristotle's Appraisal of Manly Spirit," 447.

64. Hobbes, *De Cive*, part 1, ch. 1, sect. 3, p. 25.

65. Hobbes, *De Cive*, part 1, ch. 3, sect. 13, p. 50.

66. Gabriella Slomp, *Thomas Hobbes and the Political Philosophy of Glory* (London: Macmillan Press Ltd., 2000), 98.

67. The argument appears also in Hobbes, *The Elements of Law*, part 2, ch. 4.

68. Hobbes, *De Cive*, part 2, ch. 9, sect. 1, p. 105.

69. Hobbes, *De Cive*, part 2, ch. 9, sect. 2, p. 106.

70. Hobbes, *De Cive*, part 2, ch. 9, sect. 3, p. 106.

71. Hobbes, *Leviathan*, part 2, ch. 20, para. 4, p. 152.

72. Hobbes, *Leviathan*, part 2, ch. 20, para. 4, p. 152; See also *De Cive*, ch. 9, sect. 3, pp. 106–7.

73. Hobbes, *De Cive*, part 2, ch. 9, sect. 3, pp. 106–7.

74. Hobbes, *The Elements of Law*, part 2, ch. 4, sect. 3, pp. 132–33.

75. Hobbes, *De Cive*, part 2, ch. 9, sect. 5, pp. 107–8.

76. Hobbes, *De Cive*, part 2, ch. 9, sect. 5, p. 107.

77. Hobbes, *De Cive*, part 2, ch. 9, sect. 5, p. 107.

78. Hobbes, *De Cive*, part 2, ch. 6, sect. 16, pp. 81–83.

79. Hobbes, *De Cive*, part 2, ch. 9, sect. 6, p. 108.

80. While I do not want to get into a full comparison of Hobbes with Aristotle here, there is not that much difference between the two on the issue of men and women and their relationship. Aristotle also makes the point that men's rule over women is "constitutional," that is, a matter of agreement. It also reflects what is natural, but because the woman is not so different from the man that she does not have to agree (i.e., like Aristotle's natural slave), it remains a matter of consent.

81. Hobbes, *De Cive*, part 2, ch. 9, sect. 16, p. 112.

82. Hobbes, *Leviathan*, part 2, ch. 27, para. 51, p. 228.

83. Hobbes, *Leviathan*, part 2, ch. 30, para. 11, p. 251. Robert Kraynak covers this ground of the historical role of fathers and patriarchs in the development of civilization, revealing that Hobbes clearly understood and accepted the historical origins of both families and states. "Hobbes on Barbarism and Civilization," *The Journal of Politics* 45, no. 1 (February 1983): 86–109.

84. Richard Allen Chapman, "Leviathan Writ Small: Thomas Hobbes on the Family," *The American Political Science Review* 69, no. 1 (March 1975): 76–77. See for instance Hobbes, *The Elements of Law*, part 2, ch. 4, sect. 9, p. 134.

85. Hobbes, *Leviathan*, part 2, ch. 22, para. 26, p. 177. See also *Leviathan*, part 2, ch. 25, para. 9, p. 193, "But where a man may lawfully command, as a father in his family, or a leader in an army, his exhortations and dehortations, are not only lawful, but also necessary, and laudable." Or *Leviathan*, part 3, ch. 42, para. 99, p. 407, "Making laws belongs to the lord of the family; who by his own discretion chooseth his chaplain, as also a schoolmaster to teach his children." Finally, Hobbes, *A Dialogue between a Philosopher and a Student of the Common Laws of England, the English Works of Thomas Hobbes*, vol. 6, p. 146: "And first, It is evident that dominion, government, and laws, are far more ancient than history or any other writing, and that the beginning of all dominion amongst men was in families. In which, first, the father of the family by the law of nature was absolute lord of his wife and children."

86. Hobbes, *De Cive*, part 2, ch. 8, sect. 1, p. 100. See also *Leviathan*, part 2, ch. 20, para. 15, p. 155.

87. Hobbes, *Leviathan*, part 1, ch. 13, para. 11, p. 101.

88. Hobbes, *De Cive*, part 2, ch. 6, sect. 15, note 80.

89. Hobbes, *Leviathan*, part 2, ch. 20, para. 15, p. 155.

90. Hobbes, *Leviathan*, part 1, ch. 10, para. 51, p. 77. See also *Leviathan*, part 2, ch. 22, para. 31, p. 178.

91. Chapman, "Leviathan Writ Small," 77.

92. Hobbes, *Leviathan*, part 2, ch. 30, para. 11, p. 251.

93. For a reference to kings as fathers of families, see *Leviathan*, part 3, ch. 42, para. 70, p. 394.

94. Hobbes, *Leviathan*, part 2, ch. 20, para. 4, p. 152.

95. Chapman, "Leviathan Writ Small," 78.

96. Gordon J. Schochet, "Thomas Hobbes on the Family and the State of Nature," *Political Science Quarterly* 82, no. 3 (September 1967): 432.

97. Schochet, "Thomas Hobbes on the Family," 444.

98. Schochet, "Thomas Hobbes on the Family," 444.

99. Carole Pateman, "'God Hath Ordained to Man a Helper': Hobbes, Patriarchy and Conjugal Right," *British Journal of Political Science* 19, no. 4 (October 1989): 445–63.

100. Pateman reasons that this could happen even though men and women are treated as physically equal by Hobbes for purposes of posing a threat to each other, because once a woman has a child, she is somewhat more vulnerable and more able to be conquered or submit to a man for the sake of protection for her and her child. Pateman, "'God Hath Ordained to Man a Helper,'" 454.

101. Slomp, *Thomas Hobbes and the Political Philosophy of Glory*, 100.

102. See also Carole Pateman, Nancy J. Hirschmann, and G. Bingham Powell Jr., "Political Obligation, Freedom and Feminism," *The American Political Science Review* 86, no. 1 (March 1992): 179–88, especially 182. In Pateman's part of the debate she seems to praise Hobbes in a way similar to her argument in the *British Journal of Political Science*, for at least being consistent and carrying through on his logic concerning equality in the state of nature. Indeed Pateman seems to think Hobbes's views on men, women, and the origins of marriage shed a great deal of light on the actual history of women's subjection. Can Hobbes also be credited with inadvertently providing the core logic for eventual female equality?

103. Slomp, *Thomas Hobbes and the Political Philosophy of Glory*, 104–5.

104. Slomp, *Thomas Hobbes and the Political Philosophy of Glory*, 106.

105. For a good treatment of why this code of honor in nature and in war is also rational under the circumstances, see David Boucher, "Inter-Community & International Relations in the Political Philosophy of Hobbes," *Polity* 23, no. 2 (Winter 1990): 207–32, especially 220–21. If a man (or state) enters into a confederation and then deserts it, "The most likely scenario is that you will be cast out of the confederation you deceived by breaking your covenant and left to perish as an outcast unable to procure the protection of another confederation because it is publicly known that you give your word lightly" (Boucher, "Inter-Community," 220).

106. Hobbes, *The Elements of Law*, part 1, ch. 19, sect. 2, p. 101.

107. Hobbes, *The Elements of Law*, part 1, ch. 3, sect. 5, p. 10.

108. Hobbes, *The Elements of Law*, part 1, ch. 9, sect. 4, p. 38. He also defines it as "To resolve to break through a stop unforeseen" (part 1, ch. 9, sect. 21, p. 48).

109. Hobbes, *The Elements of Law*, part 1, ch. 17, sect. 14, p. 94.

110. Hobbes, *De Cive*, part 2, ch. 13, sect. 8, p. 145.

111. Hobbes, *De Cive*, part 2, ch. 12, sect. 11, p. 137.

112. Hobbes, *Leviathan*, part 2, ch. 21, para. 11–12, p. 164.

113. Thomas S. Schrock, "The Rights to Punish and Resist Punishment in Hobbes's Leviathan," *The Western Political Quarterly* 44, no. 4 (December 1991): 860.

114. Schrock, "The Rights to Punish," 887. On the issue of sovereign authorization and the authorization of the right to punish see Clifford Orwin, "On the Sovereign Authorization," *Political Theory* 3, no. 1 (February 1975): 26–44.

115. F. C. Hood, *The Divine Politics of Thomas Hobbes: An Interpretation of Leviathan* (Oxford: Clarendon Press, 1964), 187.

116. Hobbes, *Leviathan*, part 2, ch. 21, para. 16, p. 165.

117. Hobbes, *Leviathan*, part 1, ch. 2, para. 7, p. 26.

118. Hobbes, *Leviathan*, part 2, ch. 21, para. 16, p. 165.

119. See *A Dialogue between a Philosopher and a Student of the Common Laws of England, the English Works of Thomas Hobbes*, vol. 6, pp. 154–56, for Hobbes's views on fealty. He has no difficulty supporting the idea that men are obligated to military service to the king and their lords if they have made an agreement of a certain amount of military service in exchange for their lands.

120. Clifford Orwin, "On the Sovereign Authorization," *Political Theory* 3, no. 1 (February 1975): 35.

121. Slomp, "Hobbes on Glory and Civil Strife," 181–99.

122. Hobbes, *Leviathan*, part 2, ch. 27, para. 17, pp. 220–21.

123. Hobbes, *Leviathan*, part 1, ch. 10, para. 51, p. 78.

124. Hobbes, *Leviathan*, part 1, ch. 11, para. 4, p. 81.

125. Hobbes, *Leviathan*, part 1, ch. 11, para. 16, p. 83.

126. Hobbes, *Leviathan*, part 4, conclusion, para. 2, p. 503.

127. Hayes, "Hobbes's Bourgeois Moderation," 69.

128. Hobbes, *Leviathan*, part 1, ch. 10, para. 49, p. 77.

129. Hobbes, *Leviathan*, part 2, ch. 21, para. 16, p. 165.

130. Hobbes, *Leviathan*, part 1, ch. 10, para. 39, p. 75. See also, *Leviathan*, part 1, ch. 10, para. 40, pp. 75–76. Keith Thomas's reading of this passage is more charitable, seeing within it an embracing of the duty of national defense, but without fully clearing up the contradictions between this statement and the many others that countenance self-preservation first and foremost. See Thomas, "The Social Origins of Hobbes's Political Thought," 197.

131. Hobbes, *Leviathan*, part 2, ch. 21, para. 21, p. 167.

132. Hobbes, *Leviathan*, part 2, ch. 31, para. 40, p. 269.

133. Hobbes, *Leviathan*, part 1, ch. 14, para. 32, p. 111.

134. Hobbes, *Leviathan*, part 1, ch. 15, para. 10, pp. 116–17. See also, *Leviathan*, part 2, ch. 28, para. 19, pp. 232–33.

135. Hobbes, *Leviathan*, part 4, conclusion, para. 4, p. 504.

136. Hobbes, *Leviathan*, part 2, ch. 27, para. 20, p. 222.

137. Kenneth R. Minogue, "Hobbes and the Just Man," in *Hobbes and Rousseau: A Collection of Critical Essays*, ed. Maurice Cranston and Richard S. Peters (Garden City, N.Y.: Doubleday & Co., 1972), 82.

138. Hobbes, *Behemoth*, part 3, p. 112, 303.

139. Hobbes, *Behemoth*, part 3, p. 134.

140. Hobbes, *Behemoth*, part 3, p. 136.

141. Hobbes, *Behemoth*, part 1, p. 38.

142. Thucydides, *Hobbes's Thucydides*, ed. Richard Schlatter (New Brunswick, N.J.: Rutgers University Press, 1975), book 3, p. 222.

143. Hobbes, *Leviathan*, part 1, ch. 11, para. 11, p. 82.

144. Edmund Burke, *Reflections on the Revolution in France*, ed. J. G. A. Pocock (Indianapolis: Hackett Publishing Co., 1987), 76–77.

145. Burke, *Reflections*, 66.

146. "It is now sixteen or seventeen years since I saw the queen of France, then the dauphiness, at Versailles; and surely never lighted on this orb, which she hardly

seemed to touch, a more delightful vision. I saw her just above the horizon, decorating and cheering the elevated sphere she just began to move in—glittering like the morning star, full of life and splendor and joy. Oh! what a revolution! and what a heart must I have to contemplate without emotion that elevation and that fall! Little did I dream when she added titles of veneration to those of enthusiastic, distant, respectful love, that she should ever be obliged to carry the sharp antidote against disgrace concealed in that bosom; little did I dream that I should have lived to see such disasters fallen upon her in a nation of gallant men, in a nation of men of honor and of cavaliers" (Burke, *Reflections*, 66).

147. Karen Green, "Christine De Pisan and Thomas Hobbes," *The Philosophical Quarterly* 44, no. 177 (October 1994): 463.

148. Michael Krom, "First to Flee: Fear of Death and the Hobbesian Philosopher," paper presented September 15, 2007, at Ashland University, 1.

Conclusion

Thomas Hobbes's political thought represents an intellectual turning point for honor. His thought questions the value of honor and finds it causes more problems than it solves. We now live with the societal ramifications of that rejection of honor, which not surprisingly took centuries to work its way even partly into the mentality of the average citizen. It would take another book to trace this progression into our times, and as I pointed out in my introduction, other writers have been doing this with some success. The task of this book was to attempt to expose the underlying ideas that led to the precarious situation of honor today by focusing on the early modern thinker who is pivotal on the issue of honor.

As I argued in chapter 3, the human condition, despite our best efforts, is marked by inequalities that seem intractable, but liberal theory tends to ignore such intractable or natural inequalities if it cannot reason them out of existence. Hobbes's assumptions about equality in nature, and the subsequent equal natural right to self-preservation as the motive for entering the social contract, are the chief reasons why so many scholars over the years have identified him as the first liberal political philosopher. Leo Strauss reasoned, "If we may call liberalism that political doctrine which regards as the fundamental political fact the rights, as distinguished from the duties, of man and which identifies the function of the state with the protection or the safeguarding of those rights, we must say that the founder of liberalism was Hobbes."[1] Coming from a completely different mode of analysis, C. B. Macpherson also found Hobbes to be the originator of liberal thought, but he concentrated on that aspect of liberalism that promoted "the competitive market."[2] Macpherson concluded that Hobbes's thought reflected the emerging liberal market society's "possessive individualism." Frank Coleman even went so far as to

147

argue that John Locke, normally considered much more of a direct influence on the American constitution, offered little more than warmed-over Hobbes: "Locke's view of the source, nature, and limits of public authority is in all important respects identical with Hobbes's."[3] While Coleman acknowledged that Locke and the American founders differed from Hobbes "in vesting sovereignty in a pattern of offices, a representative and hereditary assembly and monarchy, rather than a single office, monarchy," they were in agreement with Hobbes in their most important objective: "managing social conflict."[4] Coleman is interpreted by some as arguing that Hobbes goes so far as to advocate republican government.[5] If this is the case, then indeed Coleman goes too far, but the general tendency to see Hobbes as the originator of liberal ideas is well-founded.[6]

Hobbes indeed laid the groundwork for future liberal theory which moved off in directions he would no doubt disapprove. As Vickie Sullivan puts it, "although Hobbes is not a liberal himself, elements of his thought point in a liberal direction."[7] Among other liberal elements in Hobbes's thought, Sullivan notices that the sovereign's authority ultimately comes from the people through the social contract, the people are naturally equal in the state of nature, inequality is conventional and based upon agreement, and the fact that Hobbes does offer a "limited right of resistance against the powers of the state."[8] In these ways, she concludes, Hobbes's thought does provide a foundation for future liberal republicanism. He realized that times were changing, that the old way of establishing authority—namely patriarchy and divine right—would no longer work. He had come to believe that there was no ultimate eternal source of authority which was defensible—not on the basis of birth, wisdom, justice, courage, or any other intrinsic trait. The new larger gentry and merchant classes were on the rise, receiving more education, and ready to pit their new religious and political ideas against the old ones. The more competition of ideas, the less in awe people would be of any source of them. There would be more need for a different education to replace the traditional education emphasizing the authority of ancient ideas of justice and duty. Hobbes's vision for an education that could transform his society could be seen as a precursor of the Enlightenment's emphasis on education. As Kraynak explains, for Hobbes, "Enlightenment is the precondition for absolutism because it frees society from the influence of intellectual authorities and creates a scientific basis for society."[9] Anderson notes, "Hobbes's belief in the importance of education implicitly expresses more faith in our ability to control ourselves than is standardly attributed to Hobbesian agents: it shows that he believes it important to appeal to reason (as opposed to just fear), and that if properly brought up we can, under the appropriate circumstances, willingly control ourselves within the bounds required for a commonwealth to function rather than having those boundaries set entirely for us by the sovereign's big stick."[10]

Political enlightenment would teach that all are actually, for political purposes, equal. Not only that, it would teach that all opinions are, practically speaking, equal as well. In Hobbes's view, because of this, people would come to understand and accept the necessity of an all-powerful sovereign who could arbitrarily define right and wrong, honor and dishonor, gentleman and commoner. Citizens would come to accept the sovereign's order, not because they acknowledged his superiority to rule, but because they understood the necessity for someone to stop the disagreements that cause deadly conflict. The wonder is that Hobbes thought his form of enlightenment could be so controlled and directed. Once having finished off the idea of the political and social significance of inherent superiority of wisdom, character, or birth, why would a society full of ambitious and prideful beings, all too inclined to forget about the risk to their lives, willingly accept someone else's absolute authority to rule?

Many of Hobbes's most important ideas are indeed liberal. Hobbes accepts political equality as natural and ignores all remaining inequalities for the sake of peace. Other liberal ideas in Hobbes's thought include the notion that political institutions are formed for the natural right of the individual, the idea of dispelling religious authority as superstition, the rejection of the idea of truth in favor of the defining power of human perspective, the critique of political rhetoric as motivated by power and pride, the questioning of the war-making powers of the state as motivated by political or personal ambitions, the power of education to socialize citizens to accept alternative political, religious, and social schemes—all of these are liberal ideas that fully came into their own during the Enlightenment a little more than a century later. Many of these ideas have gained a great deal more ground since then. As we have seen, even the seeds of gender equality, which was entertained but certainly not universally confirmed during the Enlightenment and only was realized in Western societies in the twentieth-century, are there in Hobbes's thought.

These ideas have successfully grown and spread across a good deal of the globe. This success could be termed "progress" for most people most of the time. And yet this book has focused on one particular area of potential loss: honor. If there is something valuable about the love of honor, both personal and national, that we would like to keep despite the success of the Enlightenment liberal ideas nascent in Hobbes's thought, then we will have to engage in the hard work of reexamining these ideas, for truth and usefulness, to see whether they deserve to be critiqued, modified, or amended. Looking at the ideas of Thomas Hobbes on honor is a good place to start.

I began this book with the question of what honor meant to Hobbes, and in the process of investigation, I took a brief look at prior understandings of honor. I did this by choosing to contrast Hobbes's thought particularly with medieval ideas. Hobbes was reacting to Aristotelian philosophy mainly through its use by medieval, and his contemporary, authors. It seemed most useful to show how Hobbes rejected the medieval understanding of honor, and I chose to do this by using the exemplary work of Geoffroi de Charny. De Charny's work is representative of much medieval literature on chivalry, a literature which generally equates honor with good character traits and high social standing. Hobbes's idea that all are equal in the state of nature, that aristocratic claims represent nothing intrinsically better, but simply reveal who happens to be in power, would have struck de Charny as vulgar and obviously wrong. For de Charny, an honorable man was a good Christian, of noble blood, displaying wide-ranging knowledge, and perhaps most importantly, demonstrating courage and prowess in the military arts in the service of those who were weaker. Hobbes's "timorous" man would have represented great cowardice and thus dishonor for de Charny. Hobbes's soft, bourgeois man, who was willing to make peace in order to attain security and comfort, would have been seen as shameless.

Clearly, for the medieval advocates of chivalry, it was far better to die a noble death than to live under ignoble circumstances such as servitude or a reputation for cowardice. This is why war, as long as it was just, was considered by these writers as an opportunity to display valor and military skill, even at the risk of death. This conclusion for the battle well fought as opposed to life at any costs, was partly due to a heavy reliance on Christian faith with its promise of an afterlife, and partly due to the ancient idea that life itself was not enough—a life worth living was supposed to be the goal. Read again de Charny's thoughts on cowardly men, and think about how Hobbes might react:

> And while the cowards have a great desire to live and a great fear of dying, it is quite the contrary for the men of worth who do not mind whether they live or die, provided that their life be good enough for them to die with honor. And this is evident in the strange and perilous adventures which they seek.[11]

An examination of Hobbes's use of the term "honor" throughout his political works, from his earliest to his latest, revealed that his thoughts on honor did change somewhat over time. Strauss was essentially correct in seeing Hobbes move from a humanistic perspective, probably influenced by his early reading of the classics, to a modern "utilitarian" view in which honor is nothing more than a product of power. The early works found Hobbes still able to admire honorable men and their actions, particularly those who displayed the manly virtues of courage and skill. Honor in these works was often treated as a product, not of power, but of actual character traits and abilities. Honor was an asset in warfare, in fact the only limitation on the brutality of war. An honorable man did not do harm simply because he could, but only did what he must to achieve his just objectives. But in Hobbes's later works, much of the admiration for honor is dropped, and in its place is a growing skepticism over whether honor is at all a positive force in society and even in warfare. In Hobbes's mature thought, the man who pursues honor becomes the troublesome man, the vainglorious man, who is willing to risk his life (and even more so, others' lives) for mere trifles such as a personal insult. Hobbes's commentary on dueling, for instance, shows how silly and danger-ous he thinks are men who in engage in such practices. He places honor in the position of pride, which is a sin from the Christian perspective, and is so from Hobbes's perspective as well. In this way, though Hobbes is far from an or-thodox Christian writer, his views reflect that religion's rejection of honor-seeking as too prideful and individualistic, and as we know, Hobbes was very capable of quoting the Bible to make his case against the proud. It is not sur-prising that the religion so deeply ingrained in the psyche of his society gave him, through a selective interpretation to be sure, a way to justify his own point of view.

And yet, Hobbes's treatment of honor remained mixed throughout his ca-reer. Even in his early works, the cynical, modern rendition of honor appeared from time to time, and even in his late works, admiration for truly honorable men could still be found. Does this mean that he simply had mixed views, and was not fully reconciled to his theoretical rejection of honor? This need not be the case. In chapter 2 I examined his own experience working his way into the good graces of the aristocracy, and his analysis of the men who were in-volved on both sides of the English Civil War. This analysis showed that it was not honor per se that was the problem for Hobbes, but rather that in his experience most men were not capable of abiding by any truly honorable code, especially in times of chaos when anything and everything seemed pos-sible for men of ambition.

Hobbes himself strove to be a gentleman. Coming from obscure and even socially embarrassing origins (only because of his father's humiliation), Hobbes climbed his way out, with the help of his uncle, through his educa-tion. He was obviously brilliant, and he experienced a high degree of accept-ance from his professors and his aristocratic patrons. Though he was not of noble birth, he was granted the title of esquire, was able to converse with aris-tocrats and philosophers, and gained his own renown in their world. All of these accomplishments were due to his natural intellectual ability. While this experience might have been part of what led him to the conclusion that there is nothing intrinsically worthy about the nobility, it did not make him despise the aristocrats or the gentlemanly virtues and way of life he had come to en-joy. He did not become a radical democrat, but strove to justify the existing power structure as good for all—not because some people were inherently better than others, but because acceptance of the existing power structure was conducive to peace. Hobbes was able to admire the positive qualities of the aristocrats around him, and in particular considered Newcastle and his friend Sidney Godolphin to be true gentlemen. But he knew that the old social order was on its way out, that a new class of wealthy gentry and merchants were questioning the inherent status of the old aristocracy. This new class would no longer blindly follow the lead of the nobility in religious and political matters, and thus Hobbes understood that a new justification for social order had to be made.

The gentlemanly code of conduct of his day encompassed the older aristocratic meaning which would have disdained the idea of manual labor and which played up cultural refinement and manly valor. But it was moving toward an understanding of the gentleman as equally charitable to all, kind, religious, and at least economically productive. Hobbes's commentary on gentlemen displayed a mix of these two sets of norms. But the changes in social order mentioned above, along with the events of the English Civil War, made him reject the political and social efficacy of these gentlemanly values, even as he admired them personally. Hobbes's *Behemoth* demonstrates with awful clarity the overturning of traditional gentlemanly values *in the name of* supposed honor. Under his cynical gaze, almost no one, including King Charles, looked like a true gentleman. Presbyterian and Independent clergy, in Hobbes's view, behaved in the most fickle and self-serving ways, promoting their own power as though it were a religious principle. They were little better than Catholics (in Hobbes's view), so convinced they were of their own veracity and authority, and so little inclined to submit to civil power. Hobbes accused them of using the Bible as a mere justification for their own ambitions.

Even the Anglican clergymen were not exempt. Their own desires for supremacy made them lukewarm in their support of the king. They too wanted power for themselves. Many of the gentry and nobles, who should have known which side to support simply by considering their own financial interests and status, turned to support the cause of Parliament, due to their oversized ambitions and their resentment of those who claimed to be their superiors. Poisoned by their classical education, they came to believe that democratic reforms would improve society, but really, they too were simply thinking that they might gain money, power, and status.

Individual figures examined by Hobbes fared no better in respectability than the aforementioned groups. Charles I was portrayed much of the time as a sympathetic figure. But then again, he appeared to be weak and fickle; he betrayed his friends and unwittingly helped his enemies. The Earl of Essex felt slighted by the king and court, and thought he had much more prestige to gain with Parliament, and so he chose to be a traitor. Later spurned by Parliament, Essex learned to taste the bitterness of his own disloyalty. Similarly, Wentworth is depicted as motivated by envy and resentment of the upper nobility to side with enemies of the king. When the king made him Earl of Strafford, he easily switched sides. Later, when Parliament condemned him for treason, his friend the king did not lift a finger to help him. Likewise, Oliver Cromwell is treated as the consummate political chameleon. He changed his religious stripes when needed, first appearing as a devout Presbyterian, later an Independent, when he thought that position was politically expedient. He used religious rhetoric to motivate his supporters, but (again, in Hobbes's opinion) clearly did not take it seriously. All four of these men—Charles, Essex, Strafford, and Cromwell—are revealed as anything but true gentlemen.

From Hobbes's point of view, then, there were very few true gentlemen taking leadership roles in the Civil War, his own Earl of Newcastle a notable exception. As B says in *Behemoth*:

> According to your definition, there be few wise men now-a-days. Such wisdom is a kind of gallantry, that few are brought up to, and most think folly. Fine clothes, great feathers, civility toward men that will not swallow injuries, and injury to them that will, is the present gallantry.[12]

Echoing Thucydides' analysis of the overturning of values during the Corcyrean civil war, we sense that Hobbes does not appreciate the radical departure from traditional gentlemanly conduct that took root during the years surrounding this conflict. It was not that gallantry could not be real and admirable, but that not enough men shared that admiration for it to matter politically. Wisdom, self-restraint, humble submission to higher authorities, were now considered unmanly and foolish. Hobbes might not have been a relativist about gentlemanly values, but in his view, *many other men were*. Men like Cromwell would use value-laden language in a cynical way to manipulate their supporters, who would then convince themselves that they were doing the right thing, the Christian thing, even as they killed their fellow Englishmen. Hobbes concluded that such terms as wisdom, justice, courage, and so on, were essentially disputable words which could not form the basis for good political reasoning.

He turned his anger on the universities, which did not teach men the wisdom of obedience but the art of questioning authority. Exposure to Aristotelian philosophy had led these men to pronounce judgment on their own government and to advocate a mixed regime. Fundamentally, Aristotle and his medieval interpreters taught these men to arrive at their own definition of justice and to think that they had the authority and even the duty to criticize their government, and attempt to change it. They learned to reject absolute monarchy as "tyranny," and even to justify "tyrannicide." But Hobbes's reason and experience taught him that one man's tyrant was another's benevolent monarch.

Hobbes placed the solution for society's chaotic state squarely on the universities' shoulders. Michael Krom describes his condemnation of these institutions: "Through the schools, the philosophers disseminate their prideful and harmful teachings, corrupt the youth, and lead into madness all those who learn their useless methods of reasoning. The vain philosopher wields immense power in this manner, and Hobbes thinks it necessary that the schools be reformed if there is to be peace in the commonwealth."[13] And although the schools produce much of the problem, for Hobbes, they also represent much of the solution. As Slomp writes, "In *Leviathan* . . . Hobbes expresses a greater faith in the effectiveness of education than ever before."[14] If the universities were brought firmly under the control of the sovereign power, and their teachings brought into line with Hobbes's own philosophy, they would engender order instead of chaos. Learned men would know why it was in their interest to support peace and good order, and from whence came the obligation to remain obedient. They would understand Christianity as demanding meekness, charity, and obedience to authorities. His treatment of martyrdom took his thoughts on the value of religious convictions to their logical conclusion: Christians should be taught that there is nothing particularly admirable or right about being willing to "go to Christ by martyrdom" if it means reckless disobedience and disregard for order.[15]

Political obedience and a Christianity of meek acceptance certainly depart from the medieval emphasis on martial valor, but they also depart from the gentlemanly ideal: the man as an independent thinker, someone who acts on his own principles and is willing to take up arms if necessary for the right cause. Hobbes's treatment of Christian conviction set the tone for the liberalization of Christian teaching to make it compatible with modern republicanism.[16] Hobbes's laws of nature, seen in this light, emphasize getting along with others and passively accepting the existing political and social order. They encourage the soft, pacific aspects of human nature, not the heroic aspects that promote gallantry, courage, or valor. These laws comprise the morality which the universities should teach, in Hobbes's view. In fact, he hopes that his political science as a whole will be taught by the universities. Locke's political theory followed suit, argues Michael Rabieh, because "to the extent that the principle of self-interest rightly understood governs in those nations influenced by Locke, to the extent that morality does not demand great sacrifices of men and even promotes itself as being in their interest, Locke's [and Hobbes's] religious project seems to have succeeded."[17]

If we see Hobbes's teachings on human nature and the state of nature in the light of his conscious rejection of honor, we can see more clearly how the social contract theory that underlies much of classical liberal thought may be seen as contrary to, or even opposed to, traditional honor. A concentration on honor, for Hobbes, is a form of intoxication or drunkenness, for which the cure is a good sobering fear. Pride, born of the desire for unequal honor, lies at the very heart of the violence in the state of nature. Hobbes's natural condition of mankind is a depiction of what civilized people are like if they are thrown into a situation of anarchy. They do not automatically drop their desires for power, status, and glory. Indeed, they continue to seek them, without realizing that this quest spells doom for all concerned. He acknowledges that there are real differences among people in intelligence, talent, character, and physical strength. But he reasons that these differences are politically irrelevant. Government was not created, in his view, to preserve natural inequalities. It was created to protect our lives. Since we are roughly equal threats to each other, we must be willing to drop the demand for unequal recognition and treatment. Anything else is "madness . . . great *vain-glory*: which is commonly called *pride*, and *self-conceit*; or great *dejection* of mind."[18] Because the weakest can kill the strongest by clever planning or by making alliances, it behooves us all to submit to a power that can keep everyone in check.

So it is fear of death, specifically fear of painful, violent death, which will cure us of the drunkenness of pride or vainglory. Hobbes's state of nature is a depiction of what the world would be like without strong government, in deed what it was like, in his view, during the English Civil War. The social contract need not be seen as an actual occurrence or a necessary beginning for any government. Only the understanding of the social contract's rationale is necessary for men to accept the wisdom of obedience. They must accept the social contract now, as they are in their actual situations—whether their government is benevolent or tyrannical, whether its laws and practices actually reflect an understanding of the laws of nature or not. They must do this even if their government was imposed upon them by usurpation or conquest. Covenants based on fear are valid, and have to be, if the state of nature scenario is to be effective.

Yet in making this argument, the small vestige of the idea of duty which remains, the argument that somehow a man is bound to keep his promise because he has once made it, even under conditions of fear, rings hollow. If fear overrides all other reasons for action, a victim of crime or conquest could very reasonably renege on his agreement out of fear, not simply out of a sense of justice. Hobbes's overriding emphasis on fear seems to turn on itself.

Hobbes's thought represents a complete rejection for political purposes of Aristotle's virtuous man, the "Homeric hero," and "the aristocratic warrior society."[19] These heroic ideals formed the assumptions that underlay previous notions about government: that rank mattered, that responsibility lay with those who were in some way naturally superior, and that obedience was owed to one's betters. Contrasting with Aristotle's assumption that there are better and worse ways of life, better and worse examples of leadership, Hobbes argues that there can be no justification for obedience based upon moral or other types of superiority, except one—the superiority of physical power. While Plato and Aristotle could judge regimes largely on whether or not those in charge were selfless or selfish, whether they made decisions based upon the common interest or solely their own, Hobbes rejects this type of comparison, concluding that any regime is a good regime if it keeps its citizens safe. He argues for monarchy only because it is better to have only one self-interested person in charge instead of many, all of whom would compete with each other and cause civil conflict. While Aristotle understood the nature of pride and the damage it could do, but was nevertheless unwilling to abandon the human ideal of manly spiritedness and virtue, Hobbes sees no way to avoid abandoning it. Again, it is not that he cannot appreciate true virtue or manly spiritedness properly directed, but that he has concluded that such qualities cannot be counted upon, especially in tough times. Though we are not used to thinking in these terms, the comparison of Hobbes with Aristotle shows that Hobbes seeks peace at the expense of a certain type of manliness.

In Hobbes's time, the Aristotelian idea of separate virtues for men and women was very much the norm. The manly virtues were different from and in some ways thought superior to the womanly virtues. Yet, while not personally challenging these assumptions in his own life (he never married, so he had a limited opportunity to do so), Hobbes challenged them deeply in his political thought. In order to set political order on firmer foundations, he rejected the traditional patriarchal theory of sovereign authority and replaced it with the social contract, in which each individual approved the creation of a government, which would then control all individuals equally. With this philosophical objective in mind, he posited a radical equality in the state of nature in which no one was so different that he or she was not a credible threat to all others. Clever or dull, strong or weak, male or female, all were equal enough in the state of nature that all had to be included in the social contract. Hobbes found himself arguing that there was nothing natural about male leadership in the family or in government. The inequality that existed between men and women in these institutions, then, must come from conventional agreement. While his thought, on closer examination, is not as radical on the issue of female equality as it first appears, it does strike another blow against the traditional moral code in which natural superiors, *because* of their advantage, were said to have obligations to protect and not abuse their inferiors.

While setting the stage for future liberal arguments for gender equality that would have more traction, Hobbes's argument also sets the stage for the tendency in liberal society to impose an artificial assumption of total equality which can leave those who are weaker in some particular way, in reality, in a more vulnerable position. Indeed, using Hobbes's full logic, women come under the dominion of men through consent, yes, but this consent can be obtained by force, just as consent of whole societies can come through usurpation or conquest. Once consenting, women would be bound to obey in order to receive protection. Somehow, women go from complete equality in the state of nature to a gross inequality in society, and without the expectation that the men who now rule over them as sovereigns in the microcosm of the household will be benevolent. In fact, as we have seen, some scholars believe that Hobbes assumed that all women would be subdued by male conquest before the contract was made, so only men would actually be making the contract. Just as Hobbes hoped the monarch would be benevolent, but would not establish any means to criticize one who was not, surely Hobbes preferred the kind husband and father over the cruel master. But using his theory of obligation, there was no way to demand chivalrous or gentlemanly behavior from men once the contract was made. Seeing family, as Chapman puts it, "strictly in rational terms, as an artificial institution rather than a natural one,"[20] has its drawbacks for those who are not, after all, entirely equal in some way—as women are not the equals of men in physical strength, aggressiveness, or social status.

Under Hobbes's new thought, which lays the foundation for liberalism, the old idea of chivalry which had been held up as a moral ideal and a source of shaming for those men who mistreated women, was rejected. This code assumed the superiority of men over women, in strength, and even generally speaking in courage and wisdom. It assumed different natures for male and female, different abilities, different virtues, all based upon God-given traits inherent in the sexes. It asked those who were more advantaged in some very important ways, especially in physical strength, to behave with gentility, kindness, and moderation toward those who were their inferiors: women and all others who were assumed to be more vulnerable, including children and the elderly. Hobbes's idea that all status should be seen as conventional challenged very directly one of the central pillars of old-fashioned honor: greater responsibility based upon being gifted with greater attributes. Natural inequality provided the argument on behalf of moral obligation for those who wielded power. Without that inequality, in the traditional view of moral obligation, there would be no reason to treat anyone more gently or with more consideration than anyone else.

The question of military service brings this issue of unequal moral obligation to a head. Hobbes has a real problem dealing with national security because it

is hard to imagine a scenario in which Hobbesian soldiers would truly feel obligated to risk their lives for their country. Do soldiers, because of their position and situation, have an obligation to risk death, even knowingly sacrifice
their lives for the safety of the larger society? Hobbes sets as the foundation
of his social contract individuals who recognize and embrace as entirely rational and justified their fear of violent death. He tells his reader that if one
sovereign is no longer able to protect him, it is acceptable to switch allegiance
to one who can. He excuses men of a "timorous" nature from running away
in battle if it appears that their lives are in danger. While he still calls this running away cowardice, there is no longer the sense of dire shame associated
with this term as would have existed with Hobbes's predecessors—it may be
cowardly but it is not unjust. Indeed, running away from battle is completely
understandable; people only enter into society in the first place in order to
save their lives. In tandem with his acceptance of cowardice, Hobbes questions the value of honor in warfare, and the motivations of men who actually
seek opportunities to display their valor in battle. Through the Hobbesian
lens, able commanders are very likely cynical manipulators. They pursue
their vainglorious ambitions at the cost of others' lives, and rather than the
first responders, are actually the causes of war.

In Hobbes's mature thought, the timorous, soft, accommodating man becomes the new hero—or at least the new socially acceptable model. He values life itself over some ephemeral "good life"; he values his safety and comfort over any admiration he might imagine coming from a display of
contempt for such things. Such a man is the opposite of de Charny's model of
a man, a complete overturning of the medieval admiration for what Lindsay
calls "manly spiritedness." As Hobbes himself states it, "amongst the passions, *courage* (by which I mean the contempt of wounds, and violent death),
inclineth men to private revenges, and sometimes to endeavour the unsettling
of the public peace."[21] Courage does more harm than good. It needs to be replaced by fear, if not cowardice (which, after all, is just a word we use to express our personal disapproval of other men's opinions and actions).

Again, personally, Hobbes was still able to admire the truly gallant or val-
orous man, judging him by his courage but also by his objectives. This is why
his own Earl of Newcastle could still be admired as a courageous and able
commander who fought for the king. Likewise, he praised his friend and supporter of the king, Sidney Godolphin, who was slain in the war, for his valor
and courage. In Hobbes's view, truly gallant men like Mr. Godolphin were
confident enough in their own worth that they did not need to engage in the
type of behavior typical of the troublemakers of his day. If they went to war,
they did it for the right reasons. If they were courageous, their courage was
valuable because it was truly in the service of their country and not them-

selves. Hobbes continues to maintain that there are too few such men, and many more who do not understand real honor and courage. Most men thought of honor as something that compelled them to seek revenge for some small slight or insult. A truly gallant man was able to brush these small slights off as of no importance. It was precisely because the honorable type of character was, in Hobbes's view, rarely found, and the other type of character which took notice of small slights abounded, that Hobbes rejected honor or chivalric virtue as a foundation for his political theory. Hobbes is in some ways a tragic figure, because as an individual of good character, he had at least one foot in the chivalric or gentlemanly past. He considered himself a gentleman, and he continued to admire those men who acted like true gentlemen. But the task was to harness the base passions and selfishness of most men somehow, to make them see why they should restrain themselves, not for the sake of others, but for their own sake, not for the purity of their character and their hopes of the afterlife, but for peace and security in the here and now. But the question remains, which way of looking at the world and at life is more of a source of restraint and decency in real human situations—the old way of honor, or Hobbes's new way of fear and self-interest?

Burke famously pointed out that Enlightenment philosophers, with their insistence that everything make logical sense and relate back to self-interest, taught people to reason too much about what was right for themselves. It was better to teach them to rely on the prejudices handed down to them from their predecessors, which provided a clear sense of right and wrong, instantly accessible in times of trouble. Hobbes thought these prejudices were too unreliable—but does the argument for honor as a sort of ingrained prejudice, such as Burke's, perhaps deserve reconsideration? For Burke, one of the hallmarks of civilization was how it treated women. When we look beyond the experience of highly educated, professional women, to the experience of the majority of women, too many of whom still suffer from abusive marriages and/or male abandonment and subsequent poverty, can we so confidently reject the mechanism of shaming which used to operate to guide men's behavior in times past? Is this mechanism so obviously inferior to the modern reliance on the morality of rational self-interest?

We cannot go back to premodern ways of thinking and ways of life, and we would not want to. The benefits of equality and the politics (and economics) of self-interest have been enormous, and in many ways all people in Western societies are better off now than people have been at any other time in history. We would not be able to, and would not want to, embrace the type of permanent social stratification of feudal societies, nor the old view that men and women were almost as different as two separate species, one far better than the other. And yet, in the midst of rejecting these things, we did, with Hobbes, reject the idea of moral obligations built upon natural differences and inequalities. Despite this, there are some inequalities which appear to be enduring. Between men and women there are differences, in physical strength and levels of aggression, which have never been erased even by the advantages of labor-saving technologies or equal education and job opportunities, and which continue to cause problems for women in their relationships with men.

There is also a difference that continues to exist between those, regardless of gender, who are more intellectually able than others, without regard to gender or racial differences. It continues to be the case that some human beings come better equipped to handle the challenges of life than others. While we can argue about how much of this difference is natural and how much is a matter of circumstances and socialization, it remains, even in our highly sophisticated age, a real factor in the relative success and influence of different individuals. While we are waiting for the playing field to become completely equal in education, can we not demand that those who are blessed for whatever reason with superior abilities use them to at least not harm and hopefully to help those who are less able?

Reflecting critically on why Hobbes established equality in the state of nature, or why he saw conflict as mainly caused by pride and empty rhetoric, might help us to examine our own assumptions more critically, too. If we admitted that inequality can after all be relevant to our relationships and our political arrangements—inequalities such as those of strength, intelligence, character—would we have to admit that some individuals (and some countries) might have more responsibility for the common welfare than others, simply because of some natural advantage they possess? If we admitted that sometimes the argument for war is made for genuine and compelling reasons, such as preserving our families and a way of life that we deem better than others, and not simply for political or personal advantage, we might have to evaluate each argument more carefully and contemplate making a painful sacrifice. Hobbes begins an attitude of cynicism that has become so great and deep that it is now difficult for citizens of democracies to see the claims of anyone in leadership as worthy of objective consideration. Yet without being able to do this, do we run the risk of self-destruction? Illiberal foes know nothing of this angst born of Hobbesian and later liberal thought. But they do accept other parts of Hobbes's thought which Enlightenment liberals rejected, such as the powerful shall rule, mixed government and democratic procedures produce weakness and disunity, religion must be dictated from above. In the face of this type of foe, we may at some point have to fall back on a deeper sense of belonging and loyalty than obligation based on individual self-interest, a sense of obligation which causes people to protect their own because it is basically good and because it is their own.

As a society, we have accepted Hobbes's idea that disputes about values cannot be resolved by reason, either by us as individuals or by higher authorities in whom we have reason to trust. But we have not accepted his conclusion that we should submit to the arbitrary judgments of a sovereign power.[22] Can we reevaluate this assumption of uncertainty about basic values while still keeping a great deal of the benefits of liberalism? For instance, can we still practice tolerance while openly and confidently acknowledging that it is better to be free than to live under communist, theocratic, or authoritarian dictatorship, by all sorts of measures both quantifiable and nonquantifiable. Likewise, could we make a distinction between true honor and false puffery, thereby making it possible to demand a higher standard of conduct from men and women in everyday life, and especially those in positions of power and authority? If we are too cynical about the existence of real honor, we will not expect it or demand it in those most important to us: our parents, our spouse, our boss, and our leaders, and we will not get what we do not expect and demand.

While we would not want to establish moral obligation on the basis of discrimination, would it be possible to acknowledge moral obligation on the basis of factual and existing inequalities? Most women are weaker physically than most men, for instance. Might we not be able to make a rule that because of this fact, men generally speaking have an obligation to aid and protect women from physical danger? While this would result in a sort of latter-day chivalry with respect to relationships between men and women as groups, it could and no doubt would have to be extended beyond gender, to the idea that whomever is relatively stronger, including women when it is true for them, is so obligated. Men and women both would have to acknowledge a moral obligation to aid, protect, and foster children, the elderly, and all others who are more vulnerable, on the same basis of unequal strength and ability. Moreover, those who are more intellectually gifted or in some other way generously endowed by nature with talents that give them an advantage would, instead of seeing this as a great opportunity to take advantage of their relatively strong position, see themselves as obligated to not abuse their position and to help those in need. All of these obligations would have to rest on an acknowledgment that these remaining inequalities are not produced wholly from one's own work, but in some way are given to some human beings by God, or by Nature, or by chance. This acknowledgment of good fortune might provide the humility necessary to see other human beings as worthy of concern—equally human, unequally empowered.

While the aim of an egalitarian-minded society might be to eliminate the underlying social and economic factors which cause a lot of the inequality not grounded in nature, inasmuch as we still experience this inequality, we might expect its beneficiaries to also feel a sense of obligation to those who do not so benefit. If we acknowledge that social and economic inequalities may change *but the fact of their existence is intractable*, then there might be even more of a reason to establish moral obligation based upon inequalities as a general rule. In any case, it seems quite possible for this sense of moral obligation to be taught and encouraged in a liberal state, alongside individualism, self-interest, and utility. Such a teaching would reestablish honor—in the form of caring about and being willing to sacrifice our individual interest for the preservation of those who need us—as a price of freedom, a voluntary modification to unfettered individualism and selfishness, a modification which allows us to preserve our society more effectively. This in turn would preserve our ability to be individuals and pursue our interests, because these ultimately are only as sure as the health of liberal society as a whole. Without the counterbalance that a sense of honor provides, one could argue that liberal society risks fragmentation, for it cannot support all necessary moral obligations on the framework of enlightened self-interest. With that in mind, perhaps it is time to call for a reconsideration of the value of honor in liberal society more generally, a project for which this book can hopefully provide some small part of the foundation.

NOTES

1. Leo Strauss, *Natural Right and History* (Chicago: University of Chicago Press, 1968), 181–82.

2. C. B. Macpherson, *The Political Theory of Possessive Individualism: Hobbes to Locke* (Oxford: Clarendon Press, 1962), 38.

3. Frank M. Coleman, *Hobbes and America: Exploring the Constitutional Foundations* (Toronto: University of Toronto Press, 1977), 100.

4. Coleman, *Hobbes and America*, 100.

5. See Terry Heinrichs, "Hobbes & the Coleman Thesis," *Polity* 16, no. 4 (Summer 1984): 647–66, for a very cogent and persuasive argument against Coleman's conclusions that Hobbes somehow advocated the right to resistance in cases other than immediate physical peril and other liberal democratic ideas.

6. Not everyone agrees that Hobbes can be seen as a liberal thinker for the simple reason that he ends up advocating absolutism, with no ability for the people to continue judgment of government after the social contract is formed. For a good example of this argument see Lucien Jaume, "Hobbes and the Philosophical Sources of Liberalism," pp. 199–216 in *The Cambridge Companion to Hobbes's Leviathan*, ed. Springborg.

7. Vickie B. Sullivan, *Machiavelli, Hobbes, and the Formation of a Liberal Republicanism in England* (Cambridge: Cambridge University Press, 2004), 105.

8. Sullivan, *Machiavelli, Hobbes*, 105.

9. Robert P. Kraynak, "Hobbes's Behemoth and the Argument for Absolutism," *The American Political Science Review* 76, no. 4 (December 1982): 844.

10. Jeremy Anderson, "The Role of Education in Political Stability," *Hobbes Studies* 16 (2003): 104.

11. Geoffroi de Charny, *The Book of Chivalry*, trans. Richard W. Kaeuper and Elspeth Kennedy (Philadelphia: University of Pennsylvania Press, 1996), 127.

12. Thomas Hobbes, *Behemoth or the Long Parliament*, ed. Ferdinand Tönnies (Chicago: University of Chicago Press, 1990), part 1, p. 38.

13. Michael P. Krom, "Vain Philosophy, the Schools and Civil Philosophy," *Hobbes Studies* 20 (2007): 113.

14. Gabriella Slomp, "Hobbes on Glory and Civil Strife," *The Cambridge Companion to Hobbes's Leviathan*, ed. Patricia Springborg (Cambridge: Cambridge University Press, 2007), 193.

15. Thomas Hobbes, *De Cive*, ed. Sterling P. Lamprecht (Westport, Conn.: Greenwood Press, 1982), part 3, ch. 18, sect. 13, p. 208.

16. John W. Seaman, "Hobbes and the Liberalization of Christianity," *Canadian Journal of Political Science* 32, no. 2 (June 1999): 227–46.

17. Michael Rabieh, "The Reasonableness of Locke, or the Questionableness of Christianity," *The Journal of Politics* 53, no. 4: 955.

18. Thomas Hobbes, *Leviathan*, ed. Michael Oakeshott (Oxford: Blackwell, 1962), part 1., ch. 8, para. 18, p. 63.

19. Martin A. Bertman, "Equality in Hobbes, with Reference to Aristotle," *The Review of Politics* 38, no. 4 (October 1976): 540.

20. Richard Allen Chapman, "Leviathan Writ Small: Thomas Hobbes on the Family," *The American Political Science Review* 69, no. 1 (March 1975): 78.

21. Hobbes, *Leviathan*, review and conclusion, para. 2, p. 503.

22. For an excellent treatment of the profound uncertainty of even the natural world (leading to the belief in ghosts and gods), and the inability of human beings to communicate truth about the world to each other, see Jan H. Blits, "Hobbesian Fear," *Political Theory* 17, no. 3 (August 1989): 417–31.

Bibliography

Adamson, J. S. A. "The Baronial Context of the English Civil War." In *The English Civil War*, edited by Richard Cust and Ann Hughes, 83–110. London: Arnold, 2001.

Anderson, Jeremy. "The Role of Education in Political Stability." *Hobbes Studies* 16 (2003): 95–104.

Ashley, Maurice. *The English Civil War: A Concise History*. London: Thames and Hudson, 1974.

Ashton, Robert. *The English Civil War: Conservatism and Revolution 1603–1649*. 2nd ed. London: Weidenfeld and Nicolson, 1989.

Aubrey, John. *Brief Lives*. Edited by Oliver Lawson Dick. London: Secker and Warburg, 1950.

Barber, Richard. *The Reign of Chivalry*. London: David & Charles, 1980.

Baumgold, Deborah. "Hobbes's Political Sensibility: The Menace of Political Ambition." In *Thomas Hobbes & Political Theory*, edited by Mary G. Dietz, 74–90. Lawrence: University Press of Kansas, 1990.

Beiner, Ronald. "Machiavelli, Hobbes, and Rousseau on Civil Religion." *The Review of Politics* 55, no. 4 (Autumn 1993): 617–38.

Bertman, Martin A. "Equality in Hobbes, with Reference to Aristotle." *The Review of Politics* 38, no. 4 (October 1976): 534–44.

Blits, Jan H. "Hobbesian Fear." *Political Theory* 17, no. 3 (August 1989): 417–31.

Bornstein, Diane. *Mirrors of Courtesy*. Hamden, Conn.: Archon Books, 1975.

Boucher, David. "Inter-Community & International Relations in the Political Philosophy of Hobbes." *Polity* 23, no. 2 (Winter 1990): 207–32.

Boucher, David, and Paul Kelly, eds. *The Social Contract from Hobbes to Rawls*. New York: Routledge, 1994.

Bowman, James. *Honor: A History*. New York: Encounter Books, 2006.

Brown, Keith C., ed. *Hobbes Studies*. Oxford: Basil Blackwell, 1965.

Burchell, David. "The Disciplined Citizen: Thomas Hobbes, Neostoicism and the Critique of Classical Citizenship." *Australian Journal of Politics and History* 45, no. 4 (December 1999): 506–24.

Burke, Edmund. *Reflections on the Revolution in France*. Edited by J. G. A. Pocock. Indianapolis: Hackett Publishing Co., 1987.

Butler, Todd. "Image, Rhetoric, and Politics in the Early Thomas Hobbes." *Journal of the History of Ideas* 67, no. 3 (July 2006): 465–87.

Castiglione, Baldassare. *The courtier of Count Baldessar Castilio: Deuided into foure bookes. Verie necessarie and profitable for young gentlemen and gentlewomen abiding in court, pallace, or place, done into English by Thomas Hobby*. London: Iohn Wolfe, 1588.

Cavallo, Joann. "Joking Matters: Politics and Dissimulation in Castiglione's Book of the Courtier." *Renaissance Quarterly* 52, no. 2 (Summer 2000): 402–24.

Cavendish, Margaret. *The World's Olio*. London: J. Martin and J. Allestrye, 1655. Obtained through *EEBO: Early English Books Online*. eebo.chadwyck.com.

Chapman, Richard Allen. "Leviathan Writ Small: Thomas Hobbes on the Family." *The American Political Science Review* 69, no. 1 (March 1975): 76–90.

Charny, Geoffroi de. *The Book of Chivalry*. Edited by Richard W. Kaeuper and Elspeth Kennedy. Philadelphia: University of Pennsylvania Press, 1996.

Coleman, Frank M. *Hobbes and America: Exploring the Constitutional Foundations*. Toronto: University of Toronto Press, 1977.

Collins, Jeffrey R. *The Allegiance of Thomas Hobbes*. Oxford: Oxford University Press, 2005.

Cranston, Maurice, and Richard S. Peters, eds. *Hobbes and Rousseau: A Collection of Critical Essays*. Garden City, N.Y.: Doubleday & Co., 1972.

Cust, Richard. "Wentworth's 'Change of Sides' in the 1620s." In *The Political World of Thomas Wentworth, Earl of Strafford: 1621–1641*, edited by J. F. Merritt, 63–80. Cambridge: Cambridge University Press, 1996.

Dietz, Mary G., ed. *Thomas Hobbes & Political Theory*. Lawrence: University Press of Kansas, 1990.

Elias, Norbert. *The Civilizing Process: The History of Manners*. Translated by Edmund Jephcott. New York: Urizon Books, 1978.

Flathman, Richard E. *Thomas Hobbes: Skepticism, Individuality and Chastened Politics*. London: Sage Publications, 1993.

Fortier, John C. " Hobbes and 'A Discourse of Laws': The Perils of Wordprint Analysis." *The Review of Politics* 59, no. 4 (Autumn 1997): 861–87.

Grafstein, Robert. "The Significance of Modern State of Nature Theory." *Polity* 19, no. 4 (Summer 1987): 529–50.

Gray, Robert. "Hobbes's System and His Early Philosophical Views." *Journal of the History of Ideas* 39, no. 2 (April–June 1978): 199–215.

Green, Karen. "Christine De Pisan and Thomas Hobbes." *The Philosophical Quarterly* 44, no. 177 (October 1994): 456–75.

Hampton, Jean. *Hobbes and the Social Contract Tradition*. Cambridge: Cambridge University Press, 1986.

Hayes, Peter. "Hobbes's Bourgeois Moderation." *Polity* 31, no. 1 (Autumn 1998): 53–74.

Heinrichs, Terry. "Hobbes & the Coleman Thesis." *Polity* 16, no. 4 (Summer 1984): 647–66.

Hobbes, Thomas. *Behemoth or the Long Parliament.* Edited by Ferdinand Tönnies. Chicago: University of Chicago Press, 1990.

———. *De Cive.* Edited by Sterling P. Lamprecht. Westport, Conn.: Greenwood Press, 1982.

———. *A Dialogue between a Philosopher and a Student of the Common Laws of England.* In vol. 6 of *The English Works of Thomas Hobbes,* edited by Sir William Molesworth. Ger.: Scientia Verlag Aalen, 1962.

———. *Elements of Law.* 2nd ed. Edited by Ferdinand Tönnies. London: Frank Cass and Company Limited, 1969.

———. *Hobbes's Thucydides.* Edited by Richard Schlatter. New Brunswick, N.J.: Rutgers University Press, 1975.

———. *Leviathan.* Edited by Michael Oakeshott. Oxford: Blackwell, 1962.

———. *Man and Citizen [De Homine and De Cive].* Edited by Bernard Gert. Indianapolis: Hackett Publishing Company, 1991.

———. *Three Discourses: A Critical Modern Edition of Newly Identified Work of the Young Hobbes.* Edited by Noel B. Reynolds and Arlene W. Saxonhouse. Chicago: University of Chicago Press, 1995.

———. *The Whole Art of Rhetoric.* In vol. 6 of *The English Works of Thomas Hobbes,* edited by Sir William Molesworth. Ger.: Scientia Verlag Aalen, 1962.

Holmes, Stephen. "Political Psychology in Hobbes's *Behemoth.*" In *Thomas Hobbes & Political Theory,* edited by Mary G. Dietz, 120–52. Lawrence. University of Kansas Press, 1990.

Hood, F. C. *The Divine Politics of Thomas Hobbes: An Interpretation of Leviathan.* Oxford: Clarendon Press, 1964.

Hutton, Sara. "In Dialogue with Thomas Hobbes: Margaret Cavendish's Natural Philosophy." *Women's Writing* 4, no. 3 (October 1997): 421–32.

Jaume, Lucien. "Hobbes and the Philosophical Sources of Liberalism." In *The Cambridge Companion to Hobbes's Leviathan,* edited by Patricia Springborg, 199–216. Cambridge: Cambridge University Press, 2007.

Kraynak, Robert P. "Hobbes on Barbarism and Civilization." *The Journal of Politics* 45, no. 1 (February 1983): 86–109.

———. "Hobbes's Behemoth and the Argument for Absolutism." *The American Political Science Review* 76, no. 4 (December 1982): 837–47.

———. "Review: Speculations on the Earliest Writings of Hobbes." *The Review of Politics* 58, no. 4 (Autumn 1996): 813–16.

Krom, Michael P. "First to Flee: Fear of Death and the Hobbesian Philosopher." Paper presented September 15, 2007, Ashland University.

———. "Vain Philosophy, the Schools and Civil Philosophy." *Hobbes Studies* 20 (2007): 93–119.

Lindsay, Thomas K. "Aristotle's Appraisal of Manly Spirit: Political and Philosophic Implications." *American Journal of Political Science* 44, no. 3 (July 2000): 433–48.

———. "Liberty, Equality, Power: Aristotle's Critique of the Democratic 'Presupposition.'" *American Journal of Political Science* 36, no. 3 (August 1992): 743–61.

Locke, John. *Second Treatise of Government.* Edited by Richard H. Cox. Arlington Heights, Ill.: H. Davidson, 1982.

Macpherson, C. B. *The Political Theory of Possessive Individualism: Hobbes to Locke*. Oxford: Clarendon Press, 1964.

Malcolm, Noel. *Aspects of Hobbes*. New York: Oxford University Press, 2003.

Mansfield, Harvey C. *Manliness*. New Haven, Conn., and London: Yale University Press, 2006.

Martinich, Aloysius P. *Hobbes: A Biography*. Cambridge: Cambridge University Press, 1999.

———. *The Two Gods of Leviathan: Thomas Hobbes on Religion and Politics*. Cambridge: Cambridge University Press, 1992.

Mathie, William. "Justice and the Question of Regimes in Ancient and Modern Political Philosophy: Aristotle and Hobbes." *Canadian Journal of Political Science/ Revue canadienne de science politique* 9, no. 3 (September 1976): 449–63.

Miner, Brad. *The Compleat Gentleman: The Modern Man's Guide to Chivalry*. Dallas: Spence Publishing, 2004.

Minogue, Kenneth. "Hobbes and the Just Man." In *Hobbes and Rousseau: A Collection of Critical Essays*, edited by Maurice Cranston and Richard S. Peters. Garden City, N.Y.: Doubleday & Co., 1972.

Northrup, Douglas A. "'The Ende Therfore of a Perfect Courtier' in Baldassare Castiglione's *The Courtier*." *Philological Quarterly* 77, no. 3 (Summer 1998): 295–305.

Oakeshott, Michael. *Hobbes on Civil Association*. Indianapolis: Liberty Fund, 1975.

Orwin, Clifford. "On the Sovereign Authorization." *Political Theory* 3, no. 1 (February 1975): 26–44.

Pateman, Carole. "'God Hath Ordained to Man a Helper': Hobbes, Patriarchy and Conjugal Right." *British Journal of Political Science* 19, no. 4 (October 1989): 445–63.

Pateman, Carole, Nancy J. Hirschmann, and G. Bingham Powell Jr. "Political Obligation, Freedom and Feminism." *The American Political Science Review* 86, no. 1 (March 1992): 179–88.

Rabieh, Michael S. "The Reasonableness of Locke, or the Questionableness of Christianity." *The Journal of Politics* 53, no. 4 (November 1991): 933–57.

Reik, Miriam M. *The Golden Lands of Thomas Hobbes*. Detroit: Wayne State University Press, 1977.

Ross, George Macdonald. "Hobbes and the Authority of the Universities." *Hobbes Studies* 10 (1997): 68–80.

Rousseau, Jean-Jacques. *Discourse on the Origins of Inequality*. In *The Basic Writings*. Indianapolis: Hackett Publishing Co., 1987.

Russell, Conrad. *The Causes of the English Civil War: The Ford Lectures Delivered in the University of Oxford, 1987–1988*. Oxford: Clarendon Press, 1990.

Sarasohn, Lisa T. "Thomas Hobbes and the Duke of Newcastle: A Study in the Mutuality of Patronage before the Establishment of the Royal Society." *Isis* 90, no. 4 (December 1999): 715–37.

Saxonhouse, Arlene. "Hobbes & the Horae Subsecivae." *Polity* 13, no. 4 (Summer 1981): 541–67.

Schochet, Gordon J. "Thomas Hobbes on the Family and the State of Nature." *Political Science Quarterly* 82, no. 3 (September 1967): 427–45.

Schrock, Thomas S. "The Rights to Punish and Resist Punishment in Hobbes's Leviathan." *The Western Political Quarterly* 44, no. 4 (December 1991): 853–90.

Seaman, John W. "Hobbes and the Liberalization of Christianity." *Canadian Journal of Political Science* 32, no. 2 (June 1999): 227–46.

Shapiro, Barbara J. "The Universities and Science in Seventeenth Century England." *The Journal of British Studies* 10, no. 2 (May 1971): 47–82.

Skinner, Quentin. "The Ideological Context of Hobbes's Political Thought." *The Historical Journal* 9, no. 3 (1966): 286–317.

Slomp, Gabriella. "Hobbes on Glory and Civil Strife." In *The Cambridge Companion to Hobbes's Leviathan*, edited by Patricia Springborg, 181–98. Cambridge: Cambridge University Press, 2007.

———. *Thomas Hobbes and the Political Philosophy of Glory*. New York: St. Martin's Press, 2000.

Spragens, Thomas A. *The Politics of Motion: The World of Thomas Hobbes*. Lexington: University Press of Kentucky, 1973.

Springborg, Patricia, ed. *The Cambridge Companion to Hobbes's Leviathan*. Cambridge: Cambridge University Press, 2007.

Stauffer, Devin. "Reopening the Quarrel between the Ancients and the Moderns: Leo Strauss's Critique of Hobbes's 'New Political Science.'" *The American Political Science Review* 101, no. 2 (May 2007): 223–33.

Stone, Lawrence. *The Crisis of the Aristocracy, 1558–1641*. Oxford: Clarendon Press, 1965.

Strauss, Leo. *Natural Right and History*. Chicago: University of Chicago Press, 1953.

———. *The Political Philosophy of Thomas Hobbes: Its Basis and Genesis*. Translated by Elsa M. Sinclair. Chicago: University of Chicago Press, 1984.

Sullivan, Vickie B. *Machiavelli, Hobbes, and the Formation of Liberal Republicanism in England*. Cambridge: Cambridge University Press, 2004.

Thomas, Keith. "The Social Origins of Hobbes's Political Thought." In *Hobbes Studies*, edited by K. C. Brown, 185–236. Oxford: Basil Blackwell, 1965.

Ustick, W. Lee. "Changing Ideals of Aristocratic Character and Conduct in Seventeenth-Century England." *Modern Philology* 30, no. 2 (November 1932): 147–66.

Wall, Alison. "Patterns of Politics in England, 1558–1625." *The Historical Journal* 31, no. 4 (December 1988): 947–63.

Zagorin, Peter. "Hobbes's Early Philosophical Development." *Journal of the History of Ideas* 54, no. 3 (July 1993): 505–18.

Index

About the Author

Laurie M. Johnson Bagby is an associate professor in the Department of Political Science at Kansas State University and author of *Hobbes's Leviathan, Political Thought: A Guide to the Classics*, and *Thucydides, Hobbes, and the Interpretation of Realism.*